School Principals

PETER LANG
New York • Washington, D.C./Baltimore • Bern
Frankfurt am Main • Berlin • Brussels • Vienna • Oxford

School Principals

Jianping Shen

Amy L. Kavanaugh, Gary L. Wegenke, Liliana Rodriguez-Campos, Rigoberto Rincones-Gomez, Louann Bierlein Palmer, Cheryle Crawford, Van E. Cooley, Sue Poppink, Dorothy VanderJagt, Chia-lin Hsieh, Connie D. Ruhl-Smith, Nanette M. Keiser, & Bradley S. Portin

PETER LANG
New York • Washington, D.C./Baltimore • Bern
Frankfurt am Main • Berlin • Brussels • Vienna • Oxford

Library of Congress Cataloging-in-Publication Data

Jianping Shen.
School principals / Jianping Shen.
p. cm.
Includes bibliographical references and index.
1. School principals—United States. 2. Educational leadership—
United States. I. Shen, Jianping.
LB2831.92.S36 371.2'012—dc22 2005008142
ISBN 0-8204-5152-5

Bibliographic information published by **Die Deutsche Bibliothek**.
Die Deutsche Bibliothek lists this publication in the "Deutsche
Nationalbibliografie"; detailed bibliographic data is available
on the Internet at http://dnb.ddb.de/.

Cover design by Joni Holst

275 Seventh Avenue, 28th Floor, New York, NY 10001
www.peterlangusa.com

CONTENTS

ACKNOWLEDGMENTS

We want to thank the publishers and organizations for the permission to use the materials in the following sources:

Cooley, V. E., & Shen, J. (1999). Who will lead: The top 10 factors that influence teachers moving into administration. *NASSP Bulletin, 83* (606), 75–80. © 1999 by National Association of Secondary School Principals. www.principals.org. Reprinted with permission.

Cooley, V. E., & Shen, J. (2003). School accountability and professional job responsibilities: A perspective from secondary principals. *NASSP Bulletin, 87* (634), 10–25. (© by National Association of Secondary School Principals). For more information concerning NASSP services and/or programs, please call (703) 860–0200, or visit *www.principals.org*.

Hsieh, C., & Shen, J. (1998). Teachers', principals', and superintendents' perceptions of leadership. *School Leadership and Management, 18* (1), 107–121. (© Carfax Publishing) The Journal's web site is *http://www.tandf.co.uk/journals*.

Poppink, S., & Shen, J. (2003). Secondary principals' salaries: A national, longitudinal study. *NASSP Bulletin, 87* (634), 67–82. (© by National Association of Secondary School Principals). For more information concerning NASSP services and/or programs, please call (703) 860–0200, or visit *www.principals.org*.

Portin, B. S., & Shen, J. (1998). The changing principalship: Its current status, variability, and impact. *The Journal of Leadership Studies, 5* (3), 93–113. (© by Baker College).

Ruhl-Smith, C., Shen, J., & Cooley, V. E. (1999). Gender differences in the reasons for entering and leaving educational administration: Discriminant function analyses. *The Journal of Psychology, 133* (6), 596–604. Reprinted with permission of the Helen Dwight Reid Educational Foundation. Published by

Heldref Publications, 1319 18th Street, NW, Washington, DC 20036-1802. www.heldref.org. Copyright © (1999).

Shen, J. (2001). Teacher and Principal empowerment: National, longitudinal, and comparative perspectives. *Educational Horizons*, 79 (3), 124–129. This article originally appeared in *educational HORIZONS*, quarterly journal of Pi Lambda Theta, Inc., International Honor Society and Professional Association in Education, P.O. Box 6626, Bloomington, IN 47407-6626.

Shen, J., Cooley, V. E., Ruhl-Smith, C., & Keiser, N. (1999). Quality and impact of educational leadership programs: A national study. *The Journal of Leadership Studies*, *6* (1 & 2), 3–16. (© by Baker College).

Shen, J., Cooley, V., & Wegenke, G. (2004). Perspectives on factors influencing application of principalship: A comparative study of teachers, principals, and superintendents. *International Journal of Leadership in Education*, 7 (1), 57–70. (© by Taylor & Francis, Ltd) The Journal's web site is *http://www.tandf.co.uk/journals*.

VanderJagt, D., Shen, J., & Hsieh, C. (2001). Elementary and secondary public school principals' perceptions of school problems. *Educational Research Quarterly*, 25 (2), 39–51.

·1·

Amy L. Kavanaugh

INTRODUCTION TO PRINCIPALSHIP

This book is about school principals—Who they are, how they are prepared, what they do, and how they think and behave. Before presenting data and analysis on current principalship, we briefly review, in this chapter, the history of principalship—how the principalship came into existence, how the principalship has evolved, how principals have been prepared, and what the characteristics are for those who prepare for and become principals. It is important to understand how the principalship came into being, the knowledge that will help us understand the current status of principalship.

A Brief History of the Principalship: 1700s–Present

The Advent of the Principalship

In our nation Massachusetts was the first system of public education to be documented (Weiss, 1992). In 1789 every town in Massachusetts was required to provide schools with certified teachers. Town councils supervised the one-room schools during this time because communities were small and rural (Campbell, Fleming, Newell, & Bennion, 1987). As populations rose at the end of the eighteenth century, schools became multigraded and there was a need for onsite supervision. A head teacher or principal teacher was appointed by the council or the board to manage the complexities of the school. The position of principal was originally known as the head teacher in American schools. Just as the name implies, one of the roles of the head teacher was to teach.

The term principal was first noted in the minutes of a meeting of the Board of Education of Albany, New York in May 1867, when the board determined " ... that the several principals be allowed compensation for making fires in their respective schools during the cold season of the year" (Weiss, 1992, p. 36). It is important to note that the position of principal was not intentionally created; instead it developed in response to certain factors in education. The following factors led to the principalship: (a) population growth within cities, (b) the grading of schools, (c) removing teaching as a duty of the position, and (d) the establishment of the Department of Elementary School Principals in 1921 (Weiss, 1992). It took decades to solidify the position of principal. Rural schools continued to be led by head teachers into the twentieth century. The principal was the first to act as a supervisor within graded, urban schools. The principal's responsibilities included teaching, keeping attendance records, distributing school supplies, and maintaining the school building (Campbell, Fleming, Newell, & Bennion, 1987; Weiss, 1992). The role soon expanded to include providing professional development for teachers and promoting or retaining students.

Schools continued to grow during the nineteenth century. The urbanization of our cities made the position of principal more complex as once-rural leaders had to make the transition to managing urban schools with large enrollments. In order to assist in school management, some school boards expanded to hundreds of members (Campbell, Fleming, Newell, & Bennion, 1987). Although teachers and many board members opposed adding to school leadership, city superintendents were appointed during the mid-nineteenth century. Superintendents then began to delegate some of their building-level responsibilities to the principal; this delegation led to the deletion of teaching from the role of principal.

In their research, Beck and Murphy (1993) organized the development of the principalship by themes, values, and the tone of the position from the 1920s–1980s. Although they define the principal's roles in each decade, characteristics of the roles may overlap into another time period. Their metaphors are listed in Table 1.1 (Beck & Murphy, 1993, p. 202). The rest of this section is primarily a synthesis of Beck and Murphy's research.

1920s Values Broker

Principals, newly released from their teaching responsibilities, had to take on management and supervision with no formal training. Beck and Murphy (1993) describe the principal during the 1920s as a spiritual leader, social leader, and scientific manager. In fact the principal was referred to in some cases as a priest leading a parish (Cubberley, 1923). Supervision was undertaken as a kind of science, where the principal monitored teachers in a demo-

TABLE 1.1. Phrases to Describe the Principalship by Decade

Decade	Metaphorical Phrase
1920s	Values Broker
1930s	Scientific Manager
1940s	Democratic Leader
1950s	Theory Guided Administrator
1960s	Bureaucratic Executive
1970s	Humanistic Facilitator
1980s	Instructional Leader

cratic style. Principals were expected to organize the curriculum, help teachers develop effective teaching strategies, and observe classroom teaching. Unlike school teachers who were expected to live conservatively, principals during this time were expected to make plenty of social contacts and be actively involved in the community.

1930s Scientific Manager

By the 1930s the principalship was still marked by scientific management, but the position shifted away from spiritual leader to that of a business executive. The principal's responsibilities were administrative. It was believed, and still is in some cases, that the principal should run the school using business principles for budgeting, maintenance, and pupil accounting (Beck & Murphy, 1993). The development of principal as professional and executive mirrors the progress of principalship preparation during this time period. The 1930s marked a time when preparation programs and principals looked to research to resolve their problems. School leaders were expected to make informed decisions using current research.

1940s Democratic Leader

The 1940s were a democratic time of school leadership reflective of nationalism or the World War II sentiment. The school was considered a place to prepare youth for their role in a democratic nation, and the principal assisted with this preparation for productive living. The responsibilities of the principal came to include curriculum development, and shared decision making between principal and teacher along with supervision (Beck & Murphy, 1993; Parker, 1986). During this decade principals and teachers began to work more cooperatively to develop and implement curriculum and instruction. The principal was less of a director and more of a coordinator.

As a result of the shift to research-based decision-making in the 1930s and the introduction of state certification for administrators, principals also began to seek higher degrees (Parker, 1978). This period is considered focused on human relations and less on scientific management (Farquhar, 1977).

1950s Theory-Guided Administrator

The 1950s were a period of synthesis, combining the scientific management approach with the human relations approach. It was noted at the 1954 meeting of the National Council of Professors of Educational Administration that a turning point had been reached in educational administration because of the synthesis of the two previous approaches to school management. This idea of synthesis was proposed by Chester Barnard (1938) and it meant the role of the principal was to accomplish the goals of scientific management and organizational purpose, as well as the goals of the human relations approach and individual purpose (Getzels, 1977).

Similar to the 1930s, principals during the 1950s were expected to apply university-based research to the school setting. They used empirical data to support teaching strategies used in classrooms during this time as they defended their practice (Beck & Murphy, 1993). In addition to defending school practices, principals were expected to efficiently manage their time through the delegation of duties and reliance on clerical staff. Principals during this decade tended to be focused on details. They seemed to get caught up in the details of running a school building rather than the larger picture of leading the school.

1960s Bureaucratic Executive

The principal of the 1960s was considered a bureaucrat who held power in the school. Schools were considered to be similar to a laboratory, hospital, or factory. Therefore, principals approached their responsibilities from a technical perspective, using scientific strategies to reach measurable outcomes (Beck & Murphy, 1993). This technical perspective led to the practice that principals were evaluated based on measurable outcomes.

The 1960s were also a decade that marked the beginnings of discontent with the role of principal. There was less glory associated with the position than in previous decades as the principalship was recognized as a position that could be taught and learned. Principals began to recognize being in the tenuous position of reporting to numerous groups with different wants and needs, including the superintendent, teachers, parents, students, the business, and the community at large. The principalship witnessed the end of the management years by the end of the 1960s, and a marked shift to primarily the humanistic approach to school leadership during the 1970s.

1970s Humanistic Facilitator

The principal of the 1970s continued to wear many hats and juggle the needs of different stakeholders. During this decade the principal was a humanistic community leader who influenced others by involving them in the schools, demonstrating what was happening inside the school. The principal worked to develop mutual respect and help teachers, acting more as a team player rather than the boss. Schools began focusing on meaningful learning for students, and the principal's role was expanded to include setting school structures to support this kind of teaching and learning.

1980s Instructional Leadership

During this period the principal strived to become an instructional leader, directly involved in the teaching and learning process. The principal was expected to be a visionary with a mission and a plan of how to achieve the vision for the school. The principal began to talk with teachers and respond to the need for increasing student achievement. Responding to teachers' needs was achieved by providing resources such as professional development and solving problems that hindered classroom success. Another term used to define the principalship during this time was change agent, someone who could make the vision a reality. The idea of change agent makes perfect sense during the 1980s as *A Nation at Risk* was published in 1983 highlighting the lagging performance of American students, and there was agreement in the literature that schools needed to be improved (Barth, 1990; Goodlad, 1984; Pounder, 1987).

1990s Reaching out to the Community

The 1990s began a movement of the principal reaching out to the community. No longer was it sufficient for the principal to go into the community to teach what schools were about or control the level of community involvement in the school; principals began to work on developing stronger ties between the school and community. These relationships with external stakeholders needed to be tended to for the welfare of the school (Goldring & Sullivan, 1996). The community surrounding schools had changed drastically to include more students who speak languages other than English, growing minority enrollments, and children living in poverty.

In addition to changes in the community surrounding the school, the charter school movement began in 1991 in Minnesota. For the first time, parents could choose to send their children to a new type of public school, which meant competition for traditional public schools. Another form of competition came as private school tuition vouchers began in Wisconsin in 1990 (Noll, 1996). There was also increasing accountability with national and state standards for testing. These changes demanded the attention of those in the position of principal; they had to do all in their power to maintain enrollment, achievement, and lead the school into the 21st century.

Principalship in the 21st Century: Age of Accountability

Competition between traditional public schools, charter schools, and private schools began in the 1990s and continues, making the principalship more complex. The increase in accountability impacts principals as they are evaluated by student performance on state achievement tests. State and national funding is tied directly to student progress, and the government is scrutinizing student performance across racial and ethnic groups. Because of the level of accountability in today's schools, principals are pressing teachers to carefully cover all of the curriculum standards, base instruction on students' prior knowledge, and develop relationships with students in order to overcome cultural differences. Together principals and teachers are developing more student-centered schools connecting instruction to standards as well as real-world experiences for students. The principal's role is that of facilitator with the goal to help students achieve. The school is less of a bureaucracy and strives to become more of a learning community. As the role of principal has changed, so have the programs that prepare school leaders. A description of how preparation for the principalship has developed follows.

Preparation Programs for the Principalship

In the literature there is a general consensus on the different stages principal preparation programs have transitioned through. Murphy (1998) lists four different periods in the development of these programs. They are:

1820–1899 Ideological Era
1900–1946 Prescriptive Era
1947–1985 Scientific Era
1986–Present Dialectic Era

The Ideological Era is characterized as a time when the principalship was not considered a true profession. There was little required training during this period. The school leader simply learned on the job. Any training that was available was on the Great Man theories (Cooper & Boyd, 1987). The principal's role was simply to provide guidance to teachers, students, and parents. It wasn't until 1875 that a school superintendent by the name of William L. Payne published the first textbook on school administration, *Chapters on School Supervision*. Payne went onto a faculty position at the University of Michigan where he taught the first college course in school administration (Callahan & Button, 1964).

The next time period, 1900–1946, is considered the Prescriptive Era of preparation programs. According to Silver (1982), by the end of this period there were 125 institutions offering school leadership training, up from 0 in 1900. During this time technical skills were emphasized. Business had a heavy influence over the program content during this era and faculty were mainly former superintendents who taught using anecdotes from their own experiences in the field. Programs sought to prepare leaders for the principalship as it currently existed, not for the future of the role.

The Scientific Era from 1947–1985 was a time when the social sciences took precedence within the preparation programs. By 1985 there were approximately 500 institutions offering school leadership preparation (National Commission on Excellence in Educational Administration, 1987). Business had less input, and the emphasis was placed on theory and research. Faculty from the Prescriptive Era, with extensive practical experience, was replaced with content area specialists with little experience in the schools. Here, programs sought to remake leadership in a rational way. This era resulted in educational administration being considered its own science.

Higher education programs designed to prepare people for the role of school principal have changed in numerous ways and at the same time have managed to stay the same in other ways. The role of the principal in today's school requires knowledge of and experience with curriculum and instruction. Current principals still need to be visionaries, good decision makers, problem solvers, and delegators.

There is a current push to make preparation programs more rigorous and connected to practice (Clark, 1998; McCarthy, 1999). In order to create this link programs encourage the use of cohort groups as students progress through their course work. These cohorts help to build a sense of community and serve as support systems for students (McCarthy, 1999). Some universities are using more of a student-centered approach to learning which represents a shift in pedagogy to building more problem-based strategies. The professors are no longer considered omniscient and student involvement is encouraged.

It seems natural then that if principals are taught using this constructivist, student-centered style that they will then lead using similar strategies. Along with this new approach to teaching and learning within the preparation programs is a more authentic type of assessment—portfolios. The use of portfolios in addition to traditional methods of assessment to evaluate student learning has gained in popularity within leadership programs (Barnett, 1995). The effective use of portfolios encourages students to be more reflective learners and apply course content to field experiences.

Despite these changes, programs to prepare for the principalship have remained structurally the same. Back in the 1960s Griffiths (1966) found that programs were made up of core classes in curriculum, supervision, school finance, school law, research, and personnel, among others. For at least the past 30 years courses in these leadership programs have remained essentially the same. The programs today typically include courses in school law, education policy, education finance, personnel administration, and leadership theory (McCarthy, 1999). Of course state licensing requirements do impact course offerings within a program, a factor that can explain the consistency in courses over time. It is also true that faculty expertise often dictates courses that are developed and implemented within educational programs.

Although current preparation programs are again interested in connections with the field, there is more of an emphasis on applying leadership theory and research to problems in the field (McCarthy, 1999). This is an important difference as it is consistent with the type of faculty hired to teach within leadership preparation programs. In fact the percentage of female faculty increased from 2% to 20% between 1972 and 1994 (McCarthy, 1999). In the 1990s new faculty were also more likely to be older and to have had previous school administration experience.

The most recent era in preparation programs is labeled the Dialectic Era 1986–present. This period is marked with critical evaluations of the preparation programs leading to efforts to transform the profession. Clark (1998), in his article on searching for authentic leadership in university programs, describes that these leadership programs have a lower status than other programs. He also makes suggestions for improvement: (a) raise admission standards, (b) immerse students in leadership through cohorts, (c) focus on instruction over research for faculty evaluations, and (d) improve preparation programs by looking for advice and innovative ideas. There is a move toward more communication between the stakeholders of the programs including those in the field as well as faculty (Murphy, 1998). As previously stated, preparation programs have begun to be more student-centered, linking theory and practice through problem-based learning, and using cohorts to build learning communities for students as they learn.

In fact, standards for school leaders were developed by the Council of Chief State School Officers' Interstate School Leaders Licensure Consortium (ISLLC) in the mid-nineties to provide higher education, state agencies, and professional associations with materials for reflective discussion on quality educational leadership, and opportunity to improve current leadership (ISLLC, 1996). This group created a very workable document outlining the knowledge, dispositions, and performances of effective educational leaders. It is quite clear that the emphasis of the educational leaders should be on the success of all students as the phrase is listed in each standard. The six standards are all-encompassing and detail key ideas that preparation programs should emphasize. The ISLLC Standards for School Leaders (1996) are listed below.

A school administrator is an educational leader who promotes the success of all students by:

- Facilitating the development, articulation, implementation, and stewardship of a vision of learning that is shared and supported by the school community.
- Advocating, nurturing, and sustaining a school culture and instructional program conducive to student learning and staff professional growth.
- Ensuring management of the organization, operations, and resources for a safe, efficient, and effective learning environment.
- Collaborating with families and community members, responding to diverse community interests and needs, and mobilizing community resources.
- Acting with integrity, fairness, and in an ethical manner.
- Understanding, responding to, and influencing the larger political, social, economic, legal, and cultural context.

So if one understands the history of the principalship, the preparation required of the position, as well as the accepted standards of the role, it is natural then to consider who decides to become a principal.

Characteristics of Those Who Become School Leaders

There is much more information available on the characteristics of educational leadership faculty than there is on the types of people who seek to become principals. Twenty-five years ago most students enrolled in educational leadership programs lived nearby their institutions and many attended the same institution for their undergraduate degrees (Davis & Spuck, 1978). It seems that students selected the preparation program based on location not on the program's reputation.

Paralleling the lack of rigor of preparation programs described in the previous section, students in these preparation programs tend to do poorly on national entrance exams and are part-time students (Murphy, 1992). Scribner (1973) reported that enrollment in master's degree programs was 18% minority and 31% female. The few preparation programs that published their enrollment indicated that approximately 50% of their students were women and 20% were minority (Milstein et al., 1993).

Beginning in the 20th century women began to advocate their advancement into school leadership positions (Schmuck, 1996). As early as 1910, more than half of school leaders were women (Donovan, 1938). Interestingly, women were generally school leaders in rural areas and in elementary schools where men dominated urban school leadership.

Then the period between 1920 and 1970 marked a time of declining female leadership in schools (Schmuck, 1996). The reasons for this decline are as follows.

- The passing of the 19th amendment marked the end of the first women's movement and took the focus off of their role in schools.
- The G.I. Bill granted men a college education, many of whom selected the field of education because of reduced academic requirements.
- Schools were consolidated so the rural schools where women were leaders were joined with larger schools led by men.
- The scientific era began and the emphasis was placed on using business strategies to "manage" schools. Tyack and Hansot (1982) describe this period as a time when men managed and women taught.

Fortunately, in the 1970s, women began to return to advocating their role as school leaders. Title IX played a major role in this reckoning with the idea of equal access to educational opportunities for girls and to employment for women. Still, women have not rebounded to their previously shared role in school leadership at the start of the 20th century. In fact, 80 years later, in 1991, only 31 percent of principals were women (Schmuck, 1996).

Describing the characteristics of students in graduate educational leadership programs also helps us to understand the types of people who chose to become school administrators over the years. Perhaps for the same reason as the second listed above (G.I. Bill), after World War II the number of middle class, white, male students increased significantly. In the 1950s most students were in their 30s, had school administration experience, and did not receive assistantships or fellowships to assist with their education (Farquhar, 1977). This description of middle class, white, and male remained consistent until the mid-1970s when affirmative action guidelines were set in place (Campbell,

Fleming, Newell, & Bennion, 1987). At this point principals were mainly white and schools were becoming more and more diverse. The affirmative action guidelines led to increases in minority and female enrollment in preparation programs.

Because school administrators have higher salaries than classroom teachers, the field may initially attract educators more interested in the added income than in the role of principal (Campbell, Fleming, Newell, & Bennion, 1987). However, as teachers gain experience in the classroom and move up the salary scale, many choose not to become principals because the difference in pay is small compared to the additional responsibility. School reform has also caused school districts to look more carefully for effective principals. Some schools have their own leadership training programs or they may team with other districts through the intermediate school district to offer leadership preparation training for new or struggling principals. Schools have also shifted toward hiring external candidates as they often push for more change than internal candidates.

While there is plenty of research on what it takes to be an effective school leader, there is very little information on the types of individuals attracted to the role of school principal (Pounder & Young, 1996). We do know that traditionally middle class white males, with some teaching experience tend fill the position of school principal. More information regarding the characteristics of the people recently becoming principals is needed.

Coda

In the foregoing, we briefly reviewed the history of principalship, how principals have been prepared, and characteristics of those who prepare for and become principals. The brief historical review reveals that the principalship has been evolving. In the next few chapters we provide data and analysis on the current status of principalship. Among others, we will discuss principals' professional preparation, leadership, working environment, job responsibilities, and compensation. We welcome you to join us in investigating school principalship.

References

Barnard, C. (1938). *The functions of the executive*. Cambridge: Harvard University Press.

Barnett, B.G. (1995). Portfolio use in educational leadership preparation programs: Educational platforms and portfolios. *Innovative Higher Education*, *19*, 197–206.

Barth, R. (1990). *Improving schools from within: Teachers, parents, and principals can make the difference.* San Francisco: Jossey-Bass.

Beck, L. & Murphy, J. (1993). *Understanding the principalship: Metaphorical themes 1920s-1990s.* New York: Teachers College Press.

Callahan, R.E. & Button, H.W. (1964). Historical change of the role of the man in the organization: 1865–1950. In Griffiths, D.E. (Ed.), *Behavioral science and educational administration, Sixty-third NSSE Yearbook, Part 1* (pp. 73–92). Chicago, IL: University of Chicago Press.

Campbell, R., Fleming, T., Newell, L., & Bennion, J. (1987). *A history of thought and practice in educational administration.* New York: Teachers College Press.

Clark, D.L. (1998). Searching for authentic leadership in university graduate programs and with public school colleagues. *Journal for a Just and Caring Education, 4,* 365–373.

Cooper, B.S. & Boyd, W.L. (1987). The evolution of training for school administrators. In J. Murphy and P. Hallinger (Eds.), *Approaches to administrative training* (pp. 3–27). Albany: State University of New York Press.

Cubberley, E.P. (1923). *The principal and his school.* Boston: Houghton Mifflin.

Davis, W.J., & Spuck, D. (1978). *A comparative analysis of masters, certification, specialist, and doctoral programs for educational administrators in the U.S.* (pp. 150–177). Columbus, OH: University Council for Educational Administration.

Donovan, F. (1938). *The school Ma'am.* New York: F. Stokes Company.

Farquhar, R.H. (1977). Preparatory programs in educational administration, 1954–1974. In L.L. Cunningham, W.G. Hack, & R.D. Nystrand (Eds.), *Educational administration: The developing decades* (pp. 329–357). Berkeley, CA: McCutchan.

Getzels, J. (1977). Educational administration twenty years later, 1954–1974. In L.L. Cunningham, W. G. Hack, & R. D. Nystrand (Eds.), *Educational administration: The developing decades.* Berkeley, CA: McCutchan.

Goodlad, J.I. (1984). *A place called school: Prospects for the future.* New York: McGraw-Hill.

Goldring, E.B. & Sullivan, A.V. (1996). Beyond the boundaries: Principals, parents, and communities shaping the school environment. In K. Leithwood, J. Chapman, D. Corson, P. Hallinger, & A. Hart (Eds.). *International handbook of educational leadership and administration* (pp. 195–222). Dordrecht: Kluwer Academic Publishers.

Griffiths, D.E. (1966). *The school superintendent.* New York: Center for Applied Research in Education.

Interstate School Leaders Licensure Consortium. (1996). *Standards for school leaders.* Washington, DC: Author.

Lauder, A. (2000). The new look in principal preparation programs. *NASSP Bulletin, 84* (617), 23–28.

Lashway, L. (1999). Preparing school leaders. *National Association of Elementary School Principals Research Roundup, 15* (3), 1–4.

McCarthy, M. (1999). The evolution of educational leadership preparation programs. In J. Murphy & K. Seashore Louis (Eds.), *Handbook of Research on Educational Administration* (2nd ed.) (pp. 119–139). San Francisco: CA: Jossey-Bass.

Milstein, M., & Associates (1993). *Changing the way we prepare educational leaders: The Danforth experience*. Newbury Park, CA: Corwin.

Murphy, J. (1992). *The landscape of leadership preparation: Reframing the education of school administrators*. Newbury Park, CA: Corwin.

Murphy, J. (1998). Preparation for the school principalship: The United States' story. *School Leadership & Management, 18* (3), 359–372.

National Commission on Excellence in Education. (1983). *A nation at risk: The imperative for educational reform*. Washington, DC: Government Printing Office.

National Commission on Excellence in Educational Administration. (1987). *Leaders for America's schools*. Tempe, AZ: University Council for Educational Administration.

Noll, J.W. (1996). *Taking sides: Clashing views on controversial educational issues* (12th ed.). Guilford, CT: McGraw-Hill/Dushkin.

Parker, D.C. (1986). From conventional wisdom to concept: School administration texts 1934–1945. In T.E. Glas (Ed.), *An analysis of texts on school administration 1820–1985: The reciprocal relationship between the literature and the profession* (pp. 39–75). Danville, IL: Interstate.

Pounder, D.G. (1987). The challenge for school leaders: Attracting and retaining good teachers. In W. Greenfield (Ed.), *Instructional leadership: Concepts, issues, and controversies* (pp.287–301). Newton, MA: Allyn & Bacon.

Pounder, D.G. & Young, I.P. (1996). Recruitment and selection of educational administrators: Priorities of today's schools. In K. Leithwood, J. Chapman, D. Corson, P. Hallinger, & A. Hart (Eds.), *International handbook of educational leadership and administration* (pp. 279–305). Dordrecht: Kluwer Academic Publishers.

Schmuck, P. (1996). Women's place in educational administration: Past, present, and future. In K. Leithwood, J. Chapman, D. Corson, P. Hallinger, & A. Hart (Eds.), *International handbook of educational leadership and administration* (pp. 337–362). Dordrecht, The Netherlands: Kluwer Academic Publishers.

Scribner, J. (1973). Urban educational policy and planning: Leadership development for urban careers. *UCLA Educator, 115* (2), 26–29.

Silver, P.F. (1982). Administrator preparation. In H.E. Mitzel (Ed.), *Encyclopedia of educational research*, vol. 1 (5th ed.) (pp. 49–59). New York: Free Press.

Tyack, D., & Hansot, E. (1982). *Managers of virtue*. New York: Basic Books.

Weiss, R. S. (1992). *The elementary school principalship: An historical evolution*. Amherst, MA: University of Massachusetts at Amherst.

·2·

Gary L. Wegenke and Jianping Shen

GENDER, RACIAL, AND ETHNIC DIVERSITY AMONG PRINCIPALS

Introduction

A school leadership challenge continues to be the rapid changes taking place in student demographics in our nation's schools and the relationship of the changes to a slower rate of change in employment of people of color and females among school principals. A conversation on the issue can begin by noting current trends in migration into the United States. The most recent immigrants, including school-aged children, are coming from Latin American and the Asian countries. The new American citizens are unlike their predecessors who came primarily from European nations. According to Hodgkinson (1998), the racial makeup of future student bodies in our nation's schools needs to be considered in light of world population trends. His world population projection for 2010 shows whites consisting of 9 percent of the world's total population. By contrast, in 1997, according to Hodgkinson, the white population was nearly 17 percent. Assuming his projections are accurate, the white population in the world will become the smallest of the ethnic cultures. In 2020, our nation's schools are predicted to have half of their student population represented by students of color (Banks, 1999). Is the composition of the public school principals reflective of the above changing demographic? In this chapter, we inquired into the composition of the public school principalship in terms of gender, race, and ethnicity over a 12-year period.

A New Approach to Diversity Leadership

The type of school leader who models new theory-based approaches to diversity leadership is one who supports broad-based diffusion of leadership concepts and skills with his/her staff. This collegial focus is an important first step toward a new approach to diversity leadership (Combs, 2002). Various diversity leadership perspectives and organizational strategies will be required in our nation's schools if schools are expected to lead the way in nurturing and encouraging diversity.

Historically, the majority of staff development diversity training programs in schools have been directed toward an individual's sensitivity to and awareness of discriminatory actions toward race, ethnic, gender, socio-economic, and religious issues. These programs, while important for long-term planning in school districts, may have had only minimal effects on day-to-day behaviors and attitudes of some of the school's staff. In rural, suburban, and urban schools where diversity understanding is translated into performance behaviors, diversity self-efficacy has been emphasized. Diversity self-efficacy is defined as one's personal judgment and confidence in acquired cognitive resources to facilitate appropriate responses to diversity issues in the workplace (Bandura, 1997). The role of the school principal practicing a self-efficacy approach to diversity management would be to reflect upon human relationship areas in the school where conflict resulting from diversity issues exists. The principal's thoughts often are connected to feelings about the school's climate where diversity issues are brought to life by staff and students.

According to Madsen and Mabokela (2000), the culture within most school settings strongly influences how the European American faculty members will treat their minority colleagues. Madsen and Mabokela identify the prevailing culture within the school as a particularly important issue when the school leader's race and ethnicity is different from their followers, where importance is placed on recruiting and retaining teachers of color, and where principals are expected to create inclusive cultures. In a school where a small percentage of the faculty is of a different race, there is little opportunity for minority staff members to affect the European American norms that are in place. The result is that minority teachers feel others treat them differently in the school. Madsen and Mabokela said, "The majority culture establishes work norms, it establishes rules and regulations of which people of color are expected to comply" (Madsen & Mabokela, 2002, p. 851). Undoubtedly, the behaviors of the majority culture will limit any outward expression of the experiences and perceptions a minority faculty member brings to the school workplace. The richness of those experiences and perceptions will become lost in attempting to comply with expectations of "how business is conducted here."

In a school culture that is open to different perspectives on and approaches to actions related to multi-cultural education, a self-efficacy school leadership philosophy is critical. A major understanding when implementing multicultural education identified by Marshall (1994) is that teachers must serve as transformational agents [school leaders] who are responsible for monitoring diversity events taking place in schools and making certain "the inequitable treatment in the disempowerment of many groups" (p. 25) is not continued. An ongoing dialogue between the principal and his/her staff would assist these school leaders to begin to clarify with each other the beliefs, values, attitudes, and actions people from diverse backgrounds bring to the school. These exchanges of ideas and information would positively impact areas of understanding related to student/student and student/teacher interactions, curriculum and instruction practices, gender bias, workforce diversity, and the school's organizational structure (Smith, 1996).

Transforming school leadership that empowers others on the school's staff to become diversity leaders becomes a moral act. It highlights the importance of schooling by taking issues of diversity and making them everybody's business and concern. Kouzes and Posner (2002) encourage school leaders to find their collective voices and model the way by sharing knowledge and understanding of critical issues in their school's environment. The diversity challenge for a collection of school leaders is to create and facilitate a day-to-day environment that allows and encourages an appreciation for multi-dimensional individual backgrounds, experiences, and perceptions of individuals and their groups.

The Interstate School Leaders Licensure Consortium's Standards on Diversity

Do school leaders, including school principals, have the disposition and knowledge of how to begin designing a workplace where staff takes equal responsibility (self-efficacy) to lead their increasingly diverse student bodies? The question, in part, was responded to through the work of the Interstate School Leaders Licensure Consortium (ISLLC). Their work, sponsored by the Council of Chief State School Officers, was to design common standards for school leaders. The research design strategy focused on two compatible dimensions related to school leadership and the reshaping of our nation's schools.

The first dimension relied on the linkages between educational leadership and schools considered to be productive. Productivity was defined in terms of student outcomes. A second dimension responded to was the increasing diversity that has been taking place in the nation—racially, linguistically, and culturally (Council of Chief State School Officers, 1996). ISSLC researchers in 1996 looked for evidence of these trends in society as well as in our nation's rural, suburban, and urban educational settings. They found that current demographic trends related to student diversity have significant implications for understanding and altering traditional views of top-down educational leadership (Green, 2001). Members of the Consortium established six standards as models for what effective school leaders at all levels must be held accountable in terms of responsibilities. Each standard begins with the words, "A school administrator is an educational leader who promotes the success of all students . . ." Each of the standards addresses the knowledge, dispositions, and performances of working effectively with an ever-increasingly diverse student population.

Starratt (1996) said, "Especially in multicultural learning communities, youngsters will need to spend time becoming acquainted with the cultural traditions and perspectives of their classmates, and appreciating the unities that bridge the cultural differences among them" (p. 78). According to Starratt, in a school culture where self-efficacy is connected to teacher empowerment, individuals and groups "grow in confidence in order that they can solve their problems and achieve their goals" (p. 175). Starratt (1996) could foresee principals developing with staff such efficacy through diversity strategies aligned with problem solving, publicizing successes, praising initiatives, and providing support for teamed initiatives within each school's setting.

According to Jason (2000) when school leaders design or create "learning environments" within which dialogues seriously consider various points of view, it is more likely that such discussions will address the diverse needs of students. Jason goes on to say that this sort of dialogue will lead to more effective actions than simply basing decisions about students and the school on what appears right for the dominating cultural group.

In the foregoing, we reviewed literature on changing demographics and new leadership approach to diversity. However, one important question remains. Have new school leadership approaches and initiatives designed to address changing student demographic trends, minority/non-minority relationship issues, and school restructuring opened more doors for people of color and females to become public school principals? In this article, we studied the composition of the public school principalship between 1987–88 and 1999–2000.

The Moral Imperative to Have a Diverse Principalship

There has been a moral need to continue a race and gender conversation in America. The conversation requires movement from what we say we value in our democratic society toward specific actions. Employing qualified individuals of color and females in leadership roles as school principals is an action with a message, which states that we value and nurture diversity.

Sergiovanni (2001, p. 85) states that "acceptance of others and cooperation within differences are the universal values postmodernists claim are needed to guarantee feelings of belonging, trust, and safety that are essential to building community." The relationships formed between school leaders (principal and faculty), students, and parents are critical elements in not only addressing diversity issues in school, but concurrently serving as models for demographic changes taking place in the nation's communities. The school remains a place where students pursue their formal education, which includes opportunities to experience, understand, and learn to respect individual differences. This is an important consideration for school principals rethinking issues related to school diversity leadership and the restructuring of their school work places. Students attending our nation's schools today will influence as adults the future progress of our democratic way of life. We need to model for our students by having an environment that values and nurtures diversity. Employing females and people of color is one important step in establishing the inclusive environment.

As an example, the absence of attention to the unique problems of girls in one current diversity debate suggests that girls and boys have identical educational experiences in schools. According to Schmuck and Schmuck (1994, p. 22), high schools were originally designed by men for boys. They go on to say, "The research shows, for example, that girls' self esteem is more vulnerable to the impact of school experiences than is that of boys, and that it declines even more during high school than it does in the middle school" (Schmuck & Schmuck, 1994, p. 23). Students from rural, suburban, and urban settings must be continually encouraged to expand their mindsets about the richness of diversity and conflict they will encounter within themselves when their mental perspectives about race, gender, and other diversity issues are challenged. Fullen says, "Homogeneous cultures by definition have less diversity, but they are more boring" (Fullen, 1997, p. 32). Students, guided by school leaders (principals and teachers) whom the students identify with and trust, can effectively learn and develop behaviors and skills that are appropriate for managing conflict associated with differences found in their classmates. Upon graduation, these young people, with or without diversity leadership exposure, will be expected by society to have the knowledge and dispositions to work out new and productive ways to address diversity issues in their communities.

The "mental models" held by public school principals and staff in relation to the students they lead is a critical element in the progress on gender and racial issues students make in school. "A mental model is a device that each of us subconsciously builds in our minds over time" (Calabrese, 2002, p. 48). Senge (1990, p. 8) notes, "Mental models are deeply ingrained assumptions, generalizations . . . that influence how we understand the world and take actions." For example, a teacher notices a female high school principal dressed in a fashionable style and says to herself, "If I had her salary, I could dress the same way." Additionally, the teacher thinks that the principal's dress doesn't align with the socio-economic backgrounds of the students in the school. However, the mental model of a female student in the same school viewing the same principal may have a different perspective. The student says to herself, "When I become a successful adult, I want to dress and have a positive relationship with others just like my high school principal does." Two people observing the same person, but by viewing the principal from their own mental models, arrive at different generalizations. Possibly when placed in principal roles, females and people of color are viewed by the staff and the student body from a variety of different perspectives that have a positive lasting influence on their behaviors and attitudes toward diversity.

Mental models, which students hold about their own gender and race, become part of their own personal method for stereotyping others. Students bring their stereotypes and misconceptions about people unlike themselves to school each day. It becomes important to the student's growth and development that their misconceptions be challenged by the behaviors of school leaders they learn to trust. Trust that is displayed by the school principal provides students and faculty a safe environment to speak and take action on diversity issues. In a safe school environment, a student's mental model may be altered to the point where judgments and opinions of others are related less to an individual's skin color and gender, allowing for more attention to be placed on an individual's attitudes and actions.

School systems, in an effort to avoid legal disputes, have in place employment policies. The policies reflect laws related to non-discrimination and equal employment opportunities. Implementing the employment policies is generally a responsibility of people in the human resource department, the superintendent, and members of the school board. Aside from large, urban school systems, the major participants, or "gatekeepers," in the employment process holding key positions are frequently white males and females. Their sensitivity and courage to act in the hiring of people of color and females for school principalships are critical in making policies come alive.

In this chapter, using survey data collected from nationally representative samples of public school principals in 1987–88, 1993–94, and 1999–2000, we report the progress that has been made in diversifying the public school principalship. We display data on the variation of the progress in different kinds of schools. We also point out the areas that require our continuing efforts.

Method

The Data Source and the Sample

The current study was based on the data from Schools and Staffing Survey (SASS), the largest survey of K-12 education in the United States conducted by the National Center for Education Statistics in 1987–88, 1993–94, and 1999–2000. Among the components of the survey is a survey of public school principals. The return rates for all the surveys were above 90 percent, a rate that was very high for this kind of survey, indeed. The achieved sample sizes and weighted sample sizes for each of the three survey years were displayed in Table 2.1.

Sampling Weights and the Data Analysis Approach

NCES developed a set of sampling weights for each survey so that we can more accurately estimate the population based on the sample. Through the use of sampling weights, the results are generalizable to the state and/or the national levels. Since we have representative samples at the national and state levels for each of the three waves of SASS, the data constitute a kind of longitudinal analysis called "trend study." In other words, by having data from three rounds of surveys conducted in 1987–88, 1993–94, and 1999–2000, we are able to discuss the trend of a phenomenon—How has it been evolving? Has the situation gotten better or not? Throughout the article, descriptive statistics, adjusted by sampling weights, are used to depict the phenomenon of interest.

What We Have Found

The Overall Pattern of the Composition of the Public School Principalship in Terms of Gender, Race, and Ethnicity from 1987–88 to 1999–2000

Table 2.2 illustrates the overall trend of the composition of the public school principalship in terms of gender, race, and ethnicity. Where gender is concerned, the data indicate the percentage of female principals is almost doubled

TABLE 2.1. A Description of the Sample Size

	1987–88	1993–94	1999–2000
Actual Sample Size	8,519	9,098	8,524
Weighted Sample Size	77,890	79,618	82,802

TABLE 2.2. The Composition of the Public School Principalship in Terms of Gender, Race, and Ethnicity Between 1987–88 and 1999–2000

	1987–88	1993–94	1999–2000
Female	24.6	34.5	43.6
Male	75.4	65.5	56.4
American Indian or Alaska Native	1.1	0.8	0.8
Asian or Pacific Islander	0.6	0.9	0.8
African American	8.8	10.2	11.3
White	89.5	88.0	87.1
Hispanic	3.3	4.1	5.1
Non-Hispanic	96.7	95.9	94.9

between 1987–88 and 1999–2000. In 1987–88, 24.6 percent of the public school principals were female. The percentage increased to 34.5 in 1993–94, and 43.6 in 1999–2000. In Table 2.3 we disaggregate the data by elementary and secondary schools. The data indicate that it is much more likely to find female principals in elementary schools than in secondary schools. In 1999–2000, 51.7 percent of all public elementary school principals were female, while the corresponding statistics for the public secondary schools was 22.9. The data in Table 2.3 all indicate clearly that more and more principals were female at both the elementary and secondary levels. Therefore, we have made significant progress in terms of having females in the public school principalship. Teaching is a profession where females constitute a majority of the teaching force; to have more females become principals is movement in the right direction.

When race is concerned, the percentages of African Americans in the public school principalship increased from 8.8 in 1987–88, to 10.2 in 1993–94, and to 11.3 in 1999–2000, with a 2.5 percentage-point increase between 1987–88 and 1999–2000. Although it is encouraging to see that the percentage of African American principals has been increasing over a 12-year period, the increase is small. Correspondingly, the percentage of white public school principals has decreased slightly over the years, from 89.5 percent in 1987–88 to 87.1 percent in 1999–2000. Where ethnicity is concerned, the percentage of Hispanic principals has increased from 3.3 in 1987–88, to 4.1 in 1993–94, and to 5.1 in 1999–2000, with a 1.8 percentage-point increase over the 12-year period.

TABLE 2.3. Percentage of Public School Principals Who Were Female in 1987–88 and 1999–2000: A Comparison Between the Elementary and Secondary Levels

	1987–88	1999–2000
Elementary	30.1	51.7
Secondary	11.5	22.9

Overall the data indicate that the public school principalship has become more diversified in terms of gender, race, and ethnicity between 1987–88 and 1999–2000. However, the public school principalship has made more progress in gender diversity than in racial and ethnic diversity.

Variation in the Change of Composition of Public School Principalship between 1987–88 and 1999–2000

Tables 2.4 and 2.5 indicate the variation in the change of the composition of public school principalship between 1987–88 and 1999–2000. Where location is concerned, the general pattern is that there has been more progress in diversity in urban schools than in suburban and rural schools. The percentage-point increases for female principals between 1987–88 and 1999–2000 were 21.2 in urban schools, 17.7 in suburban schools, and 14.5 in rural schools. The percentage-point decreases for white principals were the greatest in urban schools (–5.7), but much less in suburban (–0.9) and rural (–1.5) public schools. A similar pattern holds where ethnicity is concerned. In other words, the percentage-point increases for Hispanic principals were 3.0 in urban schools, 2.2 in suburban schools, and 0.6 in rural schools.

Table 2.5 shows the variation in the change of composition of public school principalship in relation to the level of minority enrollment in schools. The data indicate that generally speaking the rate of change in diversity was greater for schools with higher levels of minority enrollment. For example, the overall percentage-point increase for female principals between 1987–88 and 1999–2000 was 19.0. The data indicate that the percentage-point increases ranged from 15.6 for schools where 0–4% of the enrollment were minority students to 19.7 for schools where 50% or more of the enrollment were minority students. Where race is concerned, there was actually an increase in the percentage of white principals in schools where 0–4% of the student were minority. As far as ethnicity is concerned, the greatest percentage increase occurred in schools where 50 percent or more of the students were minority.

TABLE 2.4. Percentage Changes in Composition of the Public School Principalship Between 1987 88 and 1999 2000 by School Location

		Location		
	Overall	Urban	Suburban	Rural
Female	19.0	21.2	17.7	14.5
White	-2.4	-5.7	-0.9	-1.5
Hispanic	1.8	3.0	2.2	0.6

TABLE 2.5. Percentage Changes in Composition of the Public School Principalship Between 1987–88 and 1999–2000 by Different Levels of Minority Enrollment in Schools

		% of Minority in Enrollment			
	Overall	0–4%	5–19%	20–49%	≥50%
Female	19.0	15.6	17.2	19.7	18.4
White	-2.4	0.6	-0.3	-0.3	-0.6
Hispanic	1.8	1.3	1.3	0.1	3.4

The Current Status of the Composition of the Public School Principalship: Perspectives from School Location and Student Composition

Tables 2.6 and 2.7 display the most current data we have on the status of the composition of the public school principalship. In Table 2.6, we can see that female, African American, and Hispanic principals were more likely to be found in urban schools. In the 1999–2000 school year, 56.5 percent of the urban principals were female while the corresponding statistics for suburban and rural schools were 45.1 and 31.7, respectively. The disparity in the distribution of African American principals is even more significant. Among urban principals, 26.1 percent were African American. The corresponding statistics were as low as 7.9 among suburban principals and 5.0 among the rural counterparts. The disparity in the distribution of Hispanic principals is also very significant. Among urban principals, 10 percent were identified as Hispanic. The corresponding statistics were 4.5 for suburban schools and 2.3 for rural schools.

Data in Table 2.7 indicate that in 1999–2000 the public school principalship was more diversified in schools where a high level of minority enrollment

TABLE 2.6. The Composition of the Public School Principalship by School Location in 1999–2000

		Location		
	Overall	Urban	Suburban	Rural
Female	43.6	56.5	45.1	31.7
Male	56.4	43.5	54.9	68.3
American Indian or Alaska Native	0.8	0.7	0.6	1.3
Asian or Pacific Islander	0.8	1.2	0.7	0.6
African American	11.3	26.1	7.9	5.0
White	87.1	72.0	90.9	93.1
Hispanic	5.1	10.0	4.5	2.3
Non-Hispanic	94.9	90.0	95.5	97.7

TABLE 2.7. The Composition of the Public School Principalship by Different Levels of Enrollment in Schools in 1999–2000

		Minority Enrollment in School			
	Overall	0–4%	5–19%	20–49%	≥50%
Female	43.6	32.6	39.9	46.3	55.3
Male	56.4	67.4	60.1	53.7	44.7
American Indian or Alaska Native	0.8	0.3	0.6	.9	1.4
Asian or Pacific Islander	0.8	0.0	0.0	.8	2.1
African American	11.3	0.3	2.6	7.9	31.8
White	87.1	99.4	96.7	90.4	64.7
Hispanic	5.1	0.4	2.5	3.1	13.5
Non-Hispanic	94.9	99.6	97.5	96.9	86.5

was found. For example, in schools where 50 percent or more students were minority, 55.3 percent of the principals were female, 31.8 percent African American, and 13.5 percent Hispanic. In contrast, in those schools where 0–4 percent of students were minority, only 32.6 percent of principals were female, 0.3 percent African American, and 0.4 Hispanic. The level of diversity in the public school principalship is very uneven when we view the data from the perspectives of urbanicity and minority enrollment levels of schools.

State Variation in the Diversity of Public School Principals

In Figures 2.1 and 2.2, we rank the states and the District of Columbia, based on the data collected in 1999–2000, in terms of the percentage of public school principals who were female and minority. It is clear that there was tremendous amount of variability across the state, and that the variability was much more in race than in gender. Where gender is concerned, in Pennsylvania 22.8 percent of the public school principals were female in 1999–2000, while the corresponding statistics were 57.9 in Florida and 62.9 in DC. As far as race is concerned, during the 1999–2000 school year less than 10 percent of the public school principals were minority in 28 states. During the 1999–2000 school year, the places where minority constituted more than 20 percent of the public school principalship included the following: Virginia (23.4), North Carolina (25.6), Alabama (26.3), South Carolina (26.5), Georgia (27.1), Louisiana (27.2), Maryland (37.4), Mississippi (41.2), Hawaii (79.6), and DC (97.0). Therefore, the data collected in 1999–2000 indicated, indeed, a significant amount of variation between states in the composition of the public school principalship in terms of gender and race. However, we should interpret the variation in a context that includes factors such as the racial composition of the work force and females' participation rate in the work force in the states.

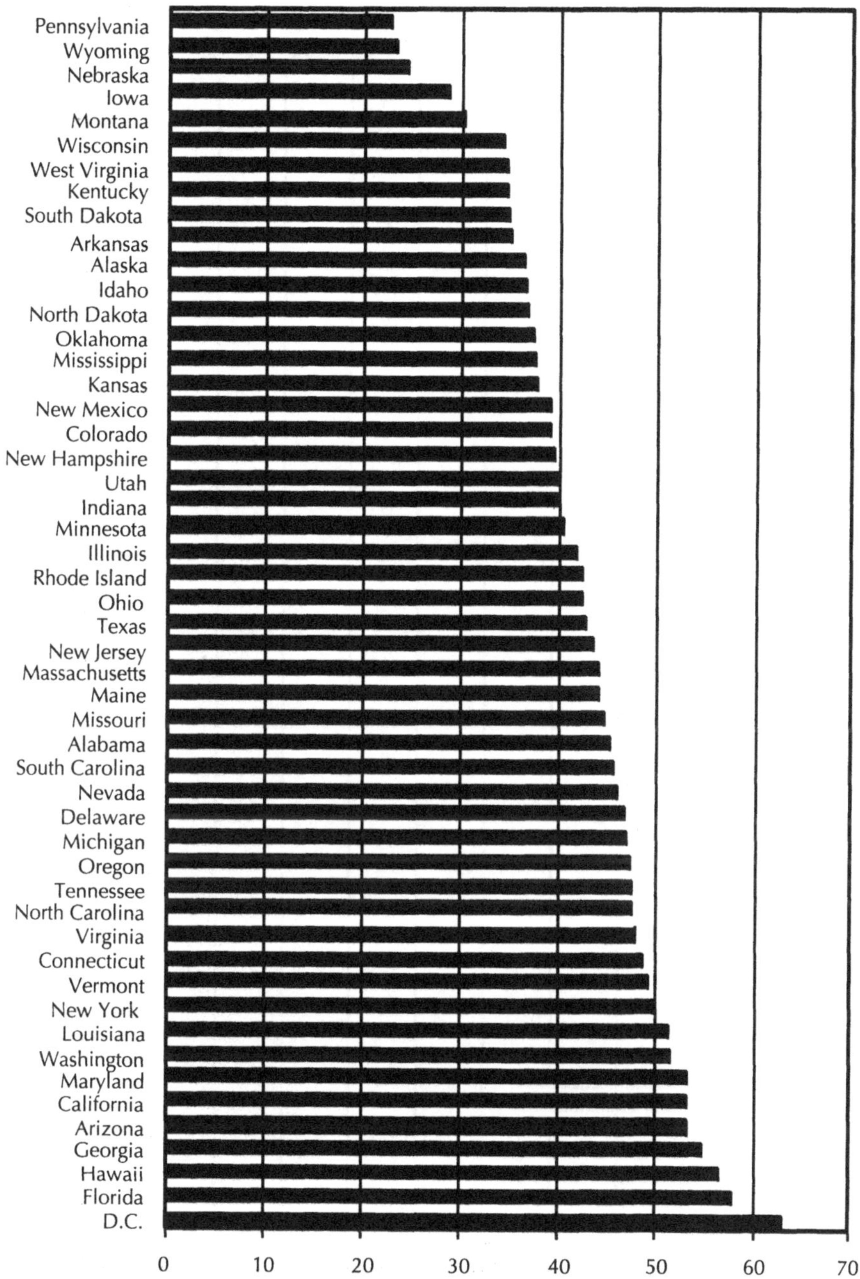

FIGURE 2.1. A State Rank of Percentage of Public School Principals Who Were Female

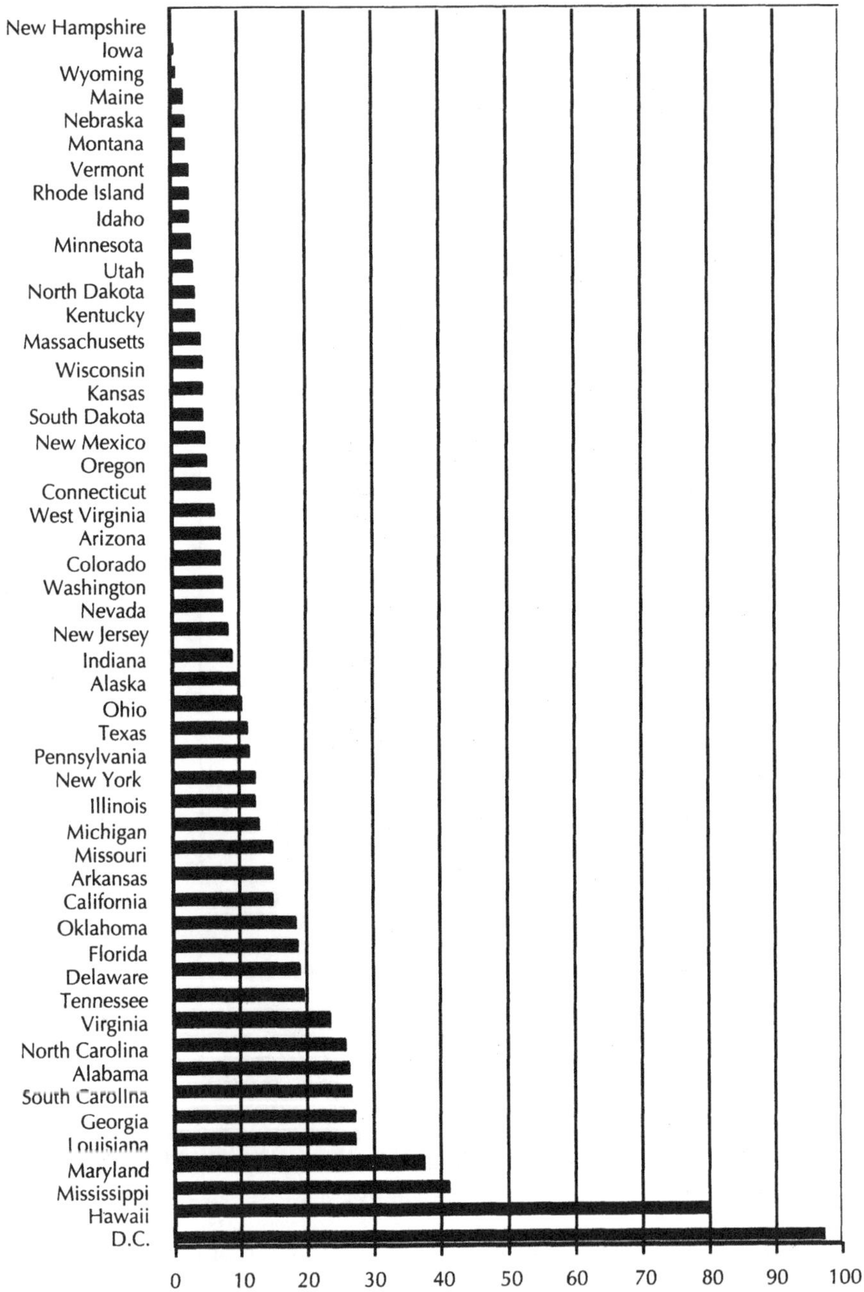

FIGURE 2.2. A State Rank of Percentage of Public School Principals Who Were Minority

Summary and Discussion

This article inquires into how the composition of the public school principalship has evolved between 1987–88 and 1999–2000, a period of 12 years. A few conclusions emerge from the data. First, overall there has been more diversity in the public school principalship in terms of gender, race, and ethnicity. Over a period of 12 years from 1987–88 to 1999–2000, the percentage of female principals increased from 24.6 percent to 43.6 percent. The same statistics for African American principals increased from 8.8 percent to 11.3 percent, and Hispanic principals from 3.3 percent to 5.1 percent. It is apparent that school systems have made more progress in appointing females than they have in addressing racial and ethnic diversification. In other words, the public school principalship as a group has made more progress in gender diversity than in racial and ethnic diversity.

Second, over the period of 12 years, we have made more progress in gender, racial, and ethnic diversification in urban schools. For example, as far as racial diversification was concerned, in urban schools the percentage of non-white principals increased by 5.7 points over the 12-year period; the corresponding statistics for suburban and rural schools were only 0.9 and 1.5 points, respectively. The pattern was the same when we consider gender and ethnic diversity. There has indeed been more progress in gender, racial, and ethnic diversity in urban schools than in suburban and rural schools.

Third, we have also found a significant amount of variation across the states and the District of Columbia in terms of the percentages of public school teachers who were female and minority in 1999–2000. The percentage of public school principals who were female ranged from 22.8 in Pennsylvania, to 57.9 in Florida and 62.9 in DC. The percentage of public school principals who were non-white varied from 0 in New Hampshire and 0.5 in Iowa to 41.2 in Mississippi, 79.6 in Hawaii, and 97.0 in DC. Although we should take into account the demographic characteristics and cultural factors when interpreting the variation, the amount of variability across the states was tremendous, indeed.

Despite the overall improvement of gender, racial, and ethnic diversification, we still have a long way to go in terms of employing public school principals and, thus reducing the disparity among schools located in different geographic areas in our nation, particularly in areas where levels of minority students are beginning and continuing to increase.

The following points may be useful for school leaders having the will to increase the representation of female and minority principals in today's public schools:

- There should be an increased awareness and a sense of urgency expressed by school officials in relation to the rapid demographic changes taking place in our nation's school-aged population and the much slower rate of change when hiring females and people of color to public school principalships.
- School officials should keep the race, gender, and ethnicity conversation at the forefront when identifying significant educational issues faced by our nation's school systems.
- School officials should reflect upon the importance of the relationship between school restructuring strategies and race, gender, and ethnic issues when taking action directed at appointing public school principals.
- School officials should challenge the "mental models" of others in the school system who influence the decision-making process in filling public school principalship positions.

As a final note, we have made some progress in diversifying the public school principalship. However, we still have a long way to go. As directions for further studies we should go beyond the demographic categories and inquire into the perspectives that female public school principals and public school principals of color bring into the workplace; we should also study the experience and perspectives of those new female and minority principals. The research and dialogue about gender, race, and ethnicity will not go away, but will continue well into the 21st century.

References

Bandura, A. (1997). *Self-efficacy: The exercise of control.* New York: W. H. Freeman and Company.

Banks, J. A. (1999). Multicultural education in the new century. *The School Administrator, 56*, 8–10.

Calabrese, R. L. (2002). *The leadership assignment.* Boston: Allyn & Bacon.

Combs, G. M. (2002). Meeting the leadership challenge of a diverse and pluralistic workplace: Implications of self-efficacy for diversity training. *Journal of Leadership Studies 8* (4), 1–16.

Council of Chief State School Officers. (1996, November). *Interstate school leaders licensure consortium: Standards for school leaders.* Washington, DC: Author.

Fullen, M. (1997). *What's worth fighting for in the principalship.* New York: Teachers College Press.

Green, R. L. (2001). *Practicing the art of leadership: A problem-based approach to implementing the ISLLC Standards.* Upper Saddle, NJ: Merrill Prentice-Hall.

Hodgkinson, H. (1996). *Bringing tomorrow into focus.* Washington, DC: Institute for Educational Leadership.

Jason, M. H. (2000, February/March). The role of the principal as transformational leader in a multicultural learning community. *The High School Journal 83* (3), 1–9.

Kouzes, J. M., & Posner, B. Z. (2002). *The leadership challenge* (3rd ed.). San Francisco: Jossey-Bass.

Madsen, J. A., & Mabokela, R. O. (2000, Winter). Organizational culture and its impact on African American teachers. *American Educational Research Journal 37* (4), 849–876.

Marshall, P. L. (1994). Four misconceptions about multicultural education that impede understanding. *Action in Teacher Education, 16* (3), 19–27.

McGee-Banks, C. A. (2000). Gender and race as factors in educational leadership and administration. *The Jossey-Bass reader on educational leadership*. San Francisco: Jossey-Bass.

Sather, S. E. (1999, Fall). Leading, lauding, and learning: Leadership in secondary schools serving diverse populations. *Journal of Negro Education 68* (4), 511–528.

Schmuck, P., & Schmuck, R. (1994). Gender equity: A critical democratic component of America's high schools. *NASSP Bulletin, 78* (558), 22–27.

Senge, P. M. (1990). *The fifth discipline: The art and practice of learning organizations.* New York: Currency-Doubleday.

Sergiovanni, T. J. (2001). *The principalship: A reflective practice perspective.* (4th ed.). Needham Heights, MA: Allyn & Bacon.

Smith, S. (1996). Leadership training for cultural diversity. *Multicultural Review, 5* (1), 33–38.

Starratt, R. J. (1996). *Transforming educational administration.* New York: The McGraw-Hill Companies, Inc.

Tirozzi, G. N. (2001, February). The artistry of leadership: The evolving role of the secondary school principal. *Phi Delta Kappan, 82* (6), 434–439.

Wheatley, M. J. (1999). *Leadership and the new science: Discovering order in a chaotic world.* San Francisco: Berrett-Koehler Publishers, Inc.

·3·

Liliana Rodriguez-Campos, Rigoberto Rincones-Gomez,

and Jianping Shen

PRINCIPALS' EDUCATIONAL ATTAINMENT, EXPERIENCE, AND PROFESSIONAL DEVELOPMENT

Introduction

Throughout the years principals have been facing new challenges, and in order to meet these challenges the principalship has been undergoing changes (Shen, Rodriguez, & Rincones, 2000). Sergiovanni (1999) argues that "the principal's greatest challenge and primary responsibility is to develop a caring community in the school, a place where strong character emerges from shared purpose that allows and encourages students to be successful learners" (p. 11). Furthermore, Haycock (1998) explains that effective principals are the ones who set direction, solve problems, and facilitate change.

Several authors have explained the role of principals as pivotal to school effectiveness (e.g., Edmonds, 1979; Hausman, Crow, & Sperry, 2000; Su, Adams, & Mininberg, 2000). One of the most consistent findings about principals is that "high-achieving schools have strong, competent leaders" (Jackson & Davis, 2000, p. 156). Although there are always individuals who seek principalship positions, some of them might not possess the necessary leadership skills. For this reason, the school communities that have the most competitive advantages are those who know how to hire and retain extraordinary leaders (Cooley & Shen, 1999). Therefore, in this chapter we report data from four waves of national surveys of elementary and secondary public school principals to investigate their (a) educational attainment, (b) work experience, and (c) professional development activities. The purpose of this chapter is to illustrate the trend of characteristics of elementary and secondary principals in the aforementioned three areas.

Literature Review

Principals serve a key role for their students, staff, and the community (Heckman, 1996; Wegenke, 2000). Because the analysis in this chapter is limited by the data of principals from the four waves conducted in 1987–88, 1990–91, 1993–94, and 1999–2000 school years, the following review focuses on three major characteristics of elementary and secondary principals: (a) educational attainment, (b) experience and instructional leadership, and (c) professional development.

Educational Attainment

Principals face situations that have been increasing in complexity throughout the years. According to Portin and Shen (1998) principals are acting more and more as decentralized decision makers, while at the same time complying with other managerial responsibilities. In addition, schools must hire principals who have the necessary skills to fulfill the high expectations that exist within educational institutions. For this reason, Shen, Rodriguez, and Rincones (2000) explain that principals are expected to continuously upgrade their educational skills because of the increasing challenges schools face.

Lauder (2000) suggests that successful principals possess a strong knowledge base and the skill to use that knowledge effectively in their schools. Through continuing education principals can help influence the school's success by encouraging a climate of renewal and innovation. According to Mosrie (1990), it is very important for principals to pursue further education in order to be successful in their places of work. Hence, it is apparent that principals set a model for the staff and students by having high educational attainment.

Experience and Instructional Leadership

Conventionally, the primary responsibility of principals is to manage the school operations, but lately instructional leadership has been added to the principal's responsibility (e.g., Crow, Matthews, & McCleary, 1996; Shen,

Rodriguez, & Rincones, 2000; Stronge, 1993). Individuals with rich and extensive experience in curriculum and instruction are more likely to be successful instructional leaders (Lauder, 2000). For example, in the United Kingdom principals are essentially head teachers. The average new secondary school head-teacher, in the United Kingdom, has taught for 20 years and has gone from classroom teacher to chair of a subject department, then to deputy head (vice principal), and finally to head (principal) (Weindling, 1990). Therefore, it is interesting to inquire into the positions held and the teaching experience before having the principalship.

Heck and Marcoulides (1992) indicate in their study that achievement outcomes in school performance could be predicted based on teachers' and principals' perceptions of instructional leadership. In order to be effective leaders principals must know the current instructional approaches used in the school, understand what effective approaches are, and engage the staff in continuously renewing the instructional approach. One of the most essential functions for principals is to turn followers into leaders and develop teachers into successful instructional leaders through understanding the nature of the educational processes (Hausman, Crow, & Sperry, 2000; Kirkpatrick, 2000; Parker & Day, 1997). Therefore, principals have a very important role in school improvement through behaviors that shape the instructional climate in the school (e.g., Cooley & Shen, 2000; Hallinger, 1992).

Several educational scholars have discussed extensively the role of the principal as an instructional leader, problem solver, and decision maker (Sergiovanni, 1991; Su, Adams, & Mininberg, 2000). Moreover, Parker and Day (1997) state that the principal as a leader serves multiple roles, including developing knowledge and skills, as well as facilitating effectiveness and change. Among other characteristics, the years of experience in teaching and the positions held before becoming a principal are important for successful principalship. Therefore, we inquire into elementary and secondary principals' experience and investigate whether there is a difference between experienced and novice principals in their experience prior to principalship.

Professional Development

Ash and Persall (2000) explain that effective professional development is a very important consideration when schools embark on collaborative decision-making. Also, Wegenke (2000) believes that principals have the need for ongoing professional development, because maintaining a positive school environment requires new knowledge and skills. Obviously, when principals improve their performance as a result of the new knowledge acquired through training, it has a positive effect on the school environment.

Su, Adams, and Mininberg (2000) state that in training for school principals, they would like to see a stronger connection between theory and practice, and training should have more fieldwork, using schools as the bases for experiments and for case studies. Also, several authors (Richardson & Prickett, 1994; Su, Adams, & Mininberg, 2000) explain that professional development for principals should focus more on real-life examples and systematic planning. For this reason, it is important for principals to participate in professional development activities, learning new skills and applying them to real work situations.

Another reason for principals to engage in continuing professional development is that through active participation, they set an example for others. As Daresh (1990) argues, through participating in professional training and other education opportunities, principals set a good model of life-long learning for teachers and students. In summary, professional development seems to be an effective way for elementary and secondary principals to gain new knowledge, develop new skills, and set an example of self-renewal.

Purpose of the Chapter

The purpose of this chapter is twofold. First, we describe the trend of characteristics of elementary and secondary public school principals by analyzing four waves of surveys conducted by the National Center for Education Statistics (NCES), which is a statistical branch of the U.S. Department of Education. Second, based on the trend of characteristics of elementary and secondary principals, we inquire into whether the expectations for elementary and secondary principals as reviewed in the foregoing are being materialized. The survey data collected by NCES offers an excellent opportunity for realizing the purpose of this chapter.

Method

The Data Source and the Sample

The current study was based on the data from Schools and Staffing Survey (SASS), the largest survey of K-12 education in the United States conducted by the NCES in 1987–88, 1990–91, 1993–94, and 1999–2000. Among the components of the survey is a survey of public school principals. The return rates for all the surveys were above 90 percent, a rate that was very high for this kind of survey, indeed. The achieved sample sizes and weighted sample sizes for each of the four survey years were as follows:

TABLE 3.1. Sample Size

	1987–88	1990–91	1993–94	1999–2000
Elementary Principals				
Achieved Sample Size	4,619	4,291	4,126	4,138
Weighted Sample Size	51,845	54,047	53,684	59,535
Secondary Principals				
Achieved Sample Size	3,555	4,491	4,391	4,386
Weighted Sample Size	22,743	22,732	21,009	23,267

Sampling Weights and the Data Analysis Approach

NCES developed a set of sampling weights for each survey so that we can more accurately estimate the population based on the sample. Through the use of sampling weights, the results are generalizable to the national level. Since we have representative samples at the national level for each of the four rounds of SASS, the data constitute a kind of longitudinal analysis called "trend study." In others words, by having data from four rounds of surveys we are able to discuss the trend of a phenomenon—How has it been evolving? Has the situation gotten better or not? Throughout this chapter, descriptive statistics, adjusted by sampling weights, are used to depict the phenomenon of interest.

Results

Educational Attainment

Data related to elementary and secondary school principals' highest educational attainment are displayed in Table 3.2. Responses indicate that elementary and secondary school principals are a very highly educated group. From 1987–88 to 1999–2000, 100 percent of elementary principals had bachelor's or associate's degrees. The percentage of elementary principals who had a master's degree rose from 96 percent in 1987–88 to 98 percent in 1990–91, 1993–94, and 1999–2000. Also, the percentage of elementary principals who had a doctorate increased from 8 percent in 1987–88 to 9 percent in 1990–91 and 1993–94, and then increased again to 10 percent in 1999–2000.

Results in Table 3.2 show that from 1987–88 to 1999–2000, 100 percent of secondary principals had bachelor's or associates degrees. In 1987–88, the percentage of secondary principals with a master's degree was 96 percent; in 1990–91 the corresponding percentage increased to 98 percent, and then to

TABLE 3.2. Public School Principals' Educational Attainment: A Comparison Across 1987–88, 1990–91, 1993–94, 1999–2000 (Percentage)

	1987–88	1990–91	1993–94	1999–2000
Elementary Principals				
Bachelor's or Associate's	100	100	100	100
Master's	96	98	98	98
Doctorate	8	9	9	10
Secondary Principals				
Bachelor's or Associate's	100	100	100	100
Master's	96	98	98	99
Doctorate	9	10	10	12

99 percent in 1999–2000. In addition, results show that the percentage of secondary principals with a doctorate rose from 9 percent in 1987–88 to 10 percent in 1990–91 to 12 percent in 1999–2000.

When we take the location into account, elementary principals in urban and suburban schools have higher educational attainment than their counterparts in rural schools (see Table 3.3). Specifically, 11 percent of the urban and suburban elementary principals hold a doctorate, followed by 6 percent of the rural elementary principals. Furthermore, secondary principals in urban schools have the highest educational attainment, followed by those in suburban, and then in rural schools. Specifically, 19 percent of the urban secondary principals hold a doctorate, followed by 13 percent of the suburban secondary principals, and 6 percent among the rural secondary principals. Hence, the data indicate that rural elementary and secondary principals are much less likely to have a doctorate than their counterparts in suburban and urban schools.

TABLE 3.3. Principals' Educational Attainment in 1999–2000: A Comparison Across Three Locations (Percentage)

	Urban	Suburban	Rural
Elementary Principals			
Bachelor's or Associate's	100	100	100
Master's	98	98	97
Doctorate	11	11	6
Secondary Principals			
Bachelor's or Associate's	100	100	100
Master's	99	99	98
Doctorate	19	13	6

Experience and Instructional Leadership

Throughout the last decade there has been research supporting and sustaining the idea that principals should be instructional leaders. Therefore, we inquire into two aspects that are related to instructional leadership. The first aspect is the positions held prior to the principalship, and the second is the years of teaching experience before the principalship. In order to be effective instructional leaders, we expect elementary and secondary principals to have rich instruction-related experience.

Positions Held Before Principalship. The data on school positions held before becoming an elementary principal are displayed in Table 3.4, from which a few interesting patterns emerge.

The first interesting pattern is that more and more elementary principals had experience in assistant principalship and program directorship, with an increase from 46 percent in 1987–88 to 65 percent in 1999–2000. This pattern seems to support the argument that the organizational structure and function of elementary schools have become more complex. Second, experience in curriculum and instruction is more and more important for becoming an elementary principal. Specifically, the data indicate that in 1987–88, only 22 percent of the elementary principals had been department heads or curriculum coordinators. The corresponding percentage increased to 32 percent in 1999–2000, resulting in an increase of 10 percentage points. Finally, the percentage for athletic coach increased slightly, from 22 percent in 1987–88 to 26 percent in 1999–2000, while the percentage for guidance counselor decreased slightly, from 8 percent in 1987–88 to 7 percent in 1999–2000.

TABLE 3.4. Positions Held Before Becoming a Public School Principal: A Comparison Across 1987–88, 1990–91, 1993–94, 1999–2000 (Percentage)

	1987–88	1990–91	1993–94	1999–2000
Elementary Principals				
Assistant Principal or Program Director	46	47	50	65
Athletic Coach	22	21	20	26
Department Head or Curriculum Coordinator	22	23	16	32
Guidance Counselor	8	7	6	7
Secondary Principals				
Assistant Principal or Program Director	57	59	63	71
Athletic Coach	48	47	46	54
Department Head or Curriculum Coordinator	30	29	30	48
Guidance Counselor	16	14	11	13

Data related to school positions held before becoming a secondary principal are displayed in Table 3.4. The patterns are similar to those for elementary principals. First, experience in curriculum and instruction became more and more important for becoming a secondary principal. Specifically, the data indicate that in 1987–88, only 30 percent of the secondary principals had been department heads or curriculum coordinators. The corresponding percentage increased to 48 percent in 1999–2000, resulting in an increase of 18 percentage points. As subject areas in schools have become more departmentalized, the need for secondary school specialists and departmental leaders has grown (Lester, 1997). Since more and more secondary principals had experience in being department heads or curriculum coordinators, it appears that the argument for instructional leadership is being translated into practice. The second interesting pattern is that more and more secondary principals had experience in assistant principalship and program directorship, with an increase from 57 percent in 1987–88 to 71 percent in 1999–2000. Finally, the percentage for athletic coach increased slightly, from 48 percent in 1987–88 to 54 percent in 1999–2000, while the percentage for guidance counselor decreased slightly, from 16 percent in 1987–88 to 13 percent in 1999–2000.

We also investigate whether there is a difference among urban, suburban, and rural principals in their experience. The data in Table 3.5 indicate that from urban to rural elementary principals, the percentages of those who had experience as (a) assistant principal or program director and (b) curriculum specialist or coordinator decreased, with suburban principals basically between urban and rural elementary principals. However, the data in Table 3.5 also indicate that from urban to rural elementary principals, the percentages

TABLE 3.5. Positions Held Before Becoming a Public School Principal: A Comparison Across Urban, Suburban, and Rural Schools in 1999–2000 (Percentage)

	Urban	Suburban	Rural
Elementary Principals			
Assistance Principal or Program Director	76	69	48
Department Head	29	34	32
Athletic Coach	16	25	38
Curriculum Specialist or Coordinator	33	28	18
Guidance Counselor	7	6	8
Secondary Principals			
Assistance Principal or Program Director	86	82	55
Department Head	52	46	48
Athletic Coach	36	52	64
Curriculum Specialist or Coordinator	26	21	16
Guidance Counselor	15	12	9

of those who had experience as (a) department head, and (d) guidance counselor increased, with suburban elementary principals basically between urban and rural elementary principals. Another interesting pattern in the data is that urban, suburban and rural elementary principals were most likely to hold positions as assistant principals or program directors. The corresponding percentages were 76, 69, and 48, respectively, among urban, suburban, and rural elementary principals.

Results in Table 3.5 show that from urban to rural secondary principals, the percentages of those who had experience in (a) assistant principal or program director, (b) department head, (c) curriculum specialist or coordinator, and (d) guidance counselor decreased, with suburban secondary principals basically between urban and rural secondary principals. This pattern might be related to the fact that rural schools tend to be smaller than their urban counterparts, and that there is less division of labor and, therefore, fewer kinds of positions in rural schools than in urban schools. Another interesting pattern in the data is that rural secondary principals were more likely to hold positions as athletic coach. Among rural principals, 64 percent of them had been athletic coaches. The corresponding percentages were 36 percent and 52 percent, respectively, among urban and suburban secondary principals. The data seem to indicate that there is some difference in career paths especially between urban and rural secondary principals.

We also compare the experience of new and experienced elementary and secondary principals. As shown in Table 3.6, new elementary principals were more likely to hold positions of assistant principal or program direc-

TABLE 3.6. Positions Held Before Becoming a Principal: A Comparison Between Those with (a) 4 or Fewer and (b) 15 or More Years of Principalship Experience by the 1999–2000 Survey (Percentage)

	4 or Fewer	15 or More
Elementary Principals		
Assistance Principal or Program Director	72	53
Department Head	24	28
Athletic Coach	37	23
Curriculum Specialist or Coordinator	30	18
Guidance Counselor	7	6
Secondary Principals		
Assistance Principal or Program Director	74	61
Department Head	54	54
Athletic Coach	52	39
Curriculum Specialist or Coordinator	22	17
Guidance Counselor	10	12

tor, athletic coach, and curriculum specialist or coordinator than their experienced counterparts. Obviously, the new elementary principals were more likely to have curricular and instructional experience before getting into principalship. The data also indicate that the assistant principal position had been increasingly used as a comprehensive training platform for future principals (Petzko et al., 2002). In the case of the position of guidance counselor, the percentage was very similar for new and experienced elementary principals.

The data in Table 3.6 also indicate that new secondary principals were more likely to hold positions of curriculum specialist or coordinator, among others. The trend seems to be consistent with the research of many scholars who have extensively discussed the role of the principal as an instructional leader (e.g., Hallinger, 1992; Heck & Marcoulides, 1992; Sergiovanni, 1991; Su, Adams, & Mininberg, 2000). More new secondary principals also held positions such as (a) assistant principal or program director and (b) athletic coach than their experienced counterparts did.

Teaching Experience Before the Principalship. As shown in Table 3.7, the average of total years of teaching experience for elementary and secondary principals remained stable between 1987–88 and 1999–2000. If we focus on the period from 1990–91 to 1999–2000, it appears that secondary principals had more teaching experience, a trend that is consistent with the advocacy of instructional leadership. Since it takes a long time for the population of principals to change its characteristics, we compare the new and experienced principals in their teaching experience to find out whether these two groups differ.

TABLE 3.7. Principals' Total Years of Teaching Experience: A Comparison Over a 12-Year Period

	Total Years of Teaching Experience			
	1987–88	1990–91	1993–94	1999–2000
Elementary Principals				
Mean	13	13	13	13
25th Percentile	7	7	7	7
50th Percentile	11	11	12	12
75th Percentile	18	17	17	17
Secondary Principals				
Mean	13	12	12	13
25th Percentile	7	6	7	7
50th Percentile	11	10	11	12
75th Percentile	18	16	16	17

TABLE 3.8. Public School Principals' Total Years of Teaching: A Comparison Between New and Experienced Principals in 1999–2000

	Total Years of Teaching Experience	
	New	Experienced
Elementary Principals		
Mean	15	11
25th Percentile	10	6
50th Percentile	15	9
75th Percentile	20	13
Secondary Principals		
Mean	15	11
25th Percentile	9	5
50th Percentile	14	8
75th Percentile	20	13

As shown in Table 3.8, when new and experienced elementary and secondary principals were compared, new elementary and secondary principals had, on average, 15 years of teaching experience. The corresponding statistics for experienced principals was 11 years of teaching experience. Therefore, new elementary and secondary principals had four more years of teaching experience than their experienced counterparts. This pattern was also true for the 25th, 50th, and 75th percentiles.

Given the fact that research evidence points to the importance for principals to be instructional leaders, it is encouraging to know that newly hired elementary and secondary principals have more teaching experience than their experienced counterparts. It is also encouraging to know that teaching experience seems to become an important criterion for hiring a new principal.

Professional Development

In addition to the formal schooling associated with academic degrees, Table 3.9 shows that more elementary principals participated in professional activities for aspiring school principals. The percentage of elementary principals who participated in this type of professional development activity increased from 37 percent in 1990–91, to 39 percent in 1993–94, and to 52 percent in 1999–2000. Furthermore, for the 1999–2000 school year, the percentage of principals who participated in these types of professional activities was 61 percent for the urban area, 53 percent for the suburban area, and 41 percent for the rural area. Hence, the percentage of participation was higher for principals in the urban area than those in the suburban and

TABLE 3.9. Percentage of Principals Who Participated in Programs or Activities for Aspiring School Principals

	1990–91	1993–94	1999–2000
Elementary Principals			
All	37	39	52
Urban	45	51	61
Suburban	42	44	53
Rural	30	30	41
Secondary Principals			
All	33	37	51
Urban	42	51	60
Suburban	41	40	55
Rural	28	32	44

rural areas. The patterns were similar at the secondary levels. In summary, at both the elementary and secondary levels, more and more principals participated in professional development activities for aspiring principals and the participation level was higher for urban principals than for suburban and rural ones.

Results in Table 3.10 show that essentially all elementary and secondary principals took part in professional development activities. Comparatively speaking, elementary and secondary principals in urban schools were more likely to participate in these activities than their counterparts in the suburban and rural areas. Also, elementary and secondary principals participated more in traditional professional development activities such as workshops, followed by professional association meetings, visiting to other schools, individual or collaborative research, and networking. However, fewer elementary and secondary principals participated in professional development activities that involved mentoring, peer observation and coaching for principals. Therefore, the data in Table 3.10 not only confirm elementary and secondary principals' active participation in professional development activities, but also point out the areas in which principals should have more professional development.

Discussion and Conclusion

The data presented in the results section indicate that the following expectations for elementary and secondary principals are met. First, the population of elementary and secondary principals is highly educated. As a matter of fact, in the 1999–2000 school year more than 98 percent of elementary and secondary

TABLE 3.10. Percentage of Principals Who Reported Participation in the Following Kinds of Professional Development During the 12 Months Before the Survey Conducted in 1999–2000

	All	Urban	Suburban	Rural
Elementary Principals				
Workshops or conferences related to your role as principal	96	97	95	95
Attending professional association meetings	82	82	83	82
Visits to other schools designed to improve your work as a principal	73	76	73	69
Individual/collaborative research on a topic of professional interest to you	73	75	74	68
Participating in a principal network	57	54	58	59
University course(s) related to your role as principal	40	41	38	42
Workshops of training in which you were the presenter	44	52	45	37
Mentoring and/or peer observation and coaching of principals	40	50	39	33
Secondary Principals				
Workshops or conferences related to your role as principal	97	98	97	97
Attending professional association meetings	86	86	84	87
Visits to other schools designed to improve your work as a principal	76	82	80	70
Individual/collaborative research on a topic of professional interest to you	69	70	72	64
Participating in a principal network	63	62	67	59
University course(s) related to your role as principal	42	41	40	44
Workshops of training in which you were the presenter	42	57	44	33
Mentoring and/or peer observation and coaching of principals	38	50	38	32

principals hold a master's or doctorate degree. In addition, elementary and secondary principals' educational attainment is higher in urban and suburban schools than in rural schools.

Second, the population of elementary and secondary principals has also become stronger in their teaching experience and instructional leadership. The data indicate that (a) overall more and more public school principals hold a position as a department head or curriculum coordinator, (b) new principals are more likely to have held positions of curriculum specialist or coordinator than their experienced counterparts, (c) between 1990–91 and 1999–2000, public school principals have slightly more years of experience in teaching, and (d) new principals have an average of four more years of teaching experience than their experienced counterparts. Stronger experience in curriculum- and instruction-related activities bodes well for instructional leadership.

Finally, elementary and secondary principals are active in participating in professional activities. More and more elementary and secondary principals take part in programs for aspiring principals. Elementary and secondary principals are also very active in traditional professional development activities. However, there is a need for more innovative professional activities, such as mentoring, peer observation, and coaching.

The results of this study reveal some interesting trends of the elementary and secondary principalship. Throughout the years, elementary and secondary principals have been active in attaining advanced academic degrees, have had more years of teaching experience and a stronger background in instructional leadership, and have been striving to enhance their professional skills and knowledge base while they engage in the principalship. This chapter presents data on the characteristics of elementary and secondary principalship that help us deepen our understanding of the trends of principalship. We can see how the elementary and secondary principalship changes over the years in response to the new challenges facing the school. The changing nature of the principalship as identified in this study warrants attention, because the role of the principal will continue to be central to the ongoing success of our schools (Carlin, 1992; Portin, 2000).

References

Ash, R. C. & Persall, J. M. (2000). The principal as chief learning officer: Developing teacher leaders. *NASSP Bulletin 84*(616), 15–22.

Carlin, P. M. (1992). The principal's role in urban school reform. *Education and Urban Society*, *25*(1), 45–56.

Clark, S. N., & Clark, D. C. (1992). School restructuring: A leadership challenge for middle level administrators. In S. Clark & D. Clark (Eds.), *Schools in the middle: A decade of growth and change* (pp. 200–207). Reston, VA: National Association of Secondary School Principals.

Cooley, V. & Shen, J. (1999). Who will lead? The top 10 factors that influence teachers moving into administration. *NASSP Bulletin*, *83* (606), 75–80.

Cooley, V. E., & Shen, J. (2000). Factors influencing applying for urban principalship. *Education and Urban Society*, *32*(4), 443–454.

Cross, C. T. & Rice, R. C. (2000). The role of the principal as instructional leader in a standards-driven system. *NASSP Bulletin*, *61*(620), 61–65.

Crow, G., Matthews, J., & McCleary, L. (1996). *Leadership: A relevant and realistic role for principals.* Princeton, NJ: Eye on Education.

Daresh, J. (1990). Formation: The missing ingredient in administrator preparation. *NASSP Bulletin*, 74 (526), 1–5.

Edmonds, R. (1979). Effective schools for the urban poor. *Educational Leadership, 37* (1), 15–24.

George, P. (2002). Barriers to access and success. *Principal Leadership, 9*, 23–29.

Hallinger, P. (1992). Changing norms of principal leadership in the United States. *Journal of Educational Administration, 30* (5), 35–48.

Hausman, C. S., Crow, G. M., & Sperry, D. J. (2000). Portrait of the "ideal principal": Context and self. *NASSP Bulletin, 84* (617), 5–14.

Haycock, K. (1998). Leadership by secondary school principals. *Teacher Librarian, 26* (2), 1–32.

Heck, R., & Marcoulides, G. (1992). Principal assessment: Conceptual problem, methodological problem, or both? *Peabody Journal of Education, 68* (1), 124–144.

Heckman, P. (1996). *The courage to change: Stories from successful school reform*. Thousand Oaks, CA: Corwin Press.

House, R. M. & Martin, P. H. (1998). Advocating for better futures for all students: a new vision for school counselors. *Education, 119*, 284–91.

Jackson, A. W. & Davis, G. A. (2000). *Turning points 2000: Educating adolescents in the 21st century*. New York: Teachers College Press.

Kirkpatrick, R. (2000). Recruiting and developing candidates for principal. *NASSP Bulletin, 84*(617), 38–43.

Lauder, A. (2000). The new look in principal preparation programs. *NASSP Bulletin, 84*(617), 23–28.

Lester, G. (1997). The secondary school assistant principal as education leader: The New York City experience. *NASSP Bulletin, 81*(588), 100–105.

Mosrie, D. (1990). An effective principal training and support system. *NASSP Bulletin, 74*(526), 12–15.

Norton, J. (2000). Important developments in middle-grades reform. *Phi Delta Kappan, 81*(10), k2-k4.

Parker, S. A. & Day, V. P. (1997). Promoting inclusion through instructional leadership: The roles of the secondary school principal. *NASSP Bulletin, 81*(587), 83–89.

Petzko, V. N., Clark, D. C., Valentine, J. W., Hackmann, D. G., Nori, J. R., & Lucas, S. E. (June 2002). Leaders and leadership in middle level schools. *NASSP Bulletin, 86*(631), 13–15.

Portin, B. (2000). The changing urban principalship. *Education and Urban Society, 32*(4), 492–505.

Portin, B. & Shen, J. (1998). The changing principalship and its impact: Voices from principals. *NASSP Bulletin, 82*(602), 1–8.

Richardson, M. D. & Prickett, R. L. (1994). Recognizing how adults learn: Implications for principals. *NASSP Bulletin, 78*(558), 85–89.

Sergiovanni, T. J. (1991). *The principalship*. Boston: Allyn & Bacon.

Sergiovanni, T. J. (1999). Refocusing leadership to build community. *The High School Magazine*, 7(1), 11–15.

Shen, J., Rodriguez-Campos, L., & Rincones-Gomez, R. (2000). Characteristics of urban principalship: A national trend study. *Education and Urban Society, 32*(4), 481–491.

Stone, C. B. & Clark, M. A. (2001). School counselors and principals: Partners in support of academic achievement. *NASSP Bulletin, 85*(624), 46–53.

Stronge, J. H. (1993). Defining the principalship; Instructional leader or middle manager. *NASSP Bulletin,* 77 (553), 1–7.

Su, Z., Adams, J. P., & Mininberg, E. (2000). Profiles and preparation of urban school principals. *Education and Urban Society, 32*(4), 455–489.

Van Horn, R. (1999). Inner-city schools: A multiple-variable discussion. *Phi Delta Kappan, 81*(4), 291–297.

Wegenke, G. (2000). Principal's role in school restructuring in the Des Moines public schools. *Education and Urban Society, 32*(4), 519–534.

Weindling, D. (1990). The secondary school headteacher: New principals in the United Kingdom. *NASSP Bulletin,* 74(526), 40–45.

.4.

Jianping Shen, Louann Bierlein Palmer, and Cheryle Crawford

THE IMPORTANCE OF EDUCATIONAL GOALS AS PERCEIVED BY PRINCIPALS

Introduction

In this chapter, we report how school principals' perspectives on various educational goals evolved between 1990–91 and 1999–2000, and whether there were consistent patterns of variation among subgroups of principals. The time frame of the 1990s is significant because of its correspondence with the reform efforts of Goals 2000: Educate America Act that was passed by Congress in 1994, and the establishment of systemic accountability measures at the state and local levels during the 1990s. As precursors to the current No Child Left Behind federal reform efforts (enacted in 2002), data on perceptional changes of principals during the reform efforts of the 1990s are still relevant today.

Data collected by National Center for Education Statistics from nationally representative samples of school principals in 1990–91, 1993–94, and 1999–2000 provided an assessment of how principals' perspectives on educational goals changed in the 1990s' context of educational reform. During three consecutive surveys administered in 1990–91, 1993–94, and 1999–2000, school principals were asked what, in their opinion, the three most important educational goals were. This chapter reports on key findings from these national databases.

The movement of standards and accountability has changed the principalship. Some researchers found principals perceived that new responsibilities are "layered" on top of the traditional ones (Portin & Shen, 1998; Portin, 2000). In addition to their traditional roles, principals are now expected to be instructional leaders, fund raisers, experts in public relations, and change agents, among others. One of the most important features of the current educational system is that schools are routinely compared on the basis of test scores.

Goodlad (1984, 1994) synthesized four major groups of educational goals: (a) academic goals, (b) vocational goals, (c) social, civic, and cultural goals, and (d) personal goals. With the current predominant emphasis on academic goals by policymakers, it is interesting to inquire into whether such academic goals have been perceived as more important by school principals, and whether the emphasis on academic goals is at the expense of other goals. The answers to these questions give us a perspective on the impact of the educational reform from an important angle—school principals' perceptions on the importance of various educational goals.

Literature Review

Throughout the history of education, the concept and importance of educational goals have been changing. In *The Republic*, the Greek philosopher Plato proposed a continuum of educational goals, with the academic goals at one extreme and vocational goals at the other. According to Plato the goals of education were to offer academic education to those whose souls were occupied by rationality and vocational education to those whose souls were dominated by appetite. Plato's educational goals, both academic and vocational, were in the interest of the state. Later on, the French philosopher Jean-Jacques Rousseau proposed, in *Emile*, the idea that the goals of education were to help the young develop freely and naturally. According to Rousseau, the educational goals were constructed along a continuum from the personal to social goals.

In the United States, the most important educational goal in the 18th and 19th centuries was academic, i.e., to provide the young with academic skills. However, the beginning of the 20th century witnessed the practice of combining academic goals with vocational goals. Since that point, there has been a tension between the academic and vocational goals of education and in some cases the educational goals were conceptualized as academic versus vocational (Shen, 1997). As to the social and personal goals of education, John Dewey (1916) believed that education could serve both social and personal goals and the two goals could exist harmoniously.

During a large-scale study entitled "The Study of Schooling," Goodlad and his colleagues analyzed documents from state departments of education, scholarly pieces, and commission reports in an attempt to arrive at a typology of educational goals. Goodlad and his colleagues first sorted out about 100 goals in the literature, and then condensed them to 10 goals within four major categories. Goodlad concluded that there was sufficient evidence to suggest that a significant national agreement, relative to goals for schooling, had been reached between oversight agents and the American public. The typology, which represents a minimum repetition and at about the same level of generality, is as follows (Goodlad, 1984, pp. 51–56):

A. Academic goals
   1. Mastery of basic skills and fundamental processes
   2. Intellectual development
B. Vocational goals
   3. Career and vocational education
C. Social, civic, and cultural goals
   4. Interpersonal understandings
   5. Citizenship participation
   6. Enculturation
   7. Moral and ethical character
D. Personal goals
   8. Emotional and physical well-being
   9. Creativity and aesthetic expression
   10. Self-realization

Goodlad maintained that various educational goals are usually kept in balance until a war breaks out, the economy takes a dive, or there is a sharp criticism of the current educational practice. Throughout history there is certainly a tendency for educational goals to swing between academic and vocational goals, as well as between social and personal goals (Cuban, 1990; Goodlad, 1994a).

Over the past five decades schools have attempted to implement John Dewey's model of education that advocates schools serve both social and personal goals, thus promoting balance and harmony between the individual and the society (Dewey, 1916). Contemporary developments in immigration patterns, urbanization, and global markets have had a profound impact on educational practice and process that attempt to implement Dewey's philosophical tenets. In the present context of expanding federal, state, and local expectations, schools are attempting to act as a panacea for the social problems plaguing today's children and youth—teenage pregnancy, drug abuse, juvenile crime, adolescent suicide, and a growing AIDS epidemic, to name a few.

The educational reforms in the last fifty years could be characterized as focusing, in turn, on national security, social equity, economic security, and academic excellence. Particularly, the decade of the 1990s witnessed a predominant emphasis on academic achievement, a phenomenon that is obvious at the federal level, at the state level, and in the research community.

First, Goals 2000 at the federal level is an example. In Goals 2000: Educate America Act, eight goals were developed to offer a framework for education reform and foster systemic changes that would promote equitable educational opportunities and high levels of educational achievement. The eight educational goals outlined to frame reform efforts included the following: (a) readiness for school, (b) high school completion, (c) student achievement and citizenship, (d) science and mathematics achievement, (e) adult literacy and lifelong learning, and (f) safe, disciplined, and drug-free schools, (g) teacher education and professional development, and (h) parental participation. Essentially, all these goals were directly or indirectly related to academic achievement. Although the specific wording of the goals prescribed within the "new" federal reform legislation of No Child Left Behind (which replaced Goals 2000 in 2002) is slightly different, the focus continues to be the achievement of high academic standards, with an added twist that this must occur for all children.

Second, at the state level, all states now have an accountability system that includes a set of state developed or prescribed student assessments for core subjects of the K-12 system. Within such accountability systems, school report cards are published, depicting among other things the pass/failure rates on such assessments. Increasingly "judgments" are made about schools based upon such data, with corrective actions being put in place for schools failing to meet certain standards. The pressure on raising the academic achievement level in each school is tremendous, indeed.

Finally, in the research community and the public opinion, the academic achievement of American students has been characterized as low. For example, based on the data from the National Assessment of Education Progress, researchers summarized the achievement of students in core subjects and concluded that most students attending K-12 public schools were developing minimal academic ability necessary for democratic citizenship, lifelong learning, and productive employment in America's economic system (Mullis, Owen, & Phillips, 1990). The conclusions from the Third International Math and Science Study (e.g., Schmidt, 1999, 2001) were similar. However, we should mention that although a majority of the literature on academic achievement has criticized the academic achievement in the U.S. K-12 system, some researchers, such as Berliner and Biddle (1995) argued from a different perspective, concluding that American K-12 students' academic achievement has been improving. Overall, however, most researchers conclude that today's generation has done better academically than their parents' generation, but such improvements are not good enough, especially given the large achievement gaps amongst various student subpopulations.

Emphasis on educational goals at the local level is often determined by a variety of imposed standards and competencies from federal and state governing entities. Therefore, given the predominant emphasis on academic goals, it is interesting to inquire into whether school principals' perceptions on the importance of various educational goals changed; and if so, how their perceptions evolved. Principals now take on more and more new responsibilities, but their traditional responsibilities stay the same. In the case of educational goals, it is interesting to investigate how school principals' relative emphasis on various educational goals changed. Generally speaking, the tendency to emphasize certain aspects of educational goals in practice as a result of various reform agendas frequently takes place at the expense of less emphasized goals (Shen, 1997). Drake and Roe (1999) address the dissonance that results from school leaders' efforts to determine whose goals to achieve, how their leadership resolves the conflict between opposing forces, and provides positive learning experiences for students in all areas of knowledge, value, and behavior.

The Focus of the Study

The focus of this chapter is that given the context of educational change, how have school principals perceived the importance of various educational goals during various times within the 1990s? Are there any patterns in the evolution of school principals' perceptions?

This chapter examines data from three waves of surveys of school principals conducted by National Center for Education Statistics in 1990–91, 1993–94, and 1999–2000, each of which had a nationally representative sample of principals. The respondents were asked to choose and then rank the three most important educational goals from the following list of eight educational goals: (a) building basic literacy skills (reading, math, writing, speaking), (b) encouraging academic excellence, (c) promoting personal growth (self-esteem, self-knowledge, etc), (d) promoting good work habits and self-discipline, (e) promoting occupational or vocational skills, (f) promoting human relations skills, (g) promoting specific moral values, and (h) promoting multi-cultural awareness or understanding.

TABLE 4.1. Sample Size

	1987–88	1990–91	1993–94	1999–00
Elementary Principals				
Achieved Sample Size	4,619	4,291	4,126	4,138
Weighted Sample Size	51,845	54,047	53,684	59,535
Secondary Principals				
Achieved Sample Size	3,555	4,491	4,391	4,386
Weighted Sample Size	22,743	22,732	21,009	23,267

Method

The Data Source and the Sample

The current study was based on data from the Schools and Staffing Survey (SASS), the largest survey of K-12 education in the United States conducted periodically by the National Center for Education Statistics. Data for this study were drawn from that collected in 1990–91, 1993–94, and 1999–2000. Among the components of the larger study was a survey of public school principals. In addition to reviewing the results from all school principals as a whole, we reconstructed a sub-sample of secondary principals who were those working in public schools that were "secondary" or "combined elementary and secondary," as well as a subsection of those just working in public schools that were "elementary."

The return rates for all the surveys were above 90 percent, a rate that was very high for this kind of survey, indeed. The achieved sample sizes and weighted sample sizes for each of the four survey years were as shown in Table 4.1.

Sampling Weights and the Data Analysis Approach

NCES developed a set of sampling weights for each survey so that we can more accurately estimate the population based on the sample. Through the use of sampling weights, the results are generalizable to the state and/or the nation levels. Since we have representative samples at the national and state levels for each round of SASS, the data constitute a kind of longitudinal analysis called "trend study." In other words, by having data from three rounds of surveys conducted during the decade of the 1990s (i.e., 1990–91, 1993–94, and 1999–2000), we are able to discuss the trend of a phenomenon—How has it been evolving? Has the situation gotten better or not? Throughout the chapter, descriptive statistics, adjusted by sampling weights, are used to depict the phenomenon of interest.

Results

The Most Important Goal as Rated by School Principals in 1990–91, 1993–94, and 1999–2000

The data in Table 4.2 is a longitudinal perspective on what school principals perceived to be the most important educational goals. The data clearly indicate that academic-related goals (i.e., building basic literacy skills; encouraging academic excellence) had been the most important. If we combine the percentages for "building basic literacy skills" and "encouraging academic excellence," the percentage of all school principals who rated these academic goals as the most important was 73 in 1990–1991, 77 in 1993–1994, and 85 in 1999–2000. The data indicate that these goals were the most important overall during 1990–1991, with the percentages increasing even higher in 1999–2000.

Another noticeable change over time occurred in the level of emphasis school principals placed on "promoting personal growth." In the 1990–1991 survey, 17 percent of all school principals agreed that this was the most important goal. The corresponding statistics dropped to 11 percent in 1993–1994, and to only 4 percent in 1999–2000. This decreased emphasis on "promoting personal growth," points to a swing away from the personal goal of education (e.g., creating self esteem and self knowledge), toward an emphasis on academic-related goals.

Table 4.2 also depicts the data as broken down by elementary and secondary school principals. For both groups, there is a clear growth in combined academic-related goals of "basic literacy" and "academic excellence" goals. For elementary principals, the percentages increased from 74% in 1990–1991, to 88% in 1999–2000; and for secondary principals, they increased from 73% in 1990–1991, to 80% in 1999–2000. There is also a common decline in the importance of the "promoting personal growth" goal: for elementary principals, from 18% in 1990–1991, to 4% in 1999–2000, and for secondary principals, from 14% in 1990–1991, to 5% in 1999–2000. These findings are similar to that found across all principals as well.

Some interesting differences, however, lie in that at the elementary level the principals consistently rated the "building basic literacy skills" goal as the most important at a much higher level (63% in 1999–2000), than that of "encouraging academic excellence" (25% in 1999–2000). At the same time, the secondary principals decreased their focus somewhat on "basic literacy" skills (from 46% in 1990–1991, to 42% in 1999–2000), but increased their focus on "academic excellence" (from 27% in 1990–1991, to 38% in 1999–2000).

TABLE 4.2. Percentage of School Principals Who Rated the Goals as the Most Important: A Comparison Across Three Surveys

	Elementary			Secondary			All		
Goals	1990–91	1993–94	1999–2000	1990–91	1993–94	1999–2000	1990–91	1993–94	1999–2000
Building basic literacy skills (reading, math, writing, speaking)	53	52	63	46	41	42	50	48	57
Encouraging academic excellence	21	26	25	27	33	38	23	29	28
Promoting personal growth (self-esteem, self-knowledge, etc.)	18	12	4	14	10	5	17	11	4
Promoting good work habits and self-discipline	6	7	5	8	10	9	7	7	6
Promoting occupational or vocational skills	0	0	0	2	3	2	1	1	1
Promoting human relations skills	1	2	2	1	2	2	1	2	2
Promoting specific moral values	1	1	1	1	1	1	1	1	1
Promoting multicultural awareness or understanding	0	0	0	0	1	0	0	0	0
Total	100	100	100	100	100	100	100	100	100

Overall, the data on school principals' perceptions on the most important goals indicated that academic-related goals were important at the beginning of the 1990s, and they became even more important by 1999–2000. At the same time, the emphasis on the personal goals such as creating self-esteem diminished. Given the fact that testing has been used as the main vehicle for accountability measures and that public opinion continues to link education with productivity and economic development (i.e., focusing on the social purpose of education), the findings seem to come as no surprise.

The Three Most Important Goals as Rated by School Principals in 1990–91, 1993–94, and 1999–2000

Admittedly, the data presented in Table 4.2 were slightly arbitrary in the sense that we only reported school principals' perceptions on the most important educational goal. However, some principals might feel that the secondary or third most important goals were similarly important in comparison to the first most important. Therefore, Table 4.3 presents data on those who identified certain goals as the first, second, or third most important.

Some patterns in Table 4.3 were similar to those in Table 4.2. Again, as to the academic-related goals of "building basic literacy skills" and "encouraging academic excellence," the data indicated that these were among the most important throughout the decade. In addition, the data indicate that the goal of "promoting good work habits and self-discipline" was frequently in the top three rated goals, with its importance increasing a bit over time (from 58% in 1990–1991, to 60% in 1999–2000). Another pattern similar to that in Table 4.2 was that the percentage of all principals rating "promoting personal growth" among the three most important declined steadily over the years, from 63% in 1990–1991, to 59% in 1993–1994, to 32% in 1999–2000.

However, the data in Table 4.3 also illustrated some new and interesting patterns. First, "promoting good work habits and self-discipline" was the third most important goal after "building basic literacy skills" and "encouraging academic excellence," and its importance essentially remained steady over the years. Second, across the three surveys, increasing percentages of school principals emphasized "promoting human relations skills" (going from 18% in 1990–1991, to 25% in 1999–2000), and "promoting multi-cultural awareness or understanding" (going from 7% in 1990–1991, to 11% in 1999–2000). The trend is encouraging given the increasing diversity of the population in our country, in general, and in the school community, in particular. Third, the percentages for most of the educational goals increased over the years. This pattern indicated that principals now have a more diversified profile of job responsibilities and that principals were able to emphasize other educational

TABLE 4.3. Percentage of School Principals Who Rated the Goals as One of the Three Most Important: A Comparison Across Three Surveys

Goals	Elementary			Secondary			All		
	1990–91	1993–94	1999–2000	1990–91	1993–94	1999–2000	1990–91	1993–94	1999–2000
Building basic literacy skills (reading, math, writing, speaking)	78	75	85	72	64	69	76	72	80
Encouraging academic excellence	59	62	69	63	65	72	60	63	70
Promoting good work habits and self-discipline	58	59	60	55	56	59	58	58	60
Promoting personal growth (self-esteem, self-knowledge, etc)	66	53	33	58	44	30	63	50	32
Promoting human relations skills	19	25	26	16	23	24	18	24	25
Promoting occupational or vocational skills	7	9	7	25	32	28	13	15	13
Promoting multicultural awareness or understanding	8	12	12	6	10	10	7	11	11
Promoting specific moral values	5	6	9	6	7	9	6	6	9

goals (except for "promoting personal growth"), although they were pressured to prioritize the academic goal. The data seemed to suggest that school principals not only responded to the accountability measures related to raising academic achievement, but also paid more attention to other educational goals such as "promoting human relation skills" and "promoting multi-cultural awareness or understanding."

Table 4.3 also presents data as broken down by elementary and secondary principals. There are no distinct differences between the two groups in reference to the various trends already mentioned. The only exception is while both groups showed in increase in the importance of the two academic-related goals, secondary principals reported a slight decrease in the importance of "building basic literacy skills" (going from 72% in 1990–1991, to 69% in 1999–2000), while there was a large increase in the importance of the goal "encouraging academic excellence" (going from 63% in 1990–1991, to 72% in 1999–2000). The percentages for elementary principals for both these goals increased over time.

A Comparison Across Urban, Suburban, and Rural School Principals as to Their Perceptions in 1999–2000

Table 4.4 displays data related to urban, suburban, and rural school principals' perceptions of the three most important educational goals in 1999–2000. A few patterns were embedded in the data. The similarity among urban, suburban, and rural principals was that all three sub-groups of principals emphasized academic-related goals more than those found in vocational, social or personal categories. However, there were also a few differences. The first difference was that a slightly higher percentage of urban principals (86 percent) rated "encouraging academic excellence" among the three most important

TABLE 4.4. Percentage of School Principals Who Rated the Goals as the Three Most Important in 1999–2000: A Comparison Across Urban, Suburban, and Rural Principals

Goals	Urban	Suburban	Rural
Building basic literacy skills (reading, math, writing, speaking)	86	78	80
Encouraging academic excellence	71	71	67
Promoting good work habits and self-discipline	55	57	67
Promoting personal growth (self-esteem, self-knowledge, etc)	30	34	32
Promoting human relations skills	21	29	23
Promoting occupational or vocational skills	10	11	17
Promoting multi-cultural awareness or understanding	17	12	6
Promoting specific moral values	9	9	8

goals when compared with their counterparts in suburban (78 percent) and rural schools (80 percent). Many states have developed accountability systems that primarily focus on test scores in the core subjects. Under this kind of policy environment, urban principals have been predominantly pressured to raise academic achievement. It comes as no surprise that higher percentages of urban principals rated "encouraging academic excellence" among the three most important goals than their counterparts elsewhere.

The second difference was that a higher percentage of rural school principals (67 percent) emphasized the goal of "promoting good work habits and self-discipline," when compared with their counterparts in suburban and urban school districts (57 percent and 55 percent, respectively). A higher percentage of rural principals also emphasized "promoting occupational or vocational skills" (17 percent), than their suburban (11 percent) and urban (10 percent) counterparts. Rural principals seemed to value more of these traditional values.

The final difference was that rural principals emphasized "promoting multi-cultural awareness or understanding" much less than their urban and suburban counterparts. Only eight percent of the rural principals rated "promoting multi-cultural awareness or understanding" among the three most important goals, while the corresponding percentages for urban and suburban principals were 17 and 12, respectively. Due to the population composition, the issue of multicultural awareness and understanding appears to be more important in urban and suburban areas than in rural areas.

A Comparison Across School Principals of Different Age Groups as to Their Perceptions in 1999–2000

We investigated the possible variation among principals of different age groups as to their perceptions on the three most important goals. The related data were displayed in Table 4.5. In comparisons across different age groups, the academic goals "encouraging academic excellence" and "building basic literacy skills" had the highest level of emphasis among all age groups. All subgroups of school principals emphasized these academic-related goals more than vocational, social or personal goals.

There were, however, some noticeable differences between the 35-years-old-or-less group and others. A lower percentage of the 35-years-old-or-less group identified "encouraging academic excellence" (64 percent compared to 71, 69, and 73 percents for the other age groups) and "promoting multi-cultural awareness" (7 percent, compared to 12, 11, and 12 percents for the other age groups) as one of their top three goals. At the same time, a higher percentage of this same group identified "promoting personal growth" (42 percent, compared to 30, 32, and 33 percents for the other age groups). This

TABLE 4.5. Percentage of School Principals Who Rated the Goals as the Three Most Important in 1999–2000: A Comparison Across Different Age Groups

Goals	≤35	36–45	46–55	≥56
Building basic literacy skills (reading, math, writing, speaking)	78	80	80	81
Encouraging academic excellence	64	71	69	73
Promoting good work habits and self-discipline	63	61	60	58
Promoting personal growth (self-esteem, self-knowledge, etc)	42	30	32	33
Promoting human relations skills	25	26	26	21
Promoting occupational or vocational skills	12	12	13	15
Promoting multi-cultural awareness or understanding	7	12	11	12
Promoting specific moral values	10	10	9	7

can be interpreted to mean that the 35-years-old-or-less group was more liberal because they were more likely to emphasize "promoting personal growth," but at the same time this youngest group seemed to be more conservative because they were less likely to emphasize "promoting multi-cultural awareness or understanding." It will be interesting to follow up on the youngest groups of principals to investigate whether their perceptions change as their experience in principalship accumulates.

Summary and Discussion

In this chapter, we reported data related to school principals' perceptions on the importance of eight educational goals during the decade of the 1990s. The data pointed to the following major findings. First, the academic-related goals, which include "building basic literacy skills" and "encouraging academic excellence," were the most important goals perceived by the school principals as a whole group, as well as by its subgroups. The importance of the academic goals was predominant in comparison to other goals. Furthermore, the overall importance of these academic goals was ever increasing. The link between the evolution of school principals' perceptions and the policy environment is evident. In recent years, most states have developed comprehensive accountability systems, with test scores being a key element within these systems. It therefore comes as no surprise that school principals emphasized academic goals as their top priorities, and that this has increased over the years.

Second, although academic goals received a predominant amount of attention, between 1990–1991 and 1999–2000 a higher percentage of principals, as data in Table 4.3 suggest, also paid more and more attention to other educational goals (except for promoting personal growth). The findings seem to be consistent with conclusions that principals' job responsibilities are diversified and "layered" one on top of the other (Portin & Shen, 1998; Portin, 2000). Although principals' emphasis on the academic goal was predominant, their emphasis on other goals (except for promoting personal growth) also increased due to pressures from other interest groups. The finding that school principals emphasized "promoting personal growth" less and less, suggests the pendulum of the current educational environment has swung far away from personal goals (such as self-esteem building), and toward the academic goals. As Cuban (1990) points out, history is replete with extreme swings. If the history of education offers any guidance, personal goals may well be the focus for the next wave of educational reform. The professional community of education should resist the notion of educational "re-form" which tends to go from one extreme to the other. Rather, we should promote Goodlad's (1987, 1994b, 2004) notion of educational renewal which views change as an inherent, conscious, and daily process that focuses on the betterment of education.

Third, when we compare urban, suburban, and rural school principals, the data seem to indicate that urban principals emphasized the academic excellence goal and the goal of multicultural education more than their counterparts in suburban and rural schools. The urban principals' emphasis may be related to the fact that urban schools are under more attacks for low academic achievement and that urban schools are more diverse environments. However, rural principals emphasized the following goals—"promoting good work habits and self-discipline" and "promoting occupational or vocational skills"—more than their counterparts in urban and suburban schools. It appears that there is some difference among urban, suburban, and rural principals in their perceptions that are related to the characteristics of their work settings.

Finally, when we compare school principals of various age groups, in addition to their common emphasis on the academic goal, the data point to a surprising finding in terms of difference. It is interesting to note the 35-years-old-or-less group was more liberal because they were more likely to emphasize "promoting personal growth" than other older groups. However, at the same time the youngest group seemed to be more conservative because they were less likely to focus on "promoting multi-cultural awareness or understanding." This youngest group represents the future of the principalship. It is important and interesting to further study whether and, if so, how, the perceptions of this group changes in the future.

Principals play an important role in the success of our schools. They function as an interface between factors outside and inside of the schools. They synthesize the input from various levels and segments of the society. Therefore, their perceptions act as a barometer for the educational environment. The data in this chapter indicate that their work is, indeed, influenced by the input from various levels and segments of the society and they are responding to the demand. The data also reveal some concerns such as the swing away from the personal goals of education and some conservative opinions among the youngest school principals.

References

Berliner, D.C., & Biddle, B.J. (1995). *The manufactured crisis: Myths, fraud, and the attack on America's public schools*. Reading, MA: Addison-Wesley.

Cuban, L. (1990). Reforming again, again, and again. *Educational Researcher, 19*, 3–13.

Dewey, J. (1916). *Democracy and education*. New York: Macmillan.

Drake, T. L. & Roe, W. H. (1999). *The principalship*. Upper Saddle River, NJ: Merrill

Goodlad, J. I. (1984). *A place called school*. New York: McGraw-Hill.

Goodlad, J. I. (1994a). *What schools are for*. Bloomington: Phi Delta Kappa Educational Foundation.

Goodlad, J. I. (1994b). *Educational renewal: Better teachers, better schools*. San Francisco: Jossey-Bass.

Goodlad, J. I. (1997). *In praise of education*. New York: Teachers College Press.

Goodlad, J. I. (Ed.) (1987). *The ecology of school renewal*. Chicago: National Society for the Study of Education.

Goodlad, J. I. (2004). *Romance with schools*. New York: McGraw-Hill.

Mullis, I. V. S., Owen, E. H., and Phillips, G. W. (1990). *Accelerating academic achievement: A summary of findings from 20 years of NAEP*. Princeton, NJ: Educational Testing Service.

Portin, B. & Shen, J. (1998). The changing principalship and its impact: Voices from principals. *NASSP Bulletin, 82* (602), 1–8.

Portin, B. (2000). The changing urban principalship. *Education and Urban Society, 32*(4), 492–505.

Schmidt, W. H. (1999). *Facing the consequences: Using TIMSS for a closer look at U.S. mathematics and science education*. Dordrecht: Kluwer Academic Publishers.

Schmidt, W. H. (2001). *Why schools matter: A cross-national comparison of curriculum and learning*. San Francisco, CA: Jossey-Bass.

Shen, J. (1997). Structure of the theoretical concept of educational goals: A test of factorial validity. *The Journal of Experimental Education, 65* (4), 342–352.

·5·

Van E. Cooley and Jianping Shen

SCHOOL ACCOUNTABILITY AND PRINCIPALS' PROFESSIONAL JOB RESPONSIBILITIES

Introduction

The difficult and seemingly overwhelming responsibilities of principals continue to escalate amidst calls for increased accountability by local school boards, states, and national officials. Principals find themselves in the "eye of the storm" as a society conditioned by instant gratification expects immediate results to the latest reform (Copland, 2001; Donaldson, 2002; Taylor & Williams, 2001). This places the principal in a precarious position motivated by stakeholders' expectations to produce positive outcomes without regard to process, bureaucratic factors, or taking the right approach (Sergiovanni, 2001). The question of whether schools are equipped to address the girth of expectations is unclear (Drake & Roe, 1999). School culture is complicated by the academic and social skills that students bring to school. The social system outside of school has a major influence on the principal's role (Drake & Roe, 1999). Eisner (2002) stated that principals should spend a third of the time in the classroom and concurrently work to develop teacher leaders. Few principals have the time to spend a significant amount of time in classrooms or communicating with students about academic work. The current structure of schools may not be the best framework to promote rigorous, high academic standards (Elmore, 2000).

Dr. Lana Seivers (Seivers, L. C., personal communication, February 7, 2003), a former principal, superintendent and the current Tennessee State Commissioner of Education, stated that "Standards are here to stay and district leaders must re-examine the role of principals and teachers in the educational process. In some cases this will mean distributing responsibilities between district and community stakeholders." Seivers' perspective suggests that a change in structure must precede substantive change. Fullan (2002) believes that district policies and the school culture should be transformed to allow teachers and administrators to better serve students and increase student learning. These new organizational structures, according to Fullan, will increase organizational capacity and possibly allow principals to realistically assume the role of instructional leader.

States continue to adopt alternative methods to assess student progress. For example, Florida and Colorado now focus on what students need to learn over several elementary grades (Lueker, 2000). Although these new approaches are promising, the tide of accountability continues to rise.

The Rising Tide of Accountability

The concept of accountability has long been a hallmark of education. Historically, principal accountability involved a more general approach of doing a job well, maintaining strong teacher relationships, assuming the role of instructional leader and exhibiting sound budgeting practices (Lashman, 2000). The emphasis has shifted from accountability for how money and other resources are used to accountability for outcomes or student achievement (Elmore, Abelman, & Fuhrman, 1996). Olson (1999) reported that 48 states tested students, 36 issued report cards, and 16 states had the authority to take over failing schools. Policymakers currently mandate accountability through processes that involve student achievement targets, assessment standards, and dissemination and wide publication of test results to the media (Popham, 2001). Consequences for failing to meet targets affect student graduation from high school, teacher bonuses, district funding, and retention of principals in their positions (Bonstingl, 2001). All of these consequences place increasing pressure on principals to collaborate with teachers to insure that learning goals are linked to instructional strategies. These complex roles and the perception that schools continue to decline have resulted in a call for more effective principal leadership to address the additional accountability placed on local school districts (Christie, 2000; Portin & Shen, 1998; Portin, Shen, & Williams, 1998). This presents a dilemma for school principals who must now find timely remedies for student achievement levels which were nurtured and sustained through the students' early years in elementary and middle or junior high school. The emphasis on accountability has resulted in additional pressures and recommendations for new principals' roles (Brewer, 2001; King, 2002; Tirozzi, 2001).

Popham (2001) stressed that the emphasis on testing has resulted in curricular reductionism, and Kohn (2001) characterized schools as testing centers. Teachers under pressure from school boards and administrators now focus on what is tested. Art, music and other courses not tested have, on occasion, been removed from the curriculum. Principals, in some instances, have modified existing programs to raise test scores. Daggett (2002) indicated that teachers and administrators expressed anger and frustration resulting from pressure to teach a narrow set of skills for short-term gains in lieu of concepts that students needed to learn for long-term success. He further suggested that high-stakes testing impacted job security for teachers and administrators.

Others have called for a more diverse system for appraising accountability. Sergiovanni (2000) recommend the use of multiple measures that include state and local standards. Student portfolios and student products have also been used to assess student learning (Madaus & O'Dwyer, 1999).

The Reality of the Current Principalship

The role of the principal in this reform era continues to demand more than is reasonably possible. Echoes for instructional leadership continue with most principals unable to spend a significant amount of time in the classroom due to the daily demands of the position (Supovitz, 2000). The average workweek for principals is 62 hours with less than one-third of the time spent on curriculum and instructional activities (Schiff, 2002). The frustrations of the principal are thus captured:

> With the move toward the self-management of schools, the principal appears to have the worst of both worlds. The old world is still around with expectations to run a smooth school, and to be responsive to all; simultaneously the new world rains down on schools with disconnected demands, expecting that at the end of the day the school should be constantly showing better test results, and ideally become a learning organization. (Fullan, 2001, pp. 138–139)

Copland asserted that the role of the principal has become more complex since the 1980s. Increased responsibilities and the awareness of the demands of the position have in turn contributed to a principal shortage (Ediger, 2001). The shortage of aspiring principals is complicated by demographics, the ongoing proliferation of technology, the teacher shortage, and pressure to raise standardized test scores (Quinn, 2002; Schiff, 2002; Tirozzi, 2001).

Tirozzi indicated one challenge faced by educators is the problem of transience with forty-three million Americans moving each year. In addition, the make-up of students continues to change. It is estimated that by 2025, Hispanics and Asians will comprise 61% of the population, and that English will not be the primary language for most of these students (Tirozzi, 2001). Tirozzi also expressed concern about the impending teacher shortage and previous institutional responses to fill vacancies with individuals with limited credentials. Compounding the problem is that principals must have greater input into purchases and understand the impact of technology on instruction.

Accountability pressures have resulted in strained relationships with the districts' central offices. In a study of 40 school districts and 130 schools, Webster (1996) found that principals had limited cooperation from their peers and little support from school districts. Principals operated independently with little agreement of values, commitments, or competencies. District goals were not seen as beneficial and not incorporated into the management of schools. Goals and objectives cited were indistinct and not subject to measurement or accountability. Individual teachers headed up most improvement plans with no school-wide plans for improvement. Principals denounced educational leadership theory and philosophy, instead embracing a more pragmatic view of school leadership.

Expectations for the principal have been described as unrealistic. The concept of distributive leadership has been discussed as one way of sharing responsibility and the burden of the position so that additional time can be allocated to curriculum, instruction, and other pressing needs (Quinn, 2002; Supovitz, 2000; Schiff, 2002). Increasing accountability pressures, coupled with the changing demands of the job, require the development of a new set of skills for principals (Copland, 2001; Elmore, 2000; Fullan, 2002; Quinn, 2002; Tirozzi, 2001). The principal must engage faculty and share leadership responsibilities with them. The duties and responsibilities of the principal must be modified to meet the rising tide of accountability.

The Focus of the Chapter

Based on a national survey of elementary and secondary principals in 1999–2000, this chapter focuses on elementary and secondary school accountability, state and local sanctions for failing to meet accountability measures, and principals' engagement in major professional activities given the environment of mandate and accountability. We address five interrelated questions in the chapter.

1. To which extent do states or districts mandate performance goals?
2. Are elementary and secondary schools in the 50 states and the District of Columbia meeting performance goals developed by the state or the school district?
3. What rewards or sanctions are given for meeting or not meeting performance standards?
4. What program strategies are used to assess the school's progress on the school improvement plan?
5. How do principals perceive their engagement in major professional activities given the environment of mandate and accountability?

The results reported in this chapter provide principals' perspective on mandates, accountability, sanctions and rewards, and professional responsibilities.

Method

Data Source

This article used data from Schools and Staffing Survey (SASS) 1999–2000, the largest survey of K-12 education in the United States conducted by the National Center for Education Statistics. Among the components of the survey was a survey of public school principals.

Sample Size and Return Rate

The achieved sample size for the data for this study was 8,524, with a weighted sample size of 82,802. The return rate was above 90 percent, a rate that was very high for this kind of survey, indeed.

Among those in the sample, 43.6% of them were female, 56.4% were male. The following displayed the racial composition of the sample using the census categories at the time of the survey: American Indian or Alaska Native (0.8%), Asian or Pacific Islander (0.8%), African American (11.3%), White (87.1%). Among the sample, 5.1% were Hispanic and 94.9% non-Hispanic.

Sampling Weights and Data Analysis Approach

NCES developed a set of sampling weights for the survey so that we could more accurately estimate the population based on the sample. In other words, through the use of sampling weights, the results are generalizable to the state and/or the national levels. Throughout the chapter we used descriptive statistics, which were adjusted for sampling weights, to depict principals' perspectives on school accountability and professional job responsibilities. The high quality data of the study offered us an excellent opportunity to inquire into the important topic of the study.

What We Found

The Status of Accountability

Table 5.1 reveals similarities between elementary and secondary principals' perspective on the status of accountability. Responses were similar for both elementary and secondary principals with 91 percent of the elementary principals and 88 percent of secondary principals reporting the existence of district or state performance goals and the requirement of districts to meet these goals. Performance goals were met by over two-thirds of elementary and secondary school districts. The data suggest that it is common to require elementary and secondary schools to meet state or district performance goals and that most schools do meet the goals. Nearly 90 percent of elementary and secondary schools have developed formal school improvement plans. The measures of accountability are ubiquitous, indeed.

State Performance in Meeting Established Performances

The percentage of elementary and secondary schools in each state and the District of Columbia that failed to meet their performance goals are displayed in Table 5.2.

In presenting the data, it must be emphasized that performance standards varied with each state and the District of Columbia. Consequently, the absence of a uniform measure makes a state-by-state comparison difficult. The failure rates did not appear to be associated with a particular region of the

TABLE 5.1. Perspective on the Status of Accountability (Percentage): Perspectives of Elementary and Secondary Principals

Questions	Elementary	Secondary
Has either your district or your state established school performance goals?	91	88
Is your school required to meet district or state performance goals?	91	88
Did your school meet the minimum district or state performance goals?	67	68
Does your school have a formal school improvement plan?	89	87

TABLE 5.2. State Rank of Percentage of Elementary and Secondary Principals Who Reported Their Schools Did Not Meet Minimum District or State Performance Goals

State	Elementary Percentage	Secondary Percentage	Differences Between Elementary and Secondary	State	Elementary Percentage	Secondary Percentage	Differences Between Elementary and Secondary
Wyoming	22	31	9	Mississippi	21	30	9
Wisconsin	19	17	1	Minnesota	26	26	0
West Virginia	20	21	1	Michigan	46	22	23
Washington	48	60	12	Massachusetts	30	38	8
Virginia	69	69	0	Maryland	70	37	33
Vermont	24	41	17	Maine	29	26	4
Utah	27	19	8	Louisiana	44	47	3
Texas	10	12	2	Kentucky	23	20	4
Tennessee	37	43	6	Kansas	34	45	11
South Dakota	26	27	0	Iowa	48	32	16
South Carolina	22	22	0	Indiana	18	19	1
Rhode Island	56	51	5	Illinois	29	39	10
Pennsylvania	9	24	15	Idaho	30	24	6
Oregon	48	55	8	Hawaii	69	42	27
Oklahoma	15	15	1	Georgia	41	38	3
Ohio	73	57	16	Florida	35	41	6
North Dakota	32	16	16	Delaware	59	42	17
North Carolina	13	4	9	D.C.	68	48	21
New York	28	31	3	Connecticut	10	30	20
New Mexico	27	30	3	Colorado	44	37	8
New Jersey	29	21	8	California	45	44	1
New Hampshire	28	47	18	Arkansas	52	25	28
Nevada	31	31	1	Arizona	16	40	24
Nebraska	29	35	7	Alaska	18	26	8
Montana	19	25	6	Alabama	20	32	12
Missouri	39	30	9				

country. In 25 states, the percentage of secondary schools that did not meet the minimum performance goals exceeded that of their elementary counterparts, compared to 21 states where the percentage of elementary schools exceeded that of their secondary schools. In five states, the failure rates for elementary and secondary school were the same.

Failure rates for elementary schools ranged from a high of 73 percent in Ohio to a low of nine percent in Pennsylvania. Other states with high elementary school failure rates included Maryland (70 percent), Hawaii (69 percent),

Virginia (69 percent), and the District of Columbia (68 percent), Rhode Island (56 percent), Delaware (56 percent), and Arkansas (52 percent). States where 50 percent or more of elementary schools failed to meet performance standards included California, Louisiana, Colorado, Michigan, Idaho, Georgia, Iowa, Washington, and Oregon. States reporting elementary school failure rates from 30 to 39 percent included North Dakota, Nevada, Massachusetts, Kansas, Missouri, Florida, Tennessee, Kansas. In eighteen states, schools failing to meet performance rates ranged from 20 to 29 percent. These states included Alabama, Illinois, Maine, Minnesota, Nebraska, New Jersey, New York, New Mexico, New Hampshire, South Dakota, Vermont, Utah, Mississippi, South Carolina, Kentucky, Wyoming, and West Virginia. States with elementary schools between 13 and 19 percent not meeting state or district performance standards included North Carolina, Arizona, Indiana, Oklahoma, Alaska, Montana, and Wisconsin. States reporting the lower number of elementary schools failing to meet state or local performance standards included Texas (10 percent), Connecticut (10 percent), and Pennsylvania (9 percent).

The five states with the same percentage of elementary and secondary schools failing to meet state or district performance standards included Virginia, Nevada, Minnesota, South Carolina, and Oklahoma. In these states the percentage of schools not meeting performance standards ranged from 15 to 69 percent.

A review of secondary schools revealed a similar range in schools failing to meet state and district standards. Secondary principals in Virginia reported the highest number of schools failing to meet state or district standards, with 69 percent of respondents stating that their school failed to meet district or state performance goals. Other states in which over half of the schools failed to meet state and district standards included Washington, Ohio, Oregon and Rhode Island.

Ten states and the District of Columbia reported that between 40 and 48 percent of secondary schools failed to meet established standards. These states included New Hampshire, Louisiana, Kansas, California, Tennessee, Hawaii, Delaware, Florida, Vermont and Arizona. In 15 states, approximately one-third failed to meet district standards or state performance goals. These states included Illinois, Georgia, Massachusetts, Maryland, Nebraska, Iowa, Colorado, Alabama, Wyoming, Nevada, New York, Missouri, New Mexico, Connecticut and Mississippi. In 13 states, secondary principals reported that 20 to 27 percent of schools failed to meet district or state performance standards. These states included South Dakota, Alaska, Maine, Minnesota, Montana, Arkansas, Idaho, Pennsylvania, Michigan, South Carolina, New Jersey, West Virginia and Kentucky. The remaining states' failure rates ranged from 19 to four percent. These states included Indiana, Utah, Wisconsin, North Dakota and Oklahoma. The two states reporting the lowest percentage for meeting state or district performance standards were Texas at 12 percent and North Carolina at four percent. The reality is that in the vast majority of the states, 20 percent or more of secondary schools failed to meet minimum district or state performance goals.

The disparity between elementary and secondary schools presents an interesting comparison. Aside from the five states with identical failure rates for elementary and secondary schools, in 31 states, the difference between elementary and secondary schools was between 1 and 10 percent. In 10 states, the percentage difference between elementary and secondary schools ranged from 11 to 19 percent. States with the largest percentage difference between elementary and secondary schools included Maryland (33 percent), Arkansas (27 percent), Hawaii (28 percent), Arizona (24 percent), and Michigan (23 percent).

The failure rate is essentially a function of two factors—the quality of the school and the criterion set for the school. The enormous variation among the states, from four percent to 68 percent in the failure rate, point to, among others, the difference in the stringency of state or district performance goals. It raises the issue how to use the performance goals as a tool for school improvement rather than for a political agenda. Realistic performance goals help principals, teachers, and parents celebrate the achievement and point out direction for further improvement. Unrealistic performance goals demoralize the school community and add much stress to those in the school community, including the principal. The large percentage difference between elementary and secondary schools in some states also reveal the differential stringent levels for elementary and secondary schools, respectively.

Incentives and Corrective Measures

Incentives for elementary and secondary schools are similar. A small number of states and local school districts awarded cash bonuses to teachers and schools for meeting district and state performance standards. Among the elementary principals, about 13 percent of their teachers received cash bonuses for meeting district or school performance goals, compared to 12 percent of the secondary schools (Table 5.3). Over 18 percent of the elementary principals and 17 percent of secondary principals indicated that their school received cash bonuses or additional resources to support school activities.

Principals were also asked what happened when schools failed to meet performance goals. In over 75 percent of elementary schools and 70 percent of secondary schools, teachers and administrators wrote program improvement

TABLE 5.3. Percentage of Elementary and Secondary Principals Who Reported the Use of Following Incentives or Corrective Measures for Meeting or Not Meeting School Performance Goals

Situation	Elem.	Second.
When the school met the performance goals		
Receive cash bonuses or additional recourse that support school wide activities	18	17
Receive cash bonuses or additional recourse to distribute to teachers	13	12
When the school did not meet performance goals		
Required to write a school or program improvement plan	75	70
Put on an evaluation cycle with required targeted improvement dates	46	48
Provided with additional resources to support instructional improvement	50	44
Provided with technical assistance from outside experts on how to improve	39	42
Subject to reconstitution or takeover regulations	4	4
Required to replace the principal	4	4
Penalized by a reduction in state or district funding	3	3

plans. Nearly half of the elementary and secondary principals reported that their schools were placed on an evaluation cycle with target dates for demonstrated improvement. Fifty percent of elementary principals and 44 percent of secondary principals indicated that additional resources were allocated to support instructional improvement. Outside experts provided technical assistance to support improvement efforts in roughly 40 percent of elementary and secondary schools. Other sanctions were more punitive. Reconstitution or takeover regulations were reported by 4 percent of elementary and secondary principals, replacement of the school head by 4 percent of the principals, and reduction in state or district funding by 3 percent of the principals.

The data seem to suggest that the current school reform environment does provide incentives or corrective measures for meeting or not meeting the performance goals. The systemic nature of the reform agenda is reflected in these incentives and corrective measures. Because of these incentives and corrective measures and the media frenzy associated with the publication of information on the failure or success of the school, principals have to prioritize the work related to meeting performance goals. If a school fails to meet the performance goals, many principals reported that constructive corrective measures, such as developing a school improvement plan, providing additional resources and technical assistance, are used. Only three to four percent of elementary and secondary principals reported drastic measures such as takeover, replacement of the principal, and reduction in funding.

The Assessment of School Improvement

Principals were asked what measures were used to assess school progress on school improvement plans. Multiple measures were used by states and local districts. However, 97 percent of elementary and 93 percent of secondary school principals cited state and national tests as the most predominate measure (Table 5.4). Student and parent surveys were used by nearly 85 percent of both elementary and secondary schools. Portfolios were most prominent in elementary schools, with 65 percent of the elementary principals and 56 percent of secondary school principals stating that they used portfolios to assess student progress. It appears that testing is still the dominant vehicle for assessing school improvement. However, it is encouraging to know that other measures, such as parent or student surveys and portfolio, are also used by a high percentage of schools.

Professional Activities

Principals were asked to indicate how often they engaged in 10 basic management and leadership activities (Table 5.5). The time and attention given to each of the 10 responsibilities by elementary and secondary school principals were similar with a few exceptions. Elementary and secondary principals reported spending a major amount of time maintaining security and managing physical facilities, resources, and procedures. Eighty-seven percent of elementary principals and 84 percent of secondary principals stated they spent time each day maintaining physical security or a safe teaching and learning environment. Closely related to security issues is the management of school facilities, resources, and procedures. Ninety-five percent of elementary principals and 93 percent of secondary principals indicated that these activities were addressed daily or once or twice a week.

The amount of time elementary and secondary principals spent on instructional activities, public relations, building community, and providing leadership in curricular areas dropped significantly among elementary and secondary

TABLE 5.4. School Assessment Measures Used by Elementary and Secondary Principals

Measures	Elementary	Secondary
Using state or national tests	97	93
Parent or student surveys	84	85
Portfolio products	65	56

TABLE 5.5. Percentage of Secondary Principals Who Reported How They Spent Time on Management and Leadership Activities

Activities	Never Elementary	Never Secondary	One or twice a month Elementary	One or twice a month Secondary	Once or twice a week Elementary	Once or twice a week Secondary	Every day Elementary	Every day Secondary
Maintain the physical security of students, faculty, and other staff	1	1	4	6	8	9	87	84
Manage school facilities, resources, procedures	0	1	5	6	12	14	83	79
Facilitate student learning	1	2	15	21	28	32	52	46
Supervise and evaluate faculty and other staff	1	2	14	15	35	38	50	46
Develop public relations	1	2	22	27	28	31	50	40
Build professional community among faculty and other staff	2	3	19	33	28	30	42	35
Facilitate achievement of the school's mission	2	2	24	31	32	33	44	34
Guide the development and evaluation of curriculum and instruction	4	4	30	36	39	39	29	22
Attend district-level meetings and carry out district-level responsibilities	1	2	45	40	39	41	15	17
Provide and engage staff in professional development activities	2	2	59	62	31	29	8	8

principals. Seventy-eight percent of the principals also reported that they were engaged daily or weekly in activities that facilitated student learning. Although a significant majority of elementary and secondary principals reported spending time each day or once or twice a week on activities to facilitate student learning, 21 percent of secondary principals and 15 percent of elementary principals stated they focused on student learning only once or twice a month, and two percent of secondary principals and one percent of elementary stated that they never focused on activities that promote student learning.

Similar responses were provided on the amount of time that principals spent in the supervision and evaluation of faculty and staff. Eighty-five percent of elementary principals and 84 percent of secondary principals stated that they supervised faculty and staff either daily or weekly, contrasted with approximately 15 percent of both groups that reported they supervised or evaluated faculty and staff on a monthly basis. Half of the elementary principals and

40 percent of secondary principals indicated they spent time each day on public relations. Over 25 percent of elementary and secondary principals reported they participated in public relations activities once or twice a week. Closely associated with external public relations is building professional relationships with faculty and staff. Seventy percent of elementary principals and 65 percent of secondary principals stated that they focused on building a professional community among faculty and staff either daily or weekly, compared to 19 percent of elementary principals and 33 percent of secondary principals who reported that this activity was addressed on a monthly basis. Seventy-six percent of elementary principals and 66 percent of secondary principals devoted daily or weekly time to achieving the school mission; 24 percent of elementary principals and 31 percent of secondary principals focused on the school mission once or twice a month.

Compared to other activities, principals spent less time on the evaluation of curriculum and instruction, district level responsibilities, and professional development. Elementary principals spent more time each day guiding curriculum than their secondary counterparts. When daily and weekly activities were combined, 66 percent of elementary principals and 61 percent of secondary principals reported daily or weekly involvement in guiding the development and evaluation of curriculum and instruction, compared to 30 percent of elementary principals and 36 percent of secondary principals who reported monthly involvement. Elementary and secondary principals spent similar amounts of time participating in daily or weekly district level meetings. Fifty-four percent of elementary principals and 58 percent of secondary principals indicated they attended district meetings and implemented district responsibilities either daily or weekly, whereas over 40 percent of both groups reported monthly participation in district level meeting and carrying out district-level responsibilities. Over one-third of the principals stated that they engaged faculty and staff daily or weekly in professional development. The majority of principals described professional development as a monthly activity.

Several patterns are embedded in the data on principals' engagement in professional activities. First, as other researchers found, there appears to be a "layering" of responsibilities for principals (e.g., Portin & Shen, 1988; Portin, Shen, & Williams, 1998), i.e., additional responsibilities are added to the traditional roles. Principals are still heavily engaged in traditional roles such as managing resources and maintaining physical security. However, they are also heavily involved in school-community relationship and facilitating student learning. Second, it appears that the rhetoric of instructional leadership is being translated into practice. Many principals report that they are involved in (a) facilitating student learning and (b) guiding the development and evaluation of curriculum and instruction. Finally, it appears that management still occupies more time and energy than leadership. About 80 percent of elementary and secondary principals report that they engage in maintaining the physical security and managing the school on the daily basis. However, the same statistics for renewal-oriented activities, such as (a) building professional community among faculty and other staff and (b) facilitating achievement of the school's mission, is much lower.

Summary and Discussion

Summary

We investigated how principals perceived the status of the accountability movement and their professional job responsibilities in the context of accountability. Among others, we found the following: (a) 91 percent of elementary principals and 88 percent of secondary principals reported that the state or the school district have performance goals for the school and in excess of 67 percent indicated their schools meet the goals; (b) the percentage of schools that failed to meet the goals varied enormously among the states, ranging from 4 to 73 percent; (c) in a number of states, there was a large difference in percentage of elementary and secondary schools meeting the minimum performance goals; (d) principals reported that there were specific incentives or corrective measures for meeting or not meeting the goals, a feature that is consistent with the systemic reform movement; (e) although multiple measures were used for evaluating schools' progress, testing remained the most important measure; and (f) in the context of accountability, principals' response to their involvement in professional activities suggested that additional responsibilities were added to their traditional roles, that they paid substantial attention to instructional leadership, and that management tasks still occupied more time and energy than leadership initiatives.

Discussion

The politicized environment of educational reform. The issues of accountability and the inordinate amount of time spent by principals on daily activities are intertwined. The complexity of these two closely related constructs are impacted by a number of sociological, historical, and political forces, all of which contribute to the major issues facing school districts. Reform and accountability are growth industries, with schools blamed for the failure of students—our future workforce—to compete in a global economy, which in turn leads to economic decline. Goodlad (2002) suggested that the economic prosperity of the 1990s presented a strong argument that the purported educational decline was not an indicator that Americans could not compete in global markets. No one argues that schools cannot and should not improve and be subject to accountability measures. What becomes problematic is the political aspect of educational reform, or the lack of a sustained comprehensive program to allow school improvement measures to work. Popham (2001) discussed the political nature of testing and accountability. He suggested that several major politicians, including President Bush and California Governor Gray Davis have built careers based on the prospect of improving education. Sergiovanni (2000) described the setting of standards as political. He indicated that the setting of standards was not a scientific process. This is partially explained by the enormous variation in the percentage of schools failing to meet the performance goals is a strong indication that school reform has been politicized to an extreme extent. Benveniste (2002) characterized evaluation as "a political phenomenon that reflects agendas, tensions, and nature of political relations between political actors" (p. 89).

Many political leaders profess to possess the "magic bullet" or "potion" to transform schools. Fragmentation in program development and implementation, limited direction, and an absence of adequate support from central offices contribute to a cycle of ineffectiveness that continues to plague many school districts.

The complex and demanding work of the principal. Principals' work is complex and overwhelming. Activities in which principals engage and the amount of time allocated to each activity clearly support the above statement. Due to the demands of the school community and mandates from various authorities, many principals continue to not only fulfill their traditional roles in managing the school, but also take up new responsibilities in areas such as curriculum and instruction. Many principals find themselves mired in situations beyond their control that involve labor strife, students and parents with a myriad of social problems, and school violence. These complexities in schools and communities demand the amount of time that principals must spend on management areas just to insure the school operates at acceptable levels, at the expense of leadership initiatives.

Accountability, standards, and leadership challenges. States and local school districts have established and mandated performance goals and measures. Again, schools failing to meet performance standards ranged from 73 percent to four percent. The reality is that these measures are met by approximately 67 percent of the schools. Each state has developed its own criteria for success. The politics of the measurement criteria used to determine acceptable student success must also be considered, as state and local officials have established different standards to determine success. The variability among the states is enormous, indeed. The enormous variability certainly raises issue of the desirability of developing some kind of unified, voluntary national standards.

Accountability is here to stay. State and district leaders must systematically examine all factors that contribute both to success and to areas where improvement is indicated, and establish measurable and meaningful targets to achieve school and student success. What should "students need to know and do" to function in the 21st century? This will likely involve more than performing well on a standardized test, which is now the single most important measure for school success. Richard Florida (2002) describes the creative class or a group of individuals who create new products, processes, or designs. This group of talented individuals positively impact economic growth. This argument is germane to education in that standardized testing and accountability focus on existing conventions. New pressures for students to score high on standardized test may actually negatively impact student creativity and the long-term development of a capable workforce. This has huge implications for principals, teachers, and students—our country's future workforce.

The principal remains the key to accountability. Principal and teacher roles must be reexamined. If students and schools are to meet performance standards, collaboration, communication, and a universal understanding of the standards must occur. Principals and teachers must communicate and have the time to mutually discuss instruction and student learning on a regular basis. A genuine cultural renaissance must occur. Teachers should be encouraged to follow the curriculum they develop. Resources must be allocated to address the social and cultural problems that students bring to school. Most educators understand that all students can learn. However, the road is steeper for some than others. In those districts that experience more difficulties, additional assistance is required.

There is an axiom that if we want to improve instruction, the skills of teachers and principals must be upgraded. Professional development that focuses on the improvement of teacher and administrator skills must be conducted, and both groups are required to provide evidence of change. The overarching goal must be to establish a culture of responsibility among teachers, administrators, and school boards. This may be the most difficult task because strife and discord reduces accountability in that blame is spread to the various stakeholders

Concluding Comments

The national study on accountability and principals' professional activities provide a portrait of some of the challenges facing meaningful and lasting school reform. Cleary, principals are under the pressure of accountability and their involvement in professional job responsibilities indicate that they are working on multiple fronts. Three major concerns emerge from principals' responses. First, although several measures are used to assess schools' program, testing remains the most important. Second, principals are working in a very politicized environment. The enormous variability in the percentage of schools not meeting the performance goals clearly indicates the political nature of the criterion. Third, principals are called upon to engage in leadership initiative, such as instructional leadership, to improve schools. However, they are still mired in the managing tasks due to the immediate nature of these tasks. Principals face many challenges, indeed. We found some interesting patterns at the national and state levels. Given the different conditions across schools, particularly the difference among urban, suburban, and rural schools, one of the possible directions for further studies is to inquire into the difference among urban, suburban, and rural principals.

The long-term impact of the accountability movement must be studied to see what effects, if any, the reform initiatives have had on curriculum and student productivity in the workplace. Regrettably, for many this is the road less traveled. The linear approach to program development has experienced mixed results. The key to lasting improvement lies in the ability to systematically address multiple areas. By adopting a systematic approach, teachers and principals can develop schools that are accountable and manageable, and meet the both short- and long-term needs of students and stakeholders.

Bibliography

Benveniste, L. (2002). The political structuration of assessment: Negotiating state power and legitimacy. *Comparative Education Review 46* (1), 89–118.

Berliner, D. C., & Biddle, B. J. (1997). *The manufactured crisis: Myths, fraud and the attack on America's public schools.* White Plains, NY: Longman.

Bonstingl, J. J. (2001). Are the stakes too high? *Principal Leadership, 1* (5), 8–14.

Brewer, H. (2001). Ten steps to success. *Journal of Staff Development* 22 (1), 30–31.

Christie, K. (2000). Leadership comes around again. *Phi Delta Kappan, 82* (2), 105–106.

Copland, M. A. (2001). The myth of the superprincipal. *Phi Delta Kappan, 82* (7), 528–533.

Daggett, W. R. (2002). Moving from standards to instructional practice. *NASSP Bulletin 84* (620), 66–72.

Donaldson, G. A. (2001). The lose–lose leadership hunt, *Education Week*, October 3, 42.

Dounay, J. (2000). High-stakes testing is high-stress, too. *The Educational Digest 65* (9), 9–13.

Drake, T. L., & Roe, W. H. (1999). The principalship (5th ed.). Upper Saddle River, NJ: Prentice-Hall.

Ediger, M. (2002). Assessing the school principal. *Education 123* (1), 90–95.

Eisner, E. W. (2002). The kind of schools we need. *Phi Delta Kappan, 83* (8), 576–583.

Elmore, R. (2000). *Building a new structure for school leadership.* Washington, D.C.: Albert Shanker Institute.

Elmore, R., Abelmann, C., & Fuhrman S. (1996). The new accountability in state education policy. In H. Ladd (ed). *Performance based strategies for improving schools* (pp. 65–98). Washington, DC: Brookings Institution.

Harrington-Lueker, D. (2000). The uneasy coexistence of high stakes and developmental practice. *The School Administrator* 57 (1), 6–11.

Florida, R. (2002). The rise of the creative class. *Washington Monthly, 34* (5), 15–25.

Fullan, M. (2001). Chapter eight. The principal. *The new meaning of educational change.* New York, Teachers College Press: 137–150.

Fullan, M. (2002). The change leader. *Educational Leadership 59* (8), 16–20.

Goodlad, J.L. (2002) Kudzu, rabbits, and school reform. *Phi Delta Kappan, 84* (1), 16–23.

King, D. (2002). The changing shape of leadership. *Educational Leadership 59* (8), 61–63.

Kelly, C. (1999). Leveraging human and fiscal resources for school improvement. *Educational Administration Quarterly, 35* (4), 642–657.

Kohn, A. (2001). Fighting the test: A practical guide to rescuing our schools. *Phi Delta Kappan 82* (5), 349–357.

Lashman, L. (2000). Who's in charge? The accountability challenge. *Principal Leadership, 1* (3), 8–13.

Madaus, G. F. & O'Dwyer, L. M. (1999). A short history of performance assessment: Lessons learned. *Phi Delta Kappan 80* (9), 688–695.

Olson, L. (1999). Shining a spotlight on results. *Education Week 18* (170), 8.

Popham, W. J. (2001). *The truth about testing.* Alexandria, VA: Association for Supervision and Curriculum Development.

Portin, B. S., & Shen, J. (1998). The changing principalship: Its current status, variability, and impact. *The Journal of Leadership Studies, 5* (3), 93–113.

Portin, B., Shen, J., & Williams, R. (1998). The changing principalship and its impact: Voices from principals. *NASSP Bulletin, 82* (602), 1–8.

Quinn, T. K. (2002). Redefining leadership in the standards era. *Principal 82* (1), 16–20.

Schiff, T. (2002). Principals readiness for reform; A comprehensive approach. *Principal Leadership,* 2 (5), 21–26.

Sergiovanni, T. J. (2001). *The principalship: A reflective practice perspective* (4th ed.). Needham Heights, MA: Allyn & Bacon.

Sergiovanni, T. J. (2000). Standards and the lifeworld of leadership. *School Administrator* 57 (8), 6–12.

Supovitz, J.A. (2000). Manage less, lead more. *Principal Leadership*, *1* (3), 14–19.

Taylor, R., & Williams, R. D. (2001). Accountability: Threat or target? *School Administrator*, *56* (6), 30–33.

Tirozzi, G. N. (2001). The artistry of leadership: The evolving role of the secondary principal. *Phi Delta Kappan 82* (6), 434–439.

Webster, W. E. (1996). Effectiveness and accountability in the educational archipelago. *Thrust for Educational Leadership*, *26*, 28–31.

·6·

Sue Poppink and Jianping Shen

PRINCIPALS' SALARIES

Introduction

We based our study of principals' salaries on the self-evident postulate that salaries need to be high enough to attract and retain high quality candidates into the profession. Many have argued that principals' responsibilities have been increasing and we wanted to know if their salaries were also increasing.

There are many potential influences on principals' salaries. One is the shortage of qualified applicants for principal positions. Many have predicted that a large percentage of principals plan to retire in the next decade (Educational Research Service, 1998; Ferrandino & Tirozzi, 2000; Gilman & Lansman-Given, 2001; Long, 2000), and fewer teachers plan to apply for those jobs (Educational Research Service, 2000; Ferrandino & Tirozzi, 2000). Cooley and Shen (1999, 2000), and Cooley, Shen, and Wegenke (2004) found that teachers' decisions to assume a principalship were moderately influenced by the perceived differential in administrators' and teachers' daily salary rates.

Another influence on principals' salaries may be the increasing responsibilities in the position. Principals are now expected to be initiators of change, instructional leaders, school managers, personnel administrators, problem solvers, and boundary spanners for schools (Fullan, 2001; Leithwood & Montgomery, 1986; Sergiovanni, 1991; Vandenberghe, 1995). Instructional leadership is a relatively new role thrust on school principals but one that many consider to be of paramount importance (Bryk, Sebring, Kerbow, Rollow, & Easton, 2001; Elmore, 2000; Fullan, 2001; Glickman, 2001; Lambert,

1995; Sergiovanni, 2001). The notion of instructional leadership carries with it the idea that principals will create school cultures that encourage students' and teachers' learning and growth. This, in turn, requires that principals have the knowledge and skills to create, develop, or manage staff development opportunities around curriculum, assessment, and state standards; to develop and implement multiple forms of supervision; to use shared decision-making models, and more.

Portin and Shen (1988) and Portin (2000) found that principals' perceptions of the responsibilities are changing. They perceive that the new responsibilities mentioned above are being "layered" onto their traditional ones. In addition, though scholars are pressing for principals to focus on instructional leadership, principals reported that management, rather than leadership, was taking up a greater proportion of their time. Management has an immediate and direct impact on their working conditions and some management activities may carry legal consequences if not carried out (e.g., special education laws). Principals perceived that they pay more attention to the management aspects of their work, often at the expense of leadership. Principals also reported that their roles are becoming more ambiguous and complex because they are expected to enact in their schools new ideas, such as site-based management, without guidelines. Principals reported that their morale and enthusiasm were declining because of these multiple new responsibilities and their attendant ambiguity and complexity, coupled with the day-to-day press to manage, rather than lead, schools.

A third potential influence on principals' salaries is their changing work environment. This includes such changes as increases in federal and state policy mandates and the demographics of the student populations. Principals must now balance policy mandates, changing social mores, and their own personal values. They are responsible for creating schools that respond to dynamic social changes, such as sorting out the differences between the values and traditions of increasingly diverse demographic groups. A National Association of Secondary School Principals' (2001) press release explained that principals' work environments are also increasingly complex because of inadequate funding and the need to shoulder "responsibility that once belonged at home or in the community" (p. 1).

Finally, an influence on secondary principals' salaries is the increasing number of females in the profession. Wegenke and Shen (in press) found that between 1987–88 and 1999–2000, the percentage of female principals almost doubled. It increased from 24.6 in 1987–88, to 34.5 in 1993–94, and to 43.6 in 1999–2000. Given the lower earnings of females generally, we wondered about the gender equity of principals' salary.

The Focus of the Chapter

In this study, we asked if changes in principals' salaries are consistent with the evolving nature of the principalship. More specifically, we asked, first, what is the range and comparative value of principals' salaries, now and over time? Second, how do salaries vary by urban, suburban and rural locations? Third, what is the range and comparative value of principals' salaries by state? Finally, is there gender equity in principals' salaries?

Method

The Data Source and the Sample

This article was based on the data from Schools and Staffing Survey (SASS), the largest survey of K-12 education in the United States conducted by the National Center for Education Statistics (NCES) in 1987–88, 1990–91, 1993–94, and 1999–2000. Among the components is a survey of public school principals. The return rates for all the surveys were above 90 percent, an extraordinarily high rate for this kind of survey. The achieved sample sizes and weighted sample sizes for each of the four survey years are shown in Table 6.1.

Sampling Weights and the Data Analysis Approach

NCES developed a set of sampling weights for each survey to more accurately estimate the population based on the sample. Through the use of sampling weights, the results can be generalized to the state or national levels or both. Since we have representative samples at the national and state levels for each of the four rounds of SASS, the data constitute a kind of longitudinal analysis called a "trend study." In others words, by having data from four rounds of surveys conducted in 1987–88, 1990–91, 1993–94, and 1999–2000, we are able to discuss the trend of principals' salaries. Throughout the article, descriptive statistics, adjusted by sampling weights, are used to depict the phenomenon of interest.

TABLE 6.1. The Sample

	1987–88	1990–91	1993–94	1999–2000
Achieved Sample Size	8,519	9,054	9,098	8,524
Weighted Sample Size	77,890	78,890	79,618	82,802

Other Data Sources

In the article, we compared principals' salaries with teachers' or average workers' salaries. The data on teachers' salary were taken from the *Survey and analysis of teacher salary trends* (2000) provided by the American Federation of Teachers. The data on all workers' average pay were taken from the U.S. Bureau of the Census (2001).

Results

Trends in Principals' Salaries

Table 6.2 shows that the average unadjusted principal's salary was $41,975 in 1987–88 and $66,646 in 1999–2000, resulting in a 58.8 percent increase over the 12-year period. However, when principals' salaries were adjusted by the Consumer Price Index to the 1999–2000 level, the average salary increased only 9 percent in a twelve-year period, from $61,145 in 1987–88 to $66,646 in 1999–2000. Given the increase in responsibilities in principals' work and the economic boom in the 1990s, the real increase in principals' average salaries is easily justified.

The data in Table 6.3 show principals' salaries in contrast to the average annual pay for all workers in the U.S.—including managers and other workers—(U.S. Bureau of the Census, 2001, p. 402), and teachers' average salaries (American Federation of Teachers, p. 1). In 1990–91 principals earned an average of $41,975, and the average workers earned $26,824. Thus, in 1990–91 principals' salaries were 2.10 times than that of workers' pay. In 1999–2000 workers' pay on average was $33,313, while principals' salaries were twice (2.00) that. That is, the average salary of principals' has increased slightly less than workers' pay between 1990–91 and 1999–2000, suggesting that principals' salaries haven't increased significantly in the 1990s.

Principals' salaries have stayed steady above those of teachers'. Principals' salaries have been at least 50 percent more than teachers' salaries since 1987–88. Principals' average salaries were 56 percent more than teachers' in 1987–88, 55 percent more in 1993–94, and 59 percent more in 1999–2000.

TABLE 6.2. Principals' Average Salaries by Year, Both Unadjusted and Adjusted by the Consumer Price Index to the 1999–2000 Level

Salaries/Year	1987–88	1990–91	1993–94	1999–2000
Unadjusted	$41,975	$49,603	$54,858	$66,646
Adjusted	$61,145	$62,364	$63,302	$66,646

TABLE 6.3. Trends in Average Principals' Salaries, Workers' Pay and Teachers' Salaries (Unadjusted)

Salaries/Pay	1987–88	1990–91	1993–94	1999–2000
Principals	$41,975	$49,603	$54,858	$66,646
Workers	N/A	$23,602	N/A	$33,313
Teachers	$26,824	$31,957	$34,434	$39,981

Another way we examined principals' salaries is by their range. As Table 6.4 shows, principals at the 75th percentile earned $76,000, and those at the 25th percentile earned $56,000 in the 1999–2000 school year. The difference was $20,000. This range was about the same, between $17,763 and $20,000, over the entire 12-year period of the data represented here. The range might be influenced by whether principals work in urban, suburban or rural environments, which is explored in the next part of the paper.

Trend of Principals' Salaries by Urban, Suburban and Rural Districts

We found that on average suburban principals were paid more than urban or rural principals. However, the difference between suburban and urban principals is only about $2,000. Rural principals' average salaries were about $14,141 less in the 1999–2000 school year than suburban principals'. That is, suburban principals were paid about 29 percent more than rural principals, a pattern that fluctuates between 24 percent and 29 percent over the 12-year period investigated. These differences in salaries might be accounted for by the size of schools and by the cost of living. Rural schools are, on average, smaller than urban and suburban schools; and rural areas usually have a lower cost of living than urban and suburban areas.

Just as there is a range of principals' salaries in general, there is also a range of salaries within each—urban, suburban and rural—labor market. For in-

TABLE 6.4. Trends in Principals' Salaries Adjusted by the Consumers Price Index to the 1999–2000 Level

Salaries/Year	1987–88	1990–91	1993–94	1999–2000
Mean	$61,145	$62,364	$63,302	$66,646
25th Percentile	$52,416	$52,807	$53,080	$56,000
50th Percentile	$61,152	$61,608	$62,312	$65,000
75th Percentile	$70,179	$71,910	$72,122	$76,000

TABLE 6.5. Trends in Average Salaries for Urban, Suburban, and Rural Principals

Salaries/Year	1987–88	1990–91	1993–94	1999–2000
Urban	$45,494	$53,313	$58,023	$70,209
Suburban	$46,717	$56,418	$61,810	$72,209
Rural	$37,411	$44,293	$49,430	$56,068

stance, as Table 6.6 shows, in 1999–2000 urban principals at the 75th percentile made $78,000, while those at the 25th percentile earned $62,000, with a difference of $16,000. There is about a $12,000 difference between the 75th and 25th percentile of rural principals ($62,000 to $50,000). Between the 75th percentile and 25th percentile for suburban principals there was an even larger difference—$20,000. These differences in salaries may be related to principals' longevity in their positions, or the wealth of the districts in which they work.

There is also a range of salaries within the urban, suburban and rural labor markets and across categories. As Table 6.6 shows, in 1999–2000 for those at the 75th percentile, urban principals made about 98 percent of suburban principals' salary ($78,000 compared to $81,000). However, at the 25th percentile, urban principals earned about 102 percent of what suburban principals did ($62,000 compared to $61,000).

TABLE 6.6. Trends in Principals' Salaries by Urban, Suburban, and Rural Labor Markets, by Percentile, and by Year

Labor Market/Year	1987–88	1990–91	1993–94	1999–2000
Urban				
Mean	$45,494	$53,313	$58,023	$70,209
25th Percentile	$40,000	$46,975	$51,236	$62,000
50th Percentile	$45,000	$53,000	$58,000	$70,000
75th Percentile	$50,979	$60,000	$64,500	$78,000
Suburban				
Mean	$46,719	$56,418	$61,810	$72,104
25th Percentile	$41,000	$49,000	$52,496	$61,000
50th Percentile	$47,000	$55,800	$61,000	$71,000
75th Percentile	$52,500	$63,500	$70,000	$81,000
Rural				
Mean	$37,411	$44,293	$49,430	$56,068
25th Percentile	$32,500	$38,000	$42,000	$50,000
50th Percentile	$37,500	$43,500	$48,184	$55,000
75th Percentile	$42,000	$50,000	$55,000	$62,000

State Variation in Principals' Salaries

Another way to compare principals' salaries is by state. For this section, we created figures that show salaries displayed in four ways. These include (a) a state rank of principals' average salaries in 1999–2000, (b) a state rank of the increase of principals' median salaries between 1987–88 and 1999–2000, (c) a state rank of the ratio of principals' average salaries to the average annual pay of workers in the same state, and (d) a state rank of the ratio of principals' average salaries to that of teachers in the same state.

A state rank of principals' average salaries in 1999–2000. Figure 6.1 shows a state rank of average principals' salaries in 1999–2000. We found that just as salaries varied by the urban, suburban and rural markets, they also varied by state. North Dakota had the lowest average principals' salaries of $43,666, while New Jersey had the highest of $90,741—a $47,000 difference. In general, salaries were higher in the northeast than in other parts of the country.

A state rank of the increase of principals' median salaries between 1987–88 and 1999–2000. Figure 6.2 shows our investigation of state variation in principals' salaries from the perspective of the increase between 1987–88 and 1999–2000. Again the data revealed tremendous amounts of variability among the states. In Idaho, the increase was 76.4 percent between 1987–88 and 2000. Other states that showed strong increases included Georgia (76.1 percent), Vermont (75.7 percent), and Pennsylvania (74.4 percent). However, in the state of Alaska, the increase was only 23.3 percent between 1987–88 and 1999–2000. Other states showing the smallest increase included Wyoming (27.6 percent), Montana (36.6 percent), and Arizona (38.4 percent).

A state rank of the ratio of principals' average salaries to the average annual pay of all workers in the same state. Because the cost of living varies from state to state, in Figure 6.3, we related principals' salaries to all workers' average annual pay by creating an index that shows the ratio of principals' salaries to workers' pay. Because of the way we constructed the ratio, a ratio of "1" means that a principal and an average worker earn the same amount. Ratios that are larger than "1" show an average principal's salary is more than the average state worker's pay in the state. So, for instance, the average principal's salary, countrywide, in 1999–2000 was $66,646 and the average worker's annual pay in 1999 was $33,313. To create the ratio, we divided the principals' salary by the worker's salary and found a ratio of 2.00. This means that on average principals made about double what workers did in that year.

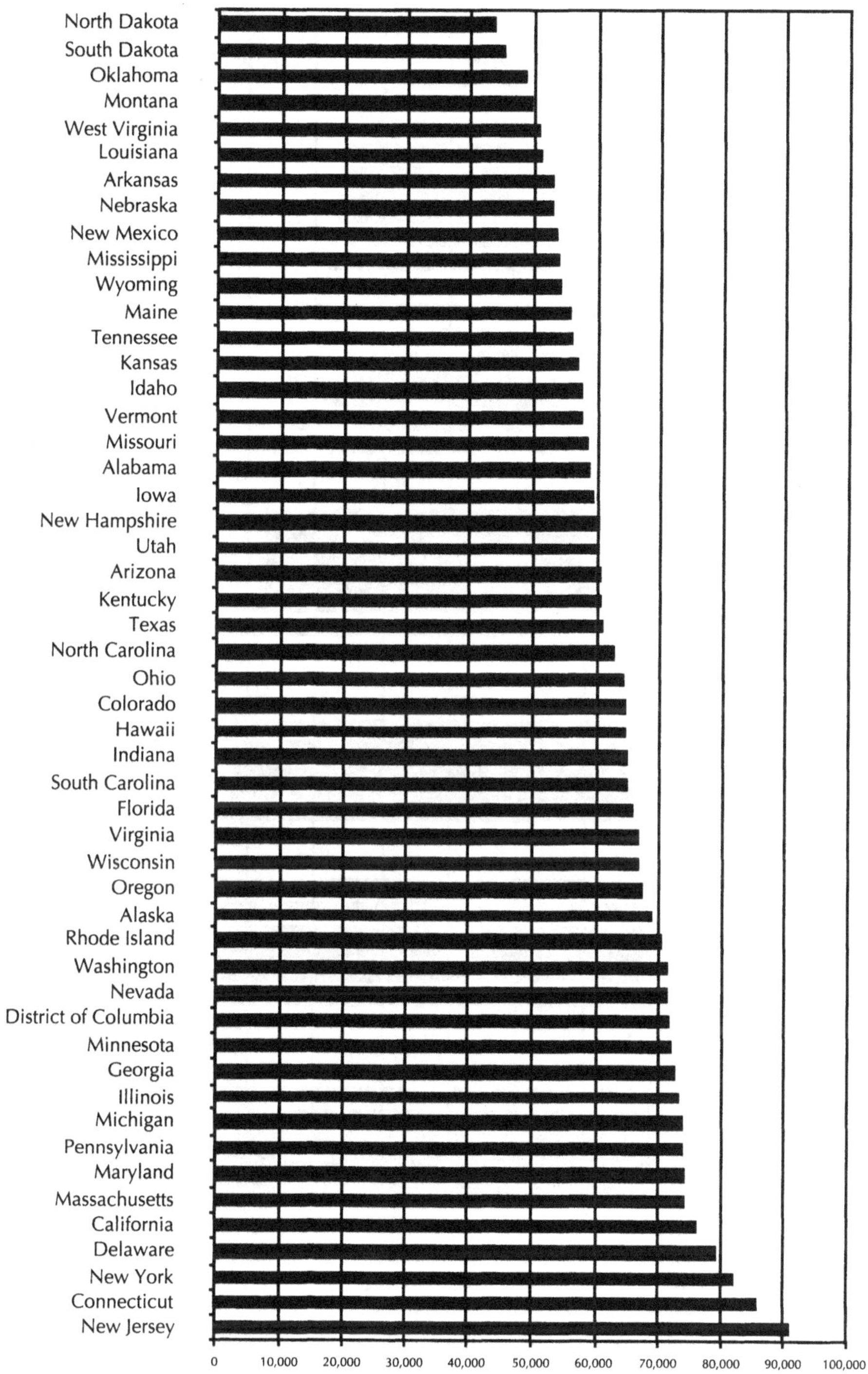

FIGURE 6.1. Principals' Annual Average Salaries in 1999–2000 (Ranked by State)

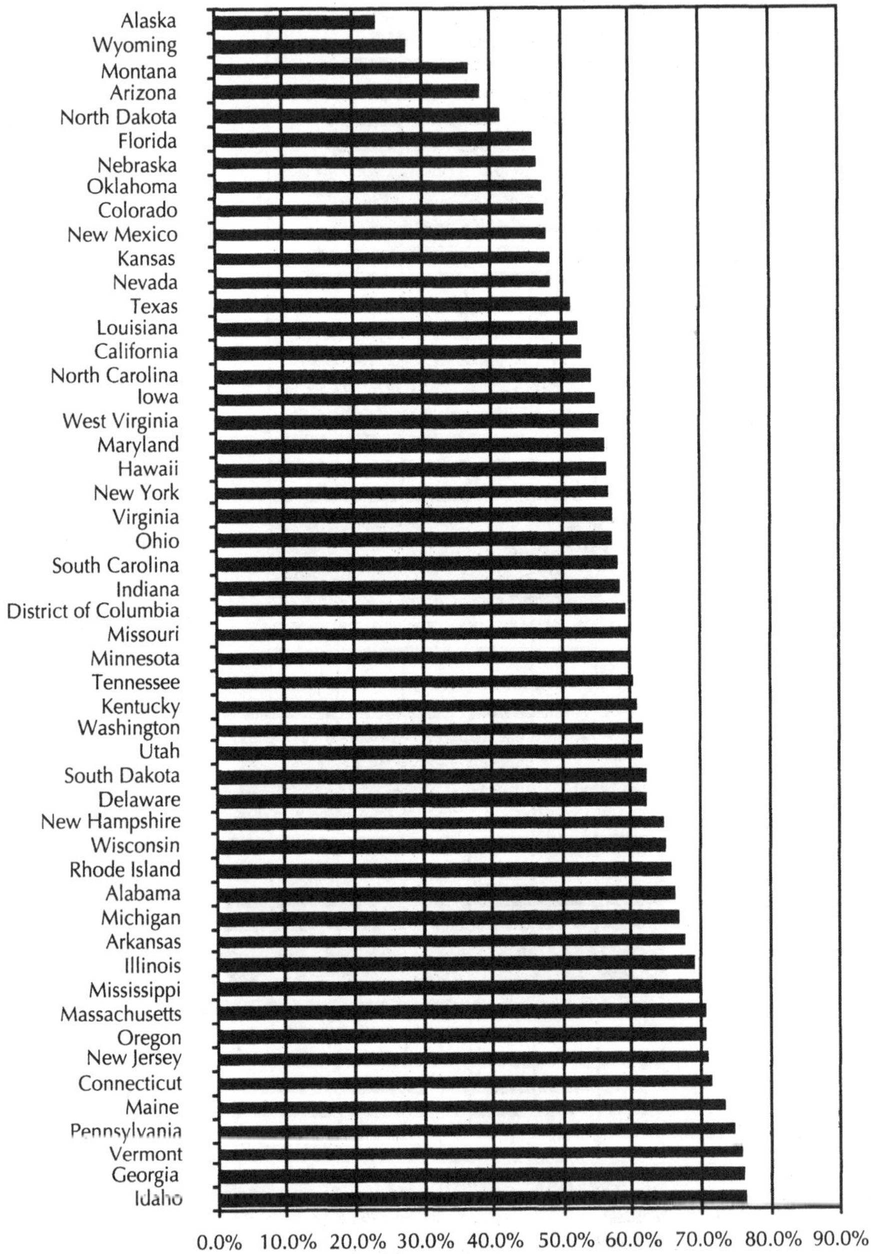

FIGURE 6.2. Percentage Increase in Principals' Annual Average Salaries Between 1987–1988 and 1999–2000 (Ranked by State)

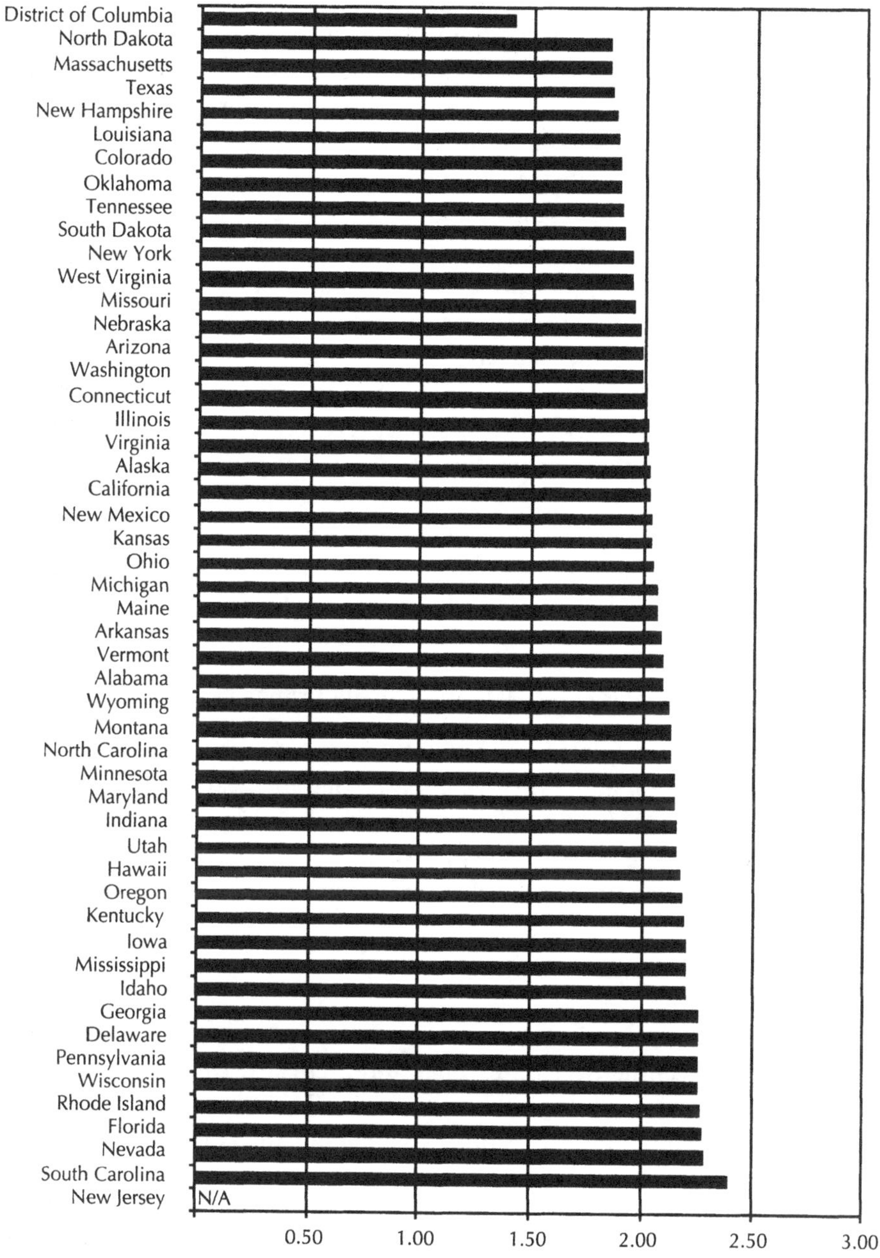

FIGURE 6.3. Ratio of Principals' Annual Average Salary to Worker's Average Annual Pay (Ranked by State)

By creating this same relatively simple index, we found substantial variation state to state. This might reflect differences in the labor markets of each state, and therefore attendant cost of living; and we are aware that there may be substantial variation within states. In three states the index was well above 2.0—South Carolina (2.39), Nevada (2.28), and Florida (2.27)—indicating that for one reason or another principals were slightly better compensated in those states than in others, when compared to workers' salaries in the state.

A state rank of the ratio of principals' average salaries to that of teachers in the same state. For Figure 6.4 we constructed a ratio of principals' average salaries to that of teachers in the same state and then listed the index for the states in an ascending order. The index shows that on average, principals earned 63 percent more than teachers, or 1.63 times what teachers made. The index shows that principals in South Carolina, Florida, New Jersey, and Delaware earned 78 percent or more than teachers, indicating, again, that principals were slightly better compensated in those states, when we compared principals' and teachers' salaries in the state. The index was relatively low in West Virginia (1.44), North Dakota (1.46) and Rhode Island (1.46).

Salaries by Male and Female Principals

As stated above, census data (2001) indicate, of those with a bachelor's degree or more, females earn about 60.6 percent of what men earn (p. 440). In contrast to this national trend, we found that female principals earned slightly more ($212) than their male counterparts in 1999–2000. In 1987–88 male principals were making more, but that trend slowed then reversed itself in the latest year for which there are data on the SASS. Females made $1,278 less 1987–88, $908 less in 1990–91, and $186 less in 1993–94, and then $212 more in 1999–2000.

Table 6.8 shows that females' salaries were about the same as men's in nearly every percentile over time. Therefore, females' average salaries were about the same as men's due to the entire distribution of female principals' salaries, and not due to the possibility that some females earned particularly high salaries.

What accounts for this surprising finding? One possibility is that principals' salaries are related to teachers' salaries, and because teachers' salaries tend to be uniform, rather than gender driven, the principals' salaries tend to vary less by sex. Second, the percentage of female principals in urban and suburban school districts is higher than in rural school districts. In 1999–2000, 21.2 percent of the urban principals and 17.7 percent of the suburban counterparts were female. In contrast, the corresponding statistics were 114.5 per-

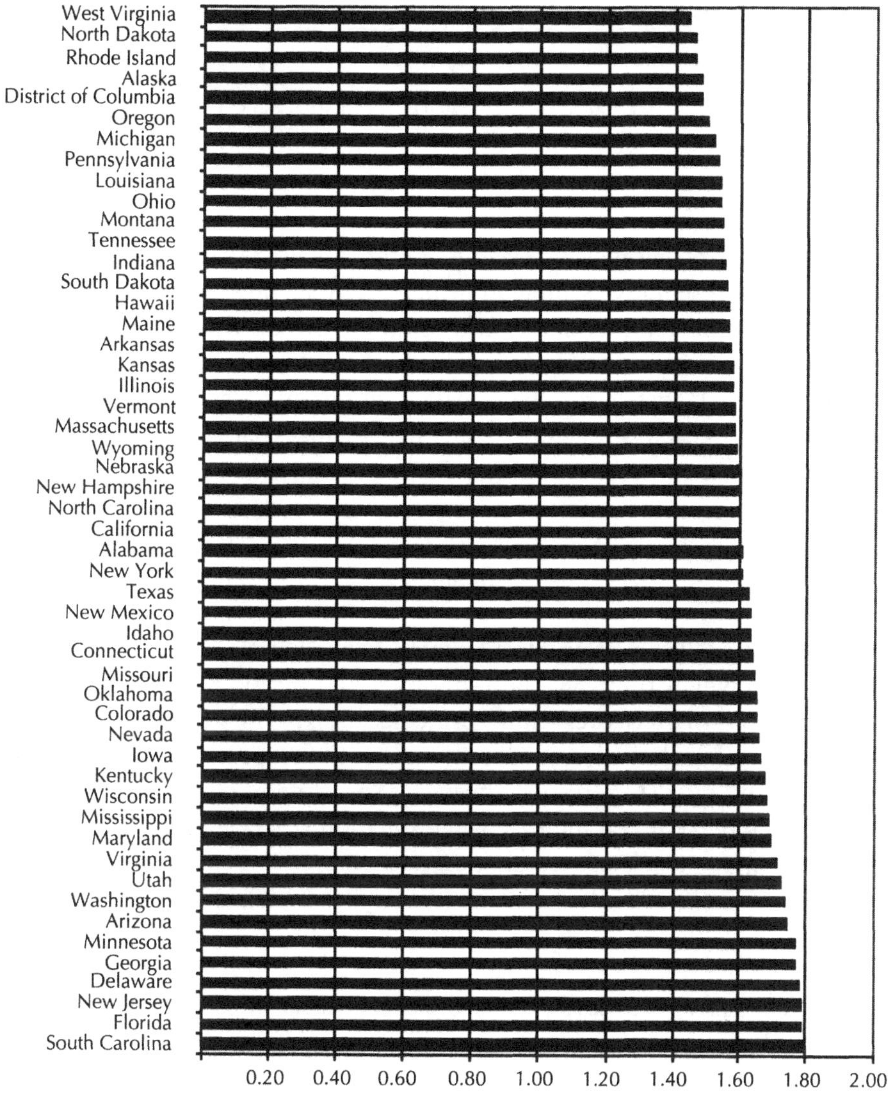

FIGURE 6.4. Ratio of Principals' Annual Average Salary to Teachers' Average Salary (Ranked by State)

cent for their rural counterparts (Wegenke & Shen, in press). As reported in the previous sections, principals in urban and suburban school districts are paid higher, so a higher percentage of female principals in urban and suburban school districts help raise the average salary for female principals. Finally, female teachers tend to teach longer before being promoted into the principal

TABLE 6.7. Average Salaries of Male and Female School Principals by Year

Average Salary/Year	1987–88	1990–91	1993–94	1999–2000
Male	$42,290	$49,875	$54,922	$66,553
Female	$41,011	$48,967	$54,736	$66,765

position, a factor that may also lead to a higher average salary for females. A nationally representative sample of principals in Schools and Staffing Survey 1999–2000 indicated that before taking up the principalship, female principals had, on average, a total of 14.4 years of teaching experience, while the corresponding statistics for their male counterparts was 11.6. Despite all these possible reasons for gender equity in principal salaries, it is encouraging to see this gender equity.

Summary

In summary, analyzing salary data from a nationally representative sample of principals drawn in 1987–88, 1990–91, 1993–94, and 1999–2000, we found a few interesting patterns regarding principals' salary. First, when we investigated principals' salaries longitudinally, we found that principals' average salaries increased by 58.8 percent between 1987–88 and 1999–2000, but there was only a 9 percent real increase when inflation was taken into account. On the average, principals earned about $5,501 more in the school year 1999–2000 than in 1987–88, after adjusting the 1987–88 salary to the 1999–2000

TABLE 6.8. Salaries of Male and Female Principals' Salaries by Year, Average, and Percentile Rank

Sex/Year	1987–88	1990–91	1993–94	1999–2000
Male				
Mean	$42,290	$49,875	$54,922	$66,553
25th Percentile	$36,000	$42,000	$46,000	$56,000
50th Percentile	$42,000	$49,000	$53,000	$65,000
75th Percentile	$48,357	$58,000	$62,500	$76,000
Female				
Mean	$41,011	$48,967	$54,736	$66,765
25th Percentile	$34,501	$42,000	$46,900	$57,000
50th Percentile	$41,900	$49,000	$54,000	$67,000
75th Percentile	$48,000	$56,000	$62,500	$76,000

level using the Consumer Price Index. Therefore, although there was an increase in principals' buying power, the increase was small.

Second, when we compared the trend of principals' salary with those of teachers and average workers, the increase for principals over the 12-year period was slightly more than that of teachers, but slightly less than that of average workers. We also found that in 1999–2000 principals' average annual salary was about 100 percent more than the average annual pay of U.S. workers and 59 percent more than the average annual pay of school teachers.

Third, we also found a substantial amount of variability in principals' salary across the states and the District of Columbia. We investigated (a) principals' average salary in the states, (b) percentage of increase of principals' median salaries between 1987–88 and 1999–2000, (c) the ratio of principals' average salary over all workers' average pay in the state, and (d) the ratio of principals' average salary over teachers' average salary in the state. All four measures revealed an enormous variability in principals' salary across the states. It appears that there is a set of dynamic factors in the states that determines principals' salaries.

Finally, our most surprising finding was that female principals make slightly more than their male counterparts in 1999–2000. Given the census finding that among those with a bachelor's degree or more, females earn about 60.6 percent of what men earn, the principalship as a profession sets an example for gender equity in salary.

As discussed in the introductory section of the article, the principalship has been evolving. There has been a shortage of qualified applicants for principal positions. Through more than a decade of research, we know that a principal is very important for the success of a school (Hallinger & Heck, 1998; Heck, Larson, & Marcoulides, 1990). This article provides some useful data on principals' salary for school board members, superintendents, principals, policy makers, and other stakeholders when they discuss matters and develop policies related to the principalship.

References

American Federation of Teachers. (2000). *Survey and analysis of teacher salary trends.* Washington, DC: American Federation of Teachers.

Bryk, A., Sebring, P., Kerbow, D., Rollow, S., & Easton, J. (1998). *Charting Chicago school reform.* Boulder, CO: Westview Press.

Cooley, V. E., & Shen, J. (1999). Who will lead: The top 10 factors that influence teachers moving into administration. *NASSP Bulletin, 83* (606), 75–80.

Cooley, V. E., & Shen, J. (2000). Factors influencing applying for urban principalship. *Education and Urban Society, 32* (4), 443–454.

Educational Research Service. (1998). Is there a shortage of qualified candidates for openings in the principalship? An exploratory study. *National Association of Elementary School Principals Online*. Retrieved February 23, 2003 from *www.naesp.org/misc/shortage.htm*.

Elmore, R. (2000). *Building a new structure for school leadership*. Washington, D.C., Albert Shanker Institute.

Ferrandino, V. L., & Tirozzi, G. N. (2000). Principals may get a share of the federal pie: Our time has come. *National Association of Elementary School Principals Online*. Retrieved February 25, 2003 from *www.naesp.org/misc/edweek_article_2–23–00.htm*

Fullan, M. (2001). The principal. *The new meaning of educational change*. New York: Teachers College Press.

Gilman, D. A., & Lansman-Given, B. (2001). Where have all the principals gone? *Educational Leadership, 58*(8) 72–74.

Glatthorn, A. A. (2000). *The principal as curriculum leader: Shaping what is taught and tested*. Thousand Oaks, CA: Corwin Press, Inc.

Glickman, C. D., Gordon, S. P., & Ross-Gordon, J. M. (2001). *Supervision and instructional leadership: A developmental approach*. Boston: Allyn & Bacon.

Goldring, E. B. (1990). Elementary school principals as boundary spanners: Their engagement with parents. *Journal of Educational Administration, 28*(1), 53–62.

Hallinger, P., & Heck, R. (1998). Exploring the Principal's Contribution to School Effectiveness: 1980–1995. *School Effectiveness and School Improvement, 9*(2), 157–191.

Heck, R., Larson, T., & Marcoulides, G. (1990). Principal instructional leadership and school achievement: Validation of a causal model. *Educational Administration Quarterly, 26*, 94–125.

Lambert, L., Walker, D., Zimmerman, D. P., Cooper, J.E., Lambert, M. D., Gardner, M. E., & Slack, P. J. F. (1995). *The constructivist leader*. New York: Teachers College Press.

Leithwood, K. A., & Montgomery, D. J. (1986). *Improving principal effectiveness: The principal profile*. Toronto: Ontario Institute for the Study of Education.

Long, A. (2000). Administrative shortage: Perceptions/reality/solutions. *Indiana Principal Leadership Academy Special Edition, 13*(4), 3.

National Association of Secondary School Principals. (2001). *The principal shortage*. Retrieved February 25, 2003 from *http://www.principals.org/publicaffairs/Shortage.html*.

Portin, B. & Shen, J. (1998). The changing principalship and its impact: Voices from principals. *NASSP Bulletin, 82* (602), 1–8.

Portin, B. (2000). The changing urban principalship. *Education and Urban Society, 32*(4), 492–505.

Sergiovanni, T. J., & R. J. Starratt (2001). *Supervision: A redefinition*. New York: McGraw-Hill.

Shen, J., Cooley, V., & Wegenke, G. (2004). Perspectives on factors influencing the application for the principalship: A comparative study of teachers, principals, and superintendents. *International Journal of Leadership in Education*, 7 (1), 57–70.

U. S. Bureau of the Census. (2001). *Statistical abstract of the United States*. Washington, D.C.: U. S. Government Printing Office.

Vandenberghe, R. (1995). Creative management of a school: A matter of vision and daily interventions. *Journal of Educational Administration, 33* (2), 31–51.

Wegenke, G. L., & Shen, J. (in press). Gender, race, and ethnic diversity among principals. In J. Shen and Associates, *School principals*. New York: Peter Lang.

·7·

Dorothy VanderJagt, Jianping Shen, and Chia-lin Hsieh

PRINCIPALS' PERCEPTIONS OF SCHOOL PROBLEMS

Introduction

It is becoming increasingly difficult for school administrators and teachers nationwide to provide America's youths with a safe environment conducive to learning. The juvenile crime rate in America is on the rise. According to Uniform Crime Reports, juvenile arrests were up 11% from 1993 to 1994. Even more disturbing is the fact that while fifteen- and sixteen-year olds make up only a small proportion of our population, they commit a large percentage of all violent crimes (Sexton, 1996).

Students need orderly surroundings to learn, but this environment is continually threatened. The National Crime Victimization Survey data show that an estimated 2.7 million violent crimes take place annually either at or near schools (Nolin, Davies, & Chandler, 1996). Violence among teens is prevalent in towns of all sizes, and many students feel schools have become more dangerous. A survey by Roper Starch Worldwide indicates that 31% of high school students think teen violence is a serious problem in their own schools, and 45% think it has become more dangerous over the past five years (USA Today, 1995).

No district or child is immune from the abuse that occurs at or around schools. According to Nolin, Davies, and Chandler (1996), substantial percentages of United States students in grades 6–12 face crime or threat at school or on the way to or from school. Fear of crime is on the rise in our nation's schools. A national poll administered by the Children's Defense Fund in 1993 found that more than half of the ten- to seventeen-year olds surveyed indicated violence was their number-one worry.

Growing up in American schools today, students have a variety of school problems in addition to violence. Substance abuse is one of the problems. Children are experimenting at a much younger age and often bring the drugs onto school grounds. As the students grow older they tend to continue to use the illegal substances. Drug use increases as the grade level increases (Morgan, 1995; Penfield & University, 1990). Many students become involved in using illegal substances because of peer pressure and others due to an emotional need. A feeling for need fulfillment may propel adolescents into the destructive behavior of substance abuse (Mainous, Martin, Oler, Richardson, & Haney, 1996; Smith & Rosenthal, 1995).

Dropping out of school is another serious school problem. Dropping out of high school is a multiply-determined process, with early influences beginning in childhood, which involves family as well as child and adolescent factors (Garnier, Stein, & Jacobs, 1997). Drop-out varies not only with anticipated opportunities and costs but also with prospects for valued participation in a socially, economically, and culturally viable community. High school students who have a valued place and a positive sense of affiliation with peers and teachers are less likely to drop out than others (Bryk & Thum, 1989). Zimmerman, Bandura, and Martinez (1992) found a significant causal path between efficacy for self-regulated learning, efficacy for academic achievement, and academic attainment. Students who perceived themselves as capable of regulating their own activities strategically are more confident about mastering academic subjects and attain higher academic performance. The goal of education is to provide students with an opportunity to become successful learners. However, educators must have students in school to help them achieve success.

As with dropouts, when opportunity and community become more difficult to find, teen pregnancy becomes more common (Bickel, Weaver, & Williams, 1997). Approximately one million teenage girls in the United States become pregnant each year (Johnson, 1992).

Through analyzing data from a nationally representative sample of public school principals, this study inquired into the extent to which various problems exist in our public schools and whether there is any difference between elementary and secondary schools in the severity of the problems. There are three main reasons for the study. First, in order to develop strategies to prevent and alleviate the school problems, we need to know the severity of those problems. Some problem management programs are enthusiastically endorsed in many school districts, but limited data exist on the validity of these programs, especially in inner-city schools where ethnically diverse students live in poverty and in the midst of violence (Johnson, Johnson, Mitchell, Cotten, Harris, & Louison, 1996).

Second, the inquiry into whether there is any difference between elementary and secondary schools in relation to school problems has implications for developing different strategies for elementary and secondary schools. If the severity of the problems intensifies as the grade levels increase, then different programs for preventing and alleviating the problems should be developed for various levels. If the trajectories of the problems are different—e.g., some problems exacerbate more quickly than others, then the findings will have implications for the focus of the programs. We should focus more on preventing those problems that exacerbate quickly.

Third, principals' perceptions are very important for understanding the problems because they not only know the intricate details of discipline and factors contributing to problems faced by children, but also have a perspective on the whole organization rather than individual classrooms. Therefore, in order to understand, prevent, and alleviate the school problems encountered by our children, it is essential to obtain information about these problems from the principals.

In summary, before schools invent and implement strategies to combat school problems, the nature and severity of the problems for both elementary and secondary schools should be identified. The possible variations at the two school levels, in different school locations, and in schools of different sizes must also be examined to determine what programs would be most conducive in certain types of schools. This study intended to contribute to our knowledge on the severity and variation of school problems.

Methods

Sample

The data were collected during the 1993–94 Schools and Staffing Survey (SASS93), a survey developed by the U.S. Department of Education's National Center for Education Statistics (NCES) and conducted by the Bureau of the Census. SASS93 was an integrated survey of public and private schools, school districts, principals, and teachers. The data collected from the principals in public schools were utilized for this study. The achieved sample of public school principals was 8,221 (weighted $N = 71{,}946$), among them 6,134 and 2,087 were at elementary and secondary levels, respectively.

Weighting

Because the sample design of the SASS93 involved stratification, disproportionate sampling of certain strata, and clustered probability sampling, the resultant SASS93 sample was not a random one. Therefore, a relative sample weight, which was based on SASS93 public principals' final weight, was used to approximate the population and adjust it down to the actual sample size of the study. After weighting, the findings of the study are generalizable to public school principals in the United States.

Instrument

Principals were asked to rate the extent to which 22 problems (please refer to Table 7.1) existed in their schools. Their answers were coded on a 4-point Likert scale—ranging from "serious (4)," to "moderate (3)," to "minor (2)," and to "not a problem (1)." The 22 items were collapsed into seven categories based on content analysis, and Cronbach's alphas were calculated for each category. It appeared that all seven categories had high internal consistency.

TABLE 7.1. Categories of School Problems

Category	Cronbach's α	Items
Truancy	.83	student tardiness
		student absenteeism
		students cutting class
		students dropping out
School Violence	.77	physical conflicts among students
		robbery or theft
		vandalism of school property
		student possession of weapons
Deviant Behavior	.87	student pregnancy
		student use of alcohol
		student drug abuse
Disrespect for Teachers	.88	verbal abuse of teachers
		student disrespect for teachers
Detrimental Family Background	.76	lack of parent involvement
		parental alcoholism and/or drug abuse
		poverty
Low Motivation	.70	student apathy
		lack of academic challenge
Lack of Preparation for Learning	.78	students come to school unprepared to learn
		poor nutrition
		poor student health
		student problems with the English language

Ratings for the items in each category were averaged for each subject to form a composite score which was used in the ensuing analysis. Please refer to Table 7.1 for the items, categories, and Cronbach's alphas.

Results

The mean and rank for each category of the school problem were displayed in Table 7.2 for both elementary and secondary school principals. Statistics related to the *t*-test for independent samples were also presented in Table 7.2. The following is a description of the patterns related to the research questions.

First, the most serious school problem at the elementary level was "detrimental family background," followed by "lack of preparation for learning," "low motivation," "disrespect for teachers," "school violence," and "truancy." "Deviant behavior" was the least serious problem at the elementary level. At the secondary level, "detrimental family background," "deviant behavior," "low motivation," and "truancy" were among the most serious problems, followed by "lack of preparation for learning," "disrespect for teachers," and "school violence." It appeared that there was no relationship between the rank order of the severity of the school problems for elementary and secondary schools. As a matter of fact, Spearman's rank order correlation between elementary and secondary school was very low ($r_s = .18, p = .70$).

Second, when we investigated the means of the school problems, it was clear that except for "lack of preparation for learning," all school problems were more severe at the secondary level than at the elementary level. The tests for equality of means between elementary and secondary schools indicated that there was a statistically significant increase from elementary to secondary schools in the severity of all school problems except for "lack of preparation for learning." Since the sample of the study was large, the null hypotheses could be

TABLE 7.2. Severity of School Problems as Perceived by Principals of Public Elementary and Secondary Schools

	Mean (Rank)				
Problem	Elementary	Secondary	*t*	*p*	Eta square
Detrimental Family Background	2.28 (1)	2.46 (1)	−9.35	.00	.01
Lack of Preparation for Learning	1.99 (2)	1.98 (5)	.60	.55	.00
Low Motivation	1.79 (3)	2.28 (3)	−27.7	.00	.08
Disrespect for Teachers	1.72 (4)	1.97 (6)	−14.3	.00	.02
School Violence	1.57 (5)	1.78 (7)	−17.3	.00	.04
Truancy	1.52 (6)	2.23 (4)	−57.9	.00	.29
Deviant Behavior	1.18 (7)	2.30 (2)	93.7	.00	.5[illegible]

easily rejected. Therefore, eta squares were displayed to indicate the effect size. As indicated in Table 7.2, effect sizes were the largest for "deviant behavior" and "truancy." Fifty-two percent of the variance in "deviant behavior" and 29% in "truancy" could be explained by the variable of school level, an indication that the severity of these two school problems increased tremendously from the elementary to secondary levels.

We also investigated whether public school principals' perceptions of school problems were related to school location. Statistics related to the one-way ANOVA for independent samples were presented in Tables 7.3 and 7.4. When we explored the mean rank of the school problems, it was clear that at both the elementary and secondary levels, the rank order of severity of school problems was essentially the same for urban, suburban, and rural schools. The rank-order correlation coefficients were all positive and statistically significant at the .01 level. When we compared the magnitude of the means, there were statistically significant differences for most of the school problems. The general pattern was that the problems were the most severe in urban schools, and least severe in suburban schools, with rural schools in the middle. However, the magnitude of the difference, as measured by eta square, tended to be small.

Finally, we examined whether public school principals' perceptions of school problems were related to school size. Statistics related to the one-way ANOVA for independent samples were presented in Tables 7.5 and 7.6. When we looked into the mean rank of the elementary school problems, it was clear that the rank order of severity of school problems was very similar in small, medium, and large schools. However, at the secondary level, there were more variations in the rank-order correlation among schools of three different sizes. The rank-order correlation between medium and small schools were .93 ($p <$ .01), while the rank-order correlation was .75 ($p > .05$) between large schools, on one hand, and medium-sized and small schools, on the other. Therefore,

TABLE 7.3. Severity of School Problems as Perceived by Public Elementary Principals in Various Locations

	Mean (Rank)					
Problem	Urban	Suburban	Rural	F	p	Eta square
Detrimental Family Background	2.47 (1)	2.06 (1)	2.32 (1)	128.02	.00	.04
Lack of Preparation for Learning	2.18 (2)	1.90 (2)	1.94 (2)	96.03	.00	.03
Disrespect for Teachers	1.85 (3)	1.65 (4)	1.69 (4)	38.62	.00	.01
Low Motivation	1.84 (4)	1.66 (3)	1.83 (3)	39.48	.00	.01
School Violence	1.69 (5)	1.53 (5)	1.52 (5)	74.81	.00	.02
Truancy	1.65 (6)	1.45 (6)	1.48 (6)	109.72	.00	.03
Deviant Behavior	1.15 (7)	1.12 (7)	1.23 (7)	50.05	.00	.02

TABLE 7.4. Severity of School Problems as Perceived by Public Secondary Principals in Various Locations

	Mean (Rank)					
Problem	Urban	Suburban	Rural	*F*	*p*	Eta square
Detrimental Family Background	2.56 (1)	2.30 (1)	2.50 (1)	18.51	.00	.02
Truancy	2.48 (2)	2.27 (2.5)	2.14 (4)	40.35	.00	.04
Low Motivation	2.33 (3)	2.19 (4)	2.29 (3)	4.50	.01	.00
Deviant Behavior	2.27 (4)	2.27 (2.5)	2.32 (2)	1.54	.22	.00
Lack of Preparation for Learning	2.22 (5)	1.95 (6)	1.91 (5)	41.47	.00	.04
Disrespect for Teachers	2.16 (6)	1.98 (5)	1.90 (6)	17.17	.00	.02
School Violence	1.97 (7)	1.87 (7)	1.68 (7)	59.79	.00	.05

large schools tended to have a different pattern from the small and medium schools. "Truancy" was the most severe problem in large schools, but was ranked the fourth in medium-sized and small schools. When means were concerned, with only one exception ("detrimental family background" at the secondary level), there were statistically significant differences among large, medium-sized, and small schools at both elementary and secondary levels. The differences among the three types of schools, as measured by eta square, tended to be larger at the secondary than at the elementary level.

Discussion

School problems are undoubtedly a concern for students, parents, educators, and the general public. The fact that teenagers are committing more violent acts at an earlier age is undoubtedly responsible for the rising growth in the

TABLE 7.5. Severity of School Problems as Perceived by Public Elementary Principals in Schools of Various Sizes*

	Mean (Rank)					
Problem	Large	Medium	Small	*F*	*p*	Eta square
Detrimental Family Background	2.41 (1)	2.27 (1)	2.25 (1)	11.79	.00	.00
Lack of Preparation for Learning	2.21 (2)	2.01 (2)	1.84 (2)	87.09	.00	.03
Disrespect for Teachers	1.97 (3)	1.73 (4)	1.59 (4)	78.34	.00	.03
Low Motivation	1.96 (4)	1.77 (3)	1.74 (3)	26.34	.00	.01
School Violence	1.81 (5)	1.58 (5)	1.44 (5)	171.49	.00	.05
Truancy	1.75 (6)	1.52 (6)	1.40 (6)	177.58	.00	.06
Deviant Behavior	1.29 (7)	1.15 (7)	1.19 (7)	49.79	.00	.02

* Small, < 300 students; medium, 300–745 students; large, >745 students.

TABLE 7.6. Severity of School Problems as Perceived by Public Secondary Principals in Schools of Various Sizes*

Problem	Mean (Rank) Large	Medium	Small	*F*	*p*	Eta square
Truancy	2.49 (1)	2.14 (4)	2.01 (4)	114.81	.00	.10
Detrimental Family Background	2.43 (2)	2.48 (1)	2.48 (1)	1.17	.31	.00
Deviant Behavior	2.41 (3)	2.26 (3)	2.21 (2)	16.46	.00	.02
Low Motivation	2.33 (4)	2.28 (2)	2.20 (3)	5.88	.00	.00
Disrespect for Teachers	2.12 (5)	1.96 (5)	1.79 (6)	37.69	.00	.04
Lack of Preparation for Learning	2.09 (6)	1.95 (6)	1.87 (5)	26.01	.00	.02
School Violence	2.00 (7)	1.75 (7)	1.53 (7)	166.66	.00	.14

* Small, < 300 students; medium, 300–745 students; large, >745 students.

nation's violent-crime rate (Sexton, 1996). This study was initiated with an aim to shed some light on the school problems as perceived by elementary and secondary principals.

Based on a nationally representative sample of elementary and secondary principals in our public schools, the data suggested that there are some problems in our public schools, and these problems tend to become more severe as the school level increases. Furthermore, there seems to be no association between the rank order of the severity of school problems in elementary and secondary schools. The problems tend to be more severe in large schools than in medium-sized and small schools, and more serious in urban schools than in suburban schools.

The findings have implications for preventing, alleviating, or solving school problems. First, since there is no association between the rank order of the severity of school problems in elementary and secondary schools, the mechanism for preventing and alleviating these problems should be different for elementary and secondary schools. The "one size fits all" approach does not seem to be meaningful. For example, although "detrimental family background" was rated as the most serious problem in both elementary and secondary schools, "deviant behavior" was ranked the second most severe problem in secondary schools but the seventh in elementary schools. The data suggest that the focus of the effort to prevent or alleviate these problems should be different for elementary and secondary schools. The finding that there was no association between the rank order of the severity of school problems in large schools, on one hand, and in medium-sized and small schools, on the other hand, also argue against the "one size fits all" approach.

Second, the problems were more serious at the secondary level than at the elementary level. Therefore, there should be a prevention strategy to deal with those problems that intensify as school level increases. Since the school problems do not exacerbate at the same trajectory, the problems that exacerbate more rapidly should become the focus of the prevention strategy.

Third, the data also illustrate the need to unite school, family, and community to combat the problems. Both elementary and secondary principals perceived "detrimental family background" as the most serious problem. "Lack of preparation to learn" and "deviant behavior" are rated the second most serious problem by elementary and secondary principals, respectively. Research suggests that parents are a major influence on children and their behavior. According to Garnier, Stein, and Jacobs (1997), children living in family environments where they are more exposed to drug use are more likely to be exposed to additional problems and have experience in drug use. However, parents could have a positive impact. For example, Trusty (1996), conducting a study on parental involvement of 9,075 high-school seniors using data from the National Educational Longitudinal Study of 1988, found that parental involvement was positively related to constructive school attitudes, favorable perceptions of the future, and productive behavior. Parental involvement was negatively related to substance use and behavior problems. Since the school problems are, to a great extent, a reflection of those in the community and particularly those in the family, we have to unite the school, family, and community to prevent or alleviate the problems (Neuman, Hagedorn, Celano, & Daly, 1995; Nolin, Davies, & Chandler, 1996).

In summary, family, community, and educators must work together in making schools safer and better environments for students. Juvenile crime reports tripled between 1990 and 1994 (Dohrn, 1997), a statistic which is a constant reminder about growing problems of violence and others. Students, parents, staff, and the community must be educated about the severity and danger of the school problems. Programs that are geared toward different school levels and include the school as well as the family and community are beneficial in preventing and alleviating the problems faced by our schools today.

References

Bickel, R., Weaver, S., & Williams, T. (1997). Opportunity, community, and teen pregnancy in an Appalachian state. *Journal of Educational Research, 90*(3), 175–181.

Bryk, A., & Thum, Y. (1989). The effects of high school organization on dropping out: An exploratory investigation. *American Educational Research Journal, 26*, 353–383.

Dohrn, B. (1997). Youth violence: False fears and hard truths. *Educational Leadership, 55* (2), 45–47.

Garnier, H. E., Stein, J. A., & Jacobs, J. K. (1997). The process of dropping out of high school: A 19-year perspective. *American Educational Research Journal, 34* (2), 395–419.

Johnson, A. (1992). *Human arrangements.* Orlando, FL: Harcourt Brace Jovanovich.

Johnson, D. W., Johnson, R., Mitchell, J., Cotten, B., Harris, D., Louison, S. (1996). Effectiveness of conflict managers in an inner-city elementary school. *Journal of Educational Research, 89* (5), 280–285.

Mainous, A. G., Martin, C. A., Oler, M. J., Richardson, E. T., & Haney, A. S. (1996). Substance use among adolescents: Fulfilling a need state. *Adolescence, 31*(124), 807–815.

Morgan, H. (1995). Drug use in high school: Race and gender issues. *Journal of Educational Research, 88* (5), 301–308.

Neuman, S. B., Hagedorn, T., Celano, D., & Daly, P. (1995). Toward a collaborative approach to parent involvement in early education: A study of teenage mothers in an African-American community. *American Educational Research Journal, 32* (4), 801–827.

Nolin, M. J., Davies, E., & Chandler, K. (1996). Student victimization at school. *Journal of School Health, 66* (6), 216–221.

Penfield, D. A., & University, R. (1990). Surveying urban inner-city high school students: An assessment of drug and alcohol abuse. *Educational Research Quarterly, 14* (4), 6–14.

Sexton, R. L. (1996). Tackling juvenile crime. *The Journal of Social, Political and Economic Studies, 21,* 191–197.

Smith, A. M., & Rosenthal, D. A. (1995). Adolescents' perceptions of their risk environment. *Journal of Adolescence, 18,* 229–245.

Trusty, J. (1996). Relationship of parental involvement in teens' career development to teens' attitudes, perceptions, and behavior. *Journal of Research and Development in Education, 30* (1), 63–69.

USA Today. (1995). "Students Cite Widespread Violence." *USA Today, 124,* 8–9.

Zimmerman, B. J., Bandura, A., & Pons-Martinez, M. (1992). Self-motivation for academic attainment: The role of self-efficacy beliefs and personal goal setting. *American Educational Research Journal, 29* (3), 663–676.

·8·

Jianping Shen

PRINCIPALS' AND TEACHERS' POWER

During the last 20 years, the educational arena has been replete with the rhetoric of decentralization, site-based management, teacher empowerment, and distributed leadership (Aieta, Barth, & O'Brien, 1988; Anderson & Dixon, 1993; Leithwood, Begley, & Cousins, 1994; Lieberman, 1992; Wasley, Hampel, & Clark, 1997). Given the continuing emphasis on the aforementioned ideas, it is imperative to investigate (a) how teachers' leadership has evolved in practice between the 1987–88 and the 1993–94 school years, (b) whether there is any variation of teacher empowerment for various kinds of teachers, and (c) whether there is a discrepancy between principals' and teachers' perceptions of teacher empowerment.

The Rationale for the Chapter

The concept of empowerment has gradually gained momentum in theory and practice since the Second World War. Empowerment of workers has been found to be positively related to enhanced job performance, increased job satisfaction, greater work efficiency, and higher motivation (Tseo & Ramos, 1995). In education, the school effectiveness research of the last 20 years repeatedly affirms the role of principal leadership in school success. Principals remain key individuals as instructional leaders, initiators of change, school managers, personnel administrators, problem solvers, and boundary spanners for the school (Fullan, 1991; Leithwood & Montgomery, 1986; Sergiovanni, 1991; Vandenberghe, 1995). As to teachers' leadership, teacher empowerment has been found to be positively related to enhanced teacher self-esteem, increased teacher knowledge of subject matter and pedagogy, stronger staff collegiality, improved curriculum and instruction, and higher student achievement (Browder, 1994; Daigle & Leclerc, 1997; Sullivan, 1995; White, 1992).

Accompanying these empirical studies is the argument that principals and teachers should be more empowered. In other words, principals and teachers should have more leadership in school-wide and classroom policies and issues. However, despite the research, we know very little about how teachers' and principals' leadership evolved in practice in the last few years. We have little empirical information as to whether teacher empowerment differs for new and experienced teachers in different kinds of schools. We know even less about whether there is a congruence between principals and teachers in terms of their perceived leadership.

There are basically two major rationales for the study. First, there has been a discrepancy between rhetoric and practice in education. It is, therefore, imperative to investigate how the rhetoric on principals' and teachers' leadership has transpired in practice over the last decade. History reminds us of the importance of comparing theory to practice. For example, in the 1960s, the educational field was filled with the rhetoric of individualized instruction. Therefore, John Goodlad and his associates developed a checklist of 10 reasonable expectations for classroom instruction to determine whether individualized instruction had been put into practice. The checklist included, for example, that schools might pay considerable attention to and make substantial provisions for individual differences, and that teachers might make rather substantial use of basic principles of learning and instruction. Goodlad and his associates then visited classrooms across the country—in their own words, "looking behind the classroom door." What they found was that the expectations for individual instruction were not met in the classrooms they visited (Goodlad & Associates, 1970).

The second rationale for the study is that there appears to be a possible tension in the recent rhetoric on teachers' and principals' leadership. On one hand, site-based management, decentralization, and instructional leadership tend to emphasize principals' leadership in improving the school, in general, and curriculum and instruction, in particular. On the other hand, the rhetoric on teacher empowerment and distributive leadership tends to focus on teachers' leadership in bettering the school and its curriculum and instruction. Ideally, these two emphases could be combined, leading to a win-win situation for enhancing both principals' and teachers' leadership. However, the dual emphases could also result in a tension between principals' and teachers' leadership. Therefore, this study investigates the impact of the rhetoric of dual emphases by comparing the evolution of principals' and teachers' leadership during the last decade.

Data Source

Since the 1987–88 school year, the National Center for Education Statistics of the U.S. Department of Education has conducted surveys of principals' and teachers' leadership in public schools. Every three school years, the staff asks a representative sample of some 9,000 principals and 50,000 public school teachers to rate, on a six-point Likert scale ranging from "no influence at all" to "a great deal of influence," their leadership on the following school-wide and classroom policy issues.

School-wide issues:

- Determining discipline policy
- Determining the content of in-service programs
- Establishing curriculum
- Hiring new full-time teachers
- Deciding how the school budget will be spent
- Evaluating teachers

Instructional issues in classroom:

- Selecting textbooks and other instructional materials
- Selecting content, topics, and skills to be taught
- Selecting teaching techniques
- Disciplining students
- Determining the amount of homework

The following trends of principals' and teachers' leadership emerged from the survey data collected between the 1987–88 and the 1993–94 school years. The National Center for Education Statistics conducted The Schools and Staffing Survey in 1987–88, 1990–91, and 1993–94. Due to lack of funds, the survey was not conducted in 1996–97. The most recent survey was conducted during 1999–2000, but the answers to the items used in this chapter employed a different scale. Therefore, I was not able to use the 1999–2000 data. However, based on the three waves of data, we can ascertain the trajectories of teacher and principal empowerment.

Teachers' Leadership: Stagnant between the 1987–88 and the 1993–94 School Years

Table 8.1 displays the percentage of teachers in each of the school years who perceived they had much influence on some school-wide and classroom issues. Three observations emerged from the data. First, teachers' leadership on school-wide issues—determining discipline policy, determining the content of in-service programs, and establishing curriculum—remained stagnant over the years. Second, in regard to classroom issues, the percentage of teachers who perceived they had much influence over determining the amount of homework and disciplining students remained the same or decreased slightly. However, the percentage of teachers who reported much influence on selecting textbooks, teaching content, and teaching techniques increased nominally between the 1987–88 and the 1993–94 school years. When we combine the evolution of teachers' leadership on school-wide and classroom issues, it is fair to say that teachers' leadership remained stagnant over the years. Third, from the 1987–88 to the 1993–94 school years, only about 35% of the teachers indicated that they had much influence on school-wide policy issues such as setting discipline policies, determining the content of in-service programs, and establishing curriculum. However, the percentage of teachers who reported they had much influence on classroom issues ranged from 54% to 87%. Therefore, despite the rhetoric of teacher empowerment and distributive leadership, teachers still perceived that they had more influence on classroom issues than school-wide ones. In summary, teachers perceived that their leadership was stagnant between the 1987–88 and the 1993–94 school years, and that they had more leadership in classroom issues than in school-wide issues.

TABLE 8.1. Percentage of Teachers Perceiving They Had Much Influence on the Following Issues

Item	1987–88	1990–91	1993–94
School-wide Issues			
Determining discipline policy	35	37	35
Establishing curriculum	35	35	35
Determining the content of in-service programs	31	33	31
Instructional Issues in Classroom			
Determining the amount of homework	87	87	87
Selecting teaching techniques	85	87	87
Disciplining students	70	72	69
Selecting content, topics, and skills to be taught	59	60	61
Selecting textbooks and other instructional materials	54	55	55

Variation in Teacher Empowerment

Given the fact that the working condition and culture differ significantly in urban, suburban, and rural schools, it is interesting to inquire into whether there is any difference in teacher empowerment in these different kinds of schools. Furthermore, the organizational structures of elementary and secondary schools differ greatly due to the nature of how instruction is delivered. Therefore, there might be a difference between elementary and secondary teachers in their perceived influence on school-wide and classroom issues. Finally, teachers' characteristics, such as full-time status, tenure, and years of experience, are expected to be related to how they perceive their influence in the school and classroom. Thus, the study investigates whether new and more experienced teachers perceive their empowerment differently.

Table 8.2 shows the variation in teacher empowerment by school location, school level, and years of experience. Some interesting patterns emerge from the data. Where school location is concerned, there are some consistent patterns for instructional issues in the classroom, but not for school-wide issues. Basically, from urban, suburban, to rural schools, teachers reported an increasing level of empowerment over instruction-related issues such as "selecting textbooks and other instructional materials," "selecting content, topics, and skills to be taught," and "determining the amount of homework." It appears that rural teachers had more power in instructional issues than their counterparts in suburban and especially urban schools. This might be related to the more formalized decision-making structure in urban schools. There is no consistent pattern as to the school-wide issues. However, it is interesting to point out that teachers in all three kinds of schools perceived that they had much less power in school-wide issues than they did in instructional issues.

As to school levels, secondary teachers reported more power than their elementary counterparts in curriculum- and instruction-related issues such as "establishing curriculum," "selecting textbooks and other instructional materials," "selecting content, topics, and skills to be taught," "selecting teaching techniques," and "determining the amount of homework." However, secondary teachers reported less influence than their elementary counterparts in "setting discipline policy" and "disciplining students," a phenomenon which can be explained by the fact that in secondary schools the principal and/or the assistant principal are usually responsible for discipline-related issues. The data also indicate that secondary school teachers tended to have less influence than their elementary counterparts over school-wide issues such as "determining the content of in-service programs," "hiring new full-time teachers," and "deciding how the school budget will be spent."

TABLE 8.2. Variation in Teacher Empowerment: Percentage of Teachers Perceiving They Had Much Influence on the Following Issues in 1993–94

Item	Urban	Suburban	Rural	Elementary	Secondary	New*	Experienced
School Issues							
Setting discipline policy	34	33	37	42	27	35	39
Determining the content of in-service programs	31	30	30	34	29	31	38
Hiring new full-time teachers	8	9	8	9	8	8	9
Deciding how the school budget will be spent	12	12	8	12	9	10	11
Evaluating teachers	3	3	3	2	3	2	5
Establishing curriculum	30	34	40	32	37	34	37
Instructional Issues in Classroom							
Selecting textbooks and other instructional materials	48	54	64	49	62	56	48
Selecting content, topics, and skills to be taught	55	60	67	54	67	61	60
Selecting teaching techniques	84	88	88	84	89	86	89
Evaluating and grading students	86	88	88	84	90	87	87
Disciplining students	67	69	70	71	64	69	72
Determining the amount of homework to be assigned	85	88	88	84	90	87	89

*New teachers were those who had five or fewer than five years of experience in teaching.

Given the tenure system and organizational culture, it is expected that junior teachers would perceive that they are less empowered than their senior counterparts. This hypothesis is confirmed by the data where school-wide issues are concerned. The results suggest a consistent pattern that experienced teachers reported more influence over school-wide issues than their junior counterparts. However, where instructional issues in their classrooms are concerned, the results were more mixed. Experienced teacher perceived that they had slightly more influence than their junior counterparts in "selecting teaching techniques," "disciplining students," and "determining the amount of homework to be assigned." However, new teachers perceived that they had slightly more power than their senior counterparts in "selecting textbooks and other instructional materials" and "selecting content, topics, and skills to be taught."

Therefore, the analysis reveals some consistent patterns related to the variation of teacher empowerment. First, when curricular and instructional issues are concerned, there is an increasing level of empowerment as perceived by teachers from urban, to suburban, and to rural schools. Second, secondary teachers felt that they had more influence over curricular and instructional issues than their elementary counterparts. Third, when some school-wide issues were concerned, experienced teachers reported more empowerment than their junior counterparts. Finally, secondary teachers indicated much less influence than their elementary counterparts in "setting discipline policy" and "disciplining students."

Principals' Leadership: Slightly Increased Between the 1987–88 and the 1993–94 School Years

Table 8.3 shows the percentage of principals who perceived they had much influence on school-wide issues in each of the three school years. It is apparent that principals had more and more influence in hiring new full-time teachers and setting discipline policies from the 1987–88 to the 1993–94 school years. The percentage of principals reporting much influence on hiring new full-time faculty increased from 75% in 1987–88 to 82% in 1990–91 and to 85% in 1993–94. The corresponding statistics for setting discipline policy increased from 81% in 1987–88 to 85% in 1990–91 and to 87% in 1993–94. However, their leadership in establishing curriculum basically remained unchanged during the same period. This might be due to the trend of state-mandated curriculum. Therefore, principals' leadership increased slightly from the 1987–88 to the 1993–94 school years in school-wide issues such as setting discipline policy and hiring new full-time teachers, a trend which is consistent with site-based management. However, only 50% of the principals indicated that they had much influence on establishing curriculum and the percentage decreased slightly over the years, a phenomenon which is consistent with the increasingly state-mandated curriculum.

Discrepancies Between How Principals and Teachers Perceived Teachers' Leadership

Some interesting patterns emerged when we compared teachers' and principals' respective perceptions of teachers' leadership on some school-wide

TABLE 8.3. Percentage of Principals Perceiving They Had Much Influence on School-wide Issues

Item	1987–88	1990–91	1993–94
Setting discipline policy	81	85	87
Hiring new full-time teachers	75	82	85
Establishing curriculum	55	49	54

issues. The first pattern, as illustrated in Table 8.4, is that principals felt teachers had more leadership than teachers perceived themselves to have. For example, in the 1993–94 school year, 35% of the teachers perceived that they had much influence on establishing curriculum and setting discipline policy, but as many as 62% and 75% of the principals, respectively, perceived that teachers had much influence on establishing curriculum and setting discipline policy. The discrepancy is even greater when school budget, in-service programs, and teacher evaluation were concerned. For example, 41% of the principals, but only 10% of the teachers, reported that teachers had much influence on determining how the school budget should be spent. Similarly, 24% of the principals, and only 3% of the teachers, reported that teachers had much influence on teacher evaluation.

The second pattern emerging from the comparison is the different trajectory of teachers' leadership perceived by principals and teachers. Between the 1987–88 and the 1993–94 school years, while teachers perceived that their leadership on school-wide issues remained stagnant, principals felt that teachers' leadership on school-wide issues increased tremendously over the 10-year period. To be more specific, for all three academic years, 35% of the teachers reported that they had much influence on establishing curriculum, but the percentage of principals who reported that teachers had much influence on establishing curriculum increased from 52% in 1987–88 to 62% in 1993–94. In regard to setting discipline policy, only about 35% of the teachers perceived that they had much influence, but the percentage of the principals who perceived teachers had much influence on setting discipline policy increased from 52% in 1987–88 to 75% in 1993–94.

It is evident that there was a discrepancy between teachers' and principals' perception of teachers' leadership development between the 1987–88 and the 1993–94 school years. Teachers perceived that their leadership remained stagnant over the years while principals perceived that teachers' leadership has increased tremendously over the same period of time.

TABLE 8.4. Percentage of Principals and Teachers Perceiving That Teachers Had Much Influence on the Following Issues in the 1993–94 School Year

Item	Principals	Teachers
Evaluating teachers	24	3
Hiring new teachers	33	8
Deciding how the budget is spent	41	10
Establishing curriculum	62	35
Setting discipline policy	75	35
Determining content of in-service programs	76	31

Summary and Discussion

The longitudinal and comparative survey data from the National Center for Education Statistics reveal the patterns of teacher and principal empowerment in our public schools. Both encouraging and discouraging patterns are found. The encouraging aspects include that teachers reported much influence over instructional issues in their classroom, and that principals felt more empowered in the process of decentralization and site-based management although the enhancement of their leadership was slight.

However, the analysis also suggests a few major issues related to the evolution of teachers' and principals' leadership over the years. The first issue is that teachers perceived that their leadership was primarily confined to classroom issues and their leadership in school-wide issues was still very weak. Furthermore, teachers perceived that their leadership remained stagnant over the years. Thus, as far as teachers' perception of their own leadership is concerned, the rhetoric of teacher empowerment and distributive leadership has not been translated into practice.

The second major issue is the discrepancy between teachers' and principals' perceptions. Principals perceived that teachers' leadership increased steadily over the years while teachers themselves indicated that their leadership remained the same. The rhetoric of teacher empowerment and shared decision-making appears to give principals the impression that the rhetoric has been translated into practice. However, teachers themselves felt that the rhetoric has not materialized in practice yet. To make the teachers' and principals' perceptions congruent is a daunting task facing us in this new era of school leadership.

The third major issue is related to teacher empowerment in urban, suburban, and rural schools. Urban teachers perceived that they were less empowered in curricular and instructional issues than their suburban and rural counterparts. The data seem to suggest that the organizational structure and decision-making mechanism tend to be more formalized in urban schools than in suburban and rural schools, which results in less empowered teachers in urban schools. The irony is that given the magnitude and nature of the problems that urban schools have, we expect urban teachers to be more empowered and take more initiatives in educational renewal. However, the expectation does not seem to be compatible with the more formalized decision-making mechanism in urban schools.

The final issue is that new teachers felt less empowered than their senior counterparts. Although the finding is not unexpected given the tenure and power structure in our public schools, the disparity between junior and senior teachers in their perceptions of empowerment does raise the equity issue in school governance. Given the fact that the turn-over rate of new teachers is extremely high, it becomes very important to empower new teachers and treat them as professionals (Shen, 1997; Whitener, Gruber, Lynch, Tingos, Perona, & Fondelier, 1997).

In summary, the findings from the national, longitudinal study indicate that although the literature is replete with the rhetoric of site-based management, teacher empowerment, and distributive leadership, teachers are still not empowered in many school-wide policy areas. The disparity between the rhetoric and practice of teacher empowerment is substantial. The findings also have implications for principals' behaviors and policy making. Specifically, awareness of the findings from this study could assist superintendents and principals in regard to their responsibilities for teacher empowerment and in maximizing teacher empowerment. For example, principals need to involve teachers more in decision-making on many school-wide issues. Principals may also need to adopt leadership behaviors and/or policies that maximize teacher empowerment. As a result, teachers, and ultimately their students and their schools, could potentially receive the full benefits of teacher empowerment. As illustrated in the literature review, the benefits of teacher empowerment include increased teacher job performance and productivity, improved teacher morale, and ultimately, higher student motivation and achievement. We have a challenging task ahead of us to restructure the governance mechanism in public schools and improve teacher empowerment.

References

Aieta, R., Barth, R., & O'Brien, S. (1988). The principal in the year 2000: A teacher's wish. *Clearing House, 62*, 18–19.

Anderson, G., & Dixon, A. (1993). Paradigm shifts and site-based management in the United States: Toward a paradigm of social empowerment. In J. Smith (Ed.), *A socially critical view of the self-managing school* (pp. 49–61). London: Falmer.

Browder, L. H. (1994). Exploring the meanings of teacher empowerment. *International Journal of Educational Reform, 3*, 137–153.

Daigle, P. D., & Leclerc, D. C. (1997). Turning a new leaf: Flex time for teachers in a restructured school. *NASSP Bulletin, 81*, 38–43.

Fullan, M. (1991). *The new meaning of educational change*. New York: Teachers College Press.

Goodlad, J. I., & Associates (1970). *Behind the classroom door*. Worthington, OH: C.A. Jones.

Leithwood, K. A., & Montgomery, D. J. (1986). *Improving principal effectiveness: The principal profile*. Toronto: Ontario Institute for the Study of Education.

Leithwood, K., Begley, P. T., Cousins, J. B. (1994). *Developing expert leadership for future schools*. London: Falmer.

Lieberman, A. (1992) (Ed.), *The changing contexts of teaching*. Chicago: National Society for the Study of Education.

Sergiovanni, T. J. (1991). *The principalship: A reflective practice perspective*. Boston: McGraw-Hill.

Shen, J. (1997). Teacher retention and attrition in public schools: Evidence from SASS91. *Journal of Educational Research, 91*, 81–88.

Sullivan, K. (1995). Stable leadership, time for reflection contribute to momentum. *Journal of Staff Development, 16*, 6–8.

Tseo, K., & Ramos, E. L. (1995). Employee empowerment: Solution to a burgeoning crisis? *Challenge, 38*, 25–31.

Vandenberghe, R. (1995). Creative management of a school: A matter of vision and daily interventions. *Journal of Educational Administration, 33*, 31–51.

Wasley, P., Hampel, R., & Clark, R. (1997). The puzzle of whole-school change. *Phi Delta Kappan, 78*, 690–697.

White, P. A. (1992). Teacher empowerment under "ideal" school-site autonomy. *Educational Evaluation and Policy Analysis, 14*, 69–82.

Whitener, S. D., Gruber, K. J., Lynch, H., Tingos, K., Perona, M., & Fondelier, S. (1997). *Characteristics of stayers, movers, and leavers: Results from the teacher followup survey: 1994–95*. Washington, DC: U.S. Department of Education.

·9·

Chia-Lin Hsieh and Jianping Shen

CONCEPTIONS OF LEADERSHIP: A COMPARISON AMONG TEACHERS, PRINCIPALS, AND SUPERINTENDENTS

Introduction

Recent years have witnessed continued development in theories of leadership (Bass, 1990), and systematic perspectives on leadership have been developed (e.g., Bolman & Deal, 1991; Bush, 1995; Carlson, 1996). For example, the personality perspectives on leadership view leadership as a function of personal characteristics including trait, behavior, attitude, style, charisma, among others. The political perspectives on leadership view leadership as a process of compromise, bargaining, and negotiation. As will be seen in the next section on various perspectives on leadership, it is constructive to analyze leadership phenomenon by employing different perspectives because a rigorous analysis from systematic perspectives provides us with a disciplined approach to leadership analysis. However, we do not know much yet whether people in different leadership positions in a system—a school system in this case—tend to have different perspectives on leadership, a topic that has its theoretical implication for explaining educational leadership phenomenon and its practical implication for educating educational leaders.

Development in leadership theory and practice provides the impetus for the study. From the theoretical perspective, how to integrate different perspectives on leadership is a challenge for the field. To associate leadership position in a system with perspective on leadership might be one of the approaches to integrating the perspectives on leadership. Recently, there have been efforts to develop standards for leadership (e.g., AASA, 1993; CCSSO, 1996; Thomson, 1992). For example, The Interstate School Leaders Licensure Consortium, a program of the Council of Chief State School Officers (CCSSO), set model standards for school leaders. The standards presented a common core of knowledge, dispositions, and performances that intends to help link leadership more forcefully to productive schools and enhanced educational outcomes (CCSSO, 1996). Nonetheless, in this line of work, there is no consideration that there might be different perceptions of leadership for leaders in different positions.

From the practical perspective, with increasing emphasis on site-based management and school restructuring (Daresh, 1994; Stakenas, 1994; Carlson, 1996), there has been a tension among teachers, principals, and superintendents as to how they perceive their leadership roles (Malen, 1994; Weiss & Cambone, 1994; Wohlstetter, Smyer, & Mohrman, 1994). Many of these difficulties seem to arise from the possibility that teachers, principals, and superintendents have different conceptions of leadership. If we understand the similarity and difference among teachers', principals', and superintendents' conceptions of leadership, we can explain the difficulties and, therefore, make the reform agenda proceed smoothly.

Therefore, the purpose of the study was to investigate two questions: (a) what are the perceptions of a good educational leader held by teachers, principals, and superintendents? and (b) what are the similarities and differences among the three groups? Three focus groups—consisting of teachers, principals, and superintendents, respectively—were conducted to address the research questions.

In the following the authors first provide a brief description of perspectives on leadership to set a conceptual context, then proceed to report the methods of the study. After displaying the results, the authors proceed to discuss the theoretical and practical implications of the study.

Conceptualization

In the current literature (e.g., Bolman & Deal, 1991; Carlson, 1996; Bush, 1995; Cheng, 1996; Cheng & Shum, 1997), systematic perspectives on leadership have been proposed. The most commonly held leadership perspectives are as follows:

1. Personality perspective. The personality perspective views leadership as a function of a leader's personality, which includes trait, attitude, behavior, skill, intellect, charisma, trustworthiness, and vision, among others.
2. Organizational perspective. The organizational perspective views leadership from the standpoint of the official and structural elements of organizations. It has the assumption that leadership is embedded in the structure of an organization. This perspective is sometimes called "structural perspective" or "formal perspective."
3. Political perspective. The political perspective views leadership as bargaining, compromising, negotiating, and exerting influence on the basis of power. Power and conflict are very important concepts in this perspective.
4. Human resources (subjective) perspective. The human resource perspective, focusing on the individual rather than the organization, views leadership as motivating individuals and helping individuals construct meanings with a purpose to synchronize the goals of individuals and the organization.
5. Symbolic perspective. The symbolic perspective casts leadership as imagery. It views the organization as a stage and a theater in which every actor plays certain roles and attempts to communicate the right impression to the right audiences. Effective symbolic leaders are artists and prophets who use symbols and stories to communicate a vision that builds faith and loyalty among an organization's employees and other stakeholders.
6. Managerial (administrative) perspective. The managerial perspective views successful leadership as creating mechanisms to coordinate groups and link individual efforts to shared goals of quality service or products. A manager is concerned with maintenance, follows the script, reflects legal and bureaucratic authority, develops schedule and budget, and exercises power of sanction and reward (Kerry & Murdock, 1993; Sergiovanni & Starratt, 1993).
7. Moral perspective. The moral perspective on leadership maintains that the relationship between the leader and the led is not one of power but is a genuine sharing of mutual needs, aspirations, and values. Moral leadership emerges from, and always returns to, the fundamental wants and needs, aspirations, and values of followers. There has been a resurgence of this perspective in the recent literature (Goodlad, Soder, & Sirotnik, 1990; Hodgkinson, 1991).

We currently have these systematic perspectives on leadership, but we do not know yet whether these perspectives are consistently related to teachers', principals', and superintendents' conceptions of leadership, a void that the current study planned to fill. The researchers asked questions about what the important skills, knowledge, and values are for education leaders, and then tried to relate three groups' perceptions with the seven perspectives.

Methods

Sample

There were three focus groups—superintendents, principals, and teachers—for the study, each of which consisted of seven people. The purposive samples were selected by consulting the Michigan Education Directory (1997). Seven superintendents were selected to represent the school district size, geographic location, sex, and age; seven principals and seven teachers, respectively, were selected to represent school level, sex, and age.

The participants of these three groups were contacted individually by phone and were informed of the established meeting times for the group interviews approximately 10–14 days before the events. It was followed by sending a personalized invitation one week before the session and phoning each person again the day before the group interviews. The participants were reimbursed for the mileage.

Design and Procedure

The current study used focus group to collect data. Three focus groups were conducted by three professors of educational leadership in a midwestern university in USA. The moderators created a permissive environment but asked focused questions, in order to encourage the discussion and expression of differing opinions about good educational leaders (Stewart & Shamdasani, 1990; Morgan, 1988). Three focus groups were conducted so that the difference and similarity in three groups' perceptions of leadership can be identified.

The primary questions for the three focus groups were: (a) what are the skills of a good educational leader? (b) what might a good educational leader need to know? and (c) what values would you expect a good educational leader to hold? At the end of the discussion for each question, the moderators asked each focus group: (a) what is the most important skill of a good educational leader? (b) what is the most important knowledge of a good educational leader? and (c) what is the most important value of a good educational leader?

The moderator first welcomed the participants, then gave an overview of the focus-group session, and finally proceeded to ask the questions. The focus groups, ranging from 1 to 2 hours in length, were conducted in a facility specially designed for focus-group discussion. An assistant controlled tape-recording during the focus-group session in an adjacent room separated by the one-way mirror.

Data Analysis

The following were the major steps in data analysis. First, the raw data, which were the discussion in the focus groups, were transcribed verbatim. Based on the literature and the data, the authors developed codes for each of the three domains—skill, knowledge, and value. The authors coded each complete sentence. Part of the data was also coded by a researcher who was not familiar with the current study, and Cohen's (1960) inter-rater reliability was .88. The final step in data analysis was to display the similarities and differences among three groups in skill, knowledge, and value domains. Some patterns emerged from data display, which were reported as research findings.

One of the limitations associated with focus-group research was that each group really represented a single observation (Stewart & Shamdasani, 1990). By definition and by design, the statements of focus group participants were influenced by the group interaction and the opinion of others. As a result of this influence statistical estimation is not possible.

What We Found

Focus-group data related to teachers', principals', and superintendents' conceptions of leadership are reported in the following. Their conceptions are compared across skill, knowledge, and value domains, respectively.

Skill Domain

Figure 1 shows skills of a good educational leader mentioned by the teachers', principals', and superintendents' groups. The figure visually displays the similarities and differences among three groups. Teachers, principals, and superintendents all held that a good educational leader should have good communication skills, problem solving skills, organizational skills, collaboration skills, modeling skills, decision making skills, listening skills, interpersonal skills, and the skill to understand the client and the community. The following excerpts illustrated the similarities among the three groups.

TEACHERS: They need to be better communicators. . . . They have to be good writers. . . . They need to have skills to step in and solve problems. . . . The leader has to be open-minded. . . . They have to see a situation from all perspectives and understand how individuals are feeling about certain things.

PRINCIPALS: . . . be able to communicate with all the population. . . . Different people come to us to seek problem solutions. . . . We have to be organized . . . have strong organization skills. . . . In our situation, we are not going to complete all of the tasks each day, so strong organizational skills are very important. . . . We have all people to work with from custodians, the superintendent, to parents . . . be able to cooperate with all the people . . . be able to stand behind the decision.

SUPERINTENDENTS: He has to be a good problem-solver . . . ability to communicate . . . understand and listen to people. . . . You need to have tremendous people skills.

In addition to the aforementioned similarities, teachers differed from the principals and superintendents on certain skills. The teachers' group seemed to focus more on humor, keeping balance, empowering staff, mediating conflict, and instructional skills.

TEACHERS: They should empower parents, staff, and students. . . . They need to have conflict-management skills. . . . At any level they need to be knowledgeable of any academic areas that are taught. . . . If they know very little about instruction, it will take a lot of efforts on teacher's part. . . . They should have a good sense of humor.

Superintendents tended to think that developing vision, building consensus, developing skills and talents of others, flexibility, ability to influence people and political skills are important for a good educational leader.

SUPERINTENDENTS: . . . be able to articulate the vision. . . . If you are not an effective politician and do not understand the politics of the board, you will not be around to be the leader. . . . You have the ability to influence the people who are going to make decisions for you. . . . The reason I am still a superintendent today is I get involved in the board election.

At the end of the discussion on leadership skills, the moderators asked each of the three groups which skill was the most important. The results are displayed in Table 9.1. The results in Table 9.1 support those in Figure 9.1. The similarities among the three groups were that they all thought communication

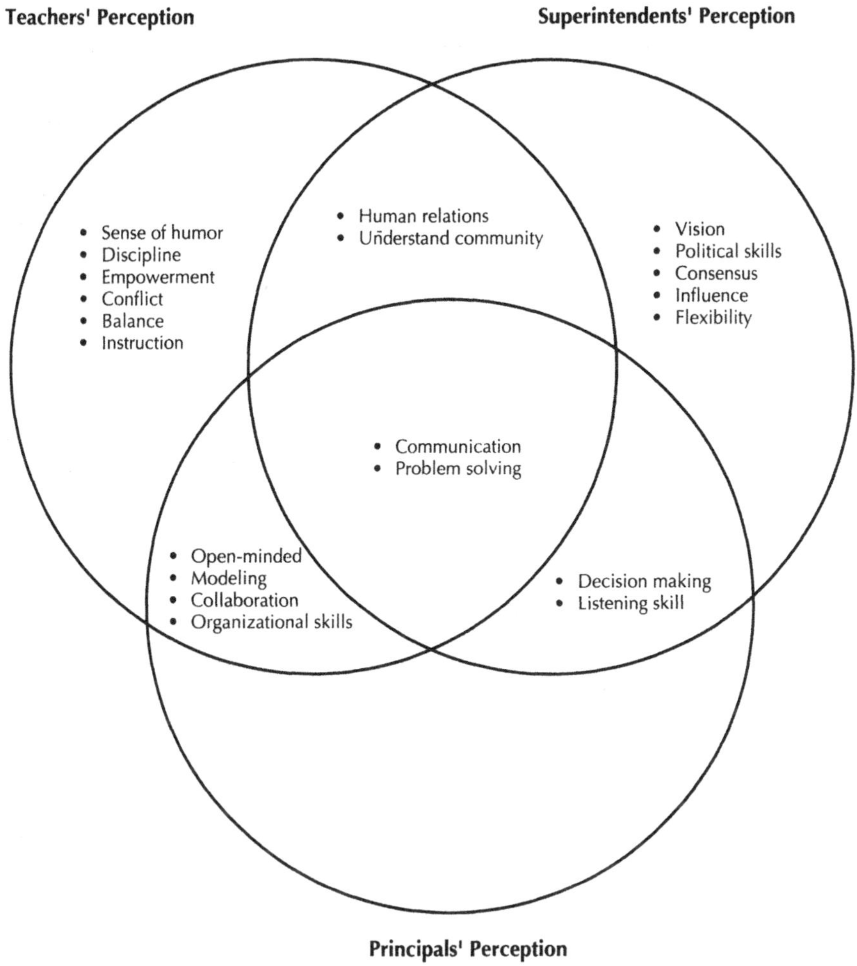

FIGURE 9.1. Skills for Educational Leaders as Mentioned by the Three Groups.

and listening skills were important. However, teachers also viewed collaboration, empowerment, and balance as the most important skills, which were not mentioned by principals and superintendents as the most important skills. Principals also included organizational skill, decision-making skill, and modeling skill as the most important ones, which were not discussed by teachers and superintendents. Superintendents included consensus-building skills as one of the most important skills, which was not mentioned by teachers and principals. It appears that teachers, principals and superintendents viewed what were important skills from the perspectives of their positions.

TABLE 9.1. The Frequency of the Most Important Items in Skill, Knowledge, and Value Domain as Mentioned by Teachers, Principals, and Superintendents

	Groups		
Domains	Teachers	Principals	Superintendents
Skill	Collaboration (2)	Listening (2)	Listening (3)
	Communication (2)	Organizing (2)	Communication (2)
	Empowerment (1)	Problem solving (1)	Problem solving (1)
	Well balanced (1)	Decision making (1)	Consensus building (1)
		Modeling (1)	
Knowledge	Learning theory (1)	Curriculum (3)	Learning theory (3)
	Lifelong learning (1)	Testing (2)	Instruction (2)
	Problem solving (1)	Budgeting (1)	Finance (2)
	Educational reform (1)	School organization (1)	Management (2)
		Connect with district (1)	Law and legislation (2)
		Helping teacher to grow (1)	
Value	Honesty (3)	Honesty (4)	Honesty (4)
	Fairness (2)	Respect (2)	Integrity (2)
	Integrity (1)	Integrity (1)	Valuing people (1)
	Care (1)	Caring (1)	
	Trust (1)	Common sense (1)	
	Morality (1)	Empathy (1)	
	Good person (1)		
	Credibility (1)		

Knowledge Domain

The similarity and difference in knowledge domain between the three groups are displayed in Figure 9.2. Teachers, principals, and superintendents agreed that knowledge about the following was important: learning theory, law and regulation, school finance, community issues, school improvement, technology, life-long learner, continuing professional development, new educational trend, business management, practicality of doing things, and responsiveness to community needs. The following are excerpts from the three groups:

TEACHERS: I expect them to know school law and financing procedure, so I can do my job. . . . They need to be knowledgeable about the community. . . . Community can be varied so differently. . . . Knowledgeable about what kids face when they go home. . . . They have to love to learn. They need to be knowledgeable, not just in local activity.

PRINCIPALS: Financing. Seeing your budget, reading your budget, meeting the needs of all your staff. . . . We have to understand the whole process of school improvement process . . . be knowledgeable about current educa-

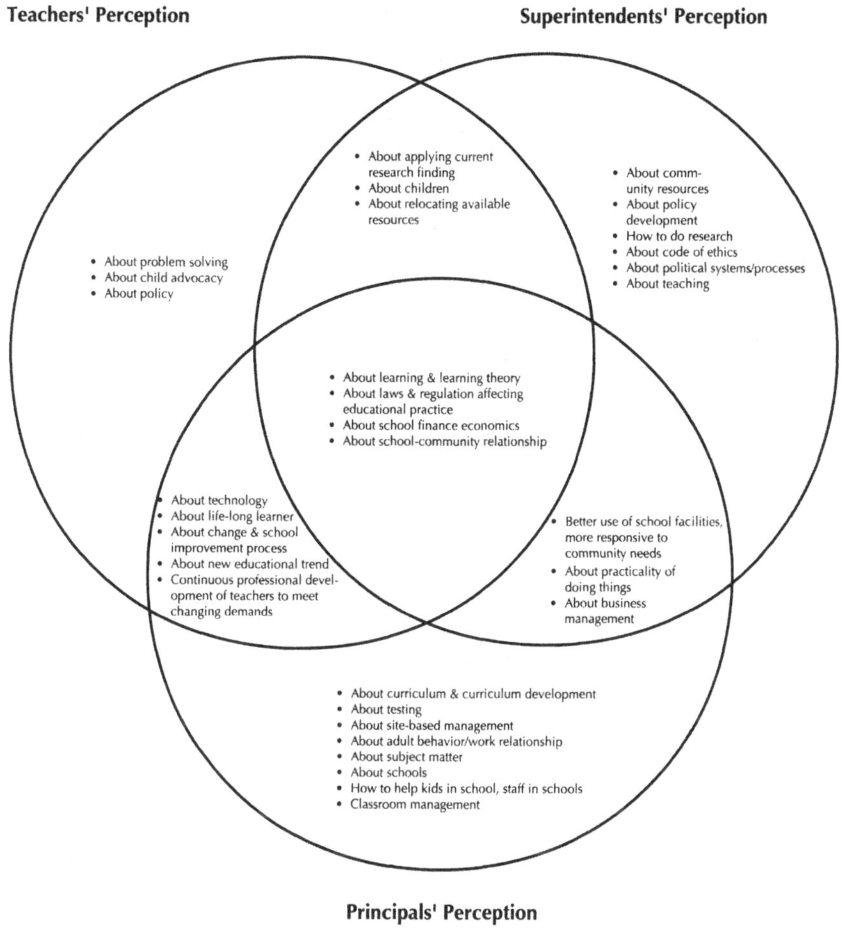

FIGURE 9.2. Knowledge for Educational Leaders as Mentioned by the Three Groups.

tional reform. . . . We need to be able to go to the classroom and use our supervision skills and then be able to move teachers to the next level . . . strong background and good educational practices.

SUPERINTENDENTS: . . . Be able to manage the finance, the legal issue, and the legislative issue . . . collective bargaining and community organization. . . . Something makes you more practical, realistic people. . . . Think about the whole business, you don't have money, you don't have the finance side, you will not be able to excel and emerge. . . . You know what you know, if you don't then hire somebody to support. . . .

As in the case of the skill domain, the three groups also differed on what knowledge educational leaders should have. In comparison to principals and superintendents, teachers emphasized that good educational leaders should have the knowledge of problem solving, child advocacy, and policy.

TEACHERS: They need to know how to solve problems. . . . They also need to be a good facilitator, be able to run school programs, and let everyone feel they are important. . . . They need to know children's rights. We often forget we are there for kids. . . . They have to be knowledgeable about the school district policy.

Principals, on the other hand, tended to focus on "building-level" knowledge which includes curriculum development, testing, site-based management, subject matter, school and classroom management, helping kids and staff, and maintaining good adult working relationships. Principals seemed to focus on knowledge about management.

PRINCIPALS: Strong site-based management. . . . If you don't know organizational management, you are going to fail. . . . We have to know what we are teaching, how to analyze test scores, work with staff . . . an understanding of school organization, including curriculum . . . be able to help teachers grow . . . recognizing what the needs are for the teacher, if you can't give her or him, find someone to do it for you.

Superintendents tended to hold that a good educational leader should have knowledge of legislation, policy development, political systems, and community resources. They seemed to focus on political knowledge.

SUPERINTENDENTS: . . . case law and how it fits to your policy development . . . understand the legislative process . . . evaluation of law and legislation related to school . . . the power of structure of the community . . . operate the negotiation within the organization . . . client issues. . . .

At the end of the discussion on leadership knowledge, the moderators asked each of the three groups which knowledge was the most important. The results are displayed in Table 9.1. The results in Table 9.1 are consistent with those in Figure 9.2. Three groups had different views on the most important knowledge. Teachers included lifelong learning, problem solving, and educational reform as among the most important knowledge bases, which were not mentioned by principals and superintendents. Principals viewed that the most important knowledge included curriculum, testing, budgeting, school organization, connection with district, and helping teachers to grow. These knowledge bases were not mentioned by teachers and superintendents. Superintendents, however, viewed that knowledge on instruction, finance, management, and legal matters were most important. These knowledge bases had not been mentioned by teachers and principals. The analysis of teachers', principals' and superintendents' similarity and difference in the most important knowledge base suggested again that their views were contingent upon their positions in the school system. Teachers were more concerned about knowledge related to effective classroom teaching, while principals and superintendents emphasized managerial and political knowledge, respectively.

Value Domain

The similarity and difference in value domain among the three groups are displayed in Figure 9.3. Teachers, principals, and superintendents agreed that good educational leaders should have the following values: honesty, valuing people, integrity, credibility, empathy, care, moral leadership, and a sense of who they are. The following are excerpts from the focus group discussions:

TEACHERS: Honesty . . . deal with me directly. Understand where they are coming from. . . . You have to be a role model.

PRINCIPALS: Put yourself in other peoples' place. . . . You got to be able to laugh somewhere. . . . If you don't have a sense of humor, something, your life is in a death. . . . be positive and humorous.

SUPERINTENDENTS: Do what you say you are going to do. . . . Establish your credibility as a leader. You have to have a strong sense of yourself. . . . You got to have a sense of being caring. . . . You got to help them to understand the problem. . . . You may not fix it, but you got to have the empathy.

In comparison to principals and superintendents, teachers emphasized fairness, acceptance of other people's values, firmness, compassion, and calmness.

TEACHERS: To be a good leader you have to stand firm, you have had your own position, your own value system about what you feel is right or wrong. . . . Accepting other people's values, not make judgments. . . . A leader is basically a fair and just person. . . . A leader should be consistent and fair.

Principals, on the other hand, stressed the following values: resiliency, common sense, high regard for other people, consistency, and love for kids.

PRINCIPALS: I value consistency . . . dealing with all kinds of people in the same consistent manner . . . care for those children. . . .

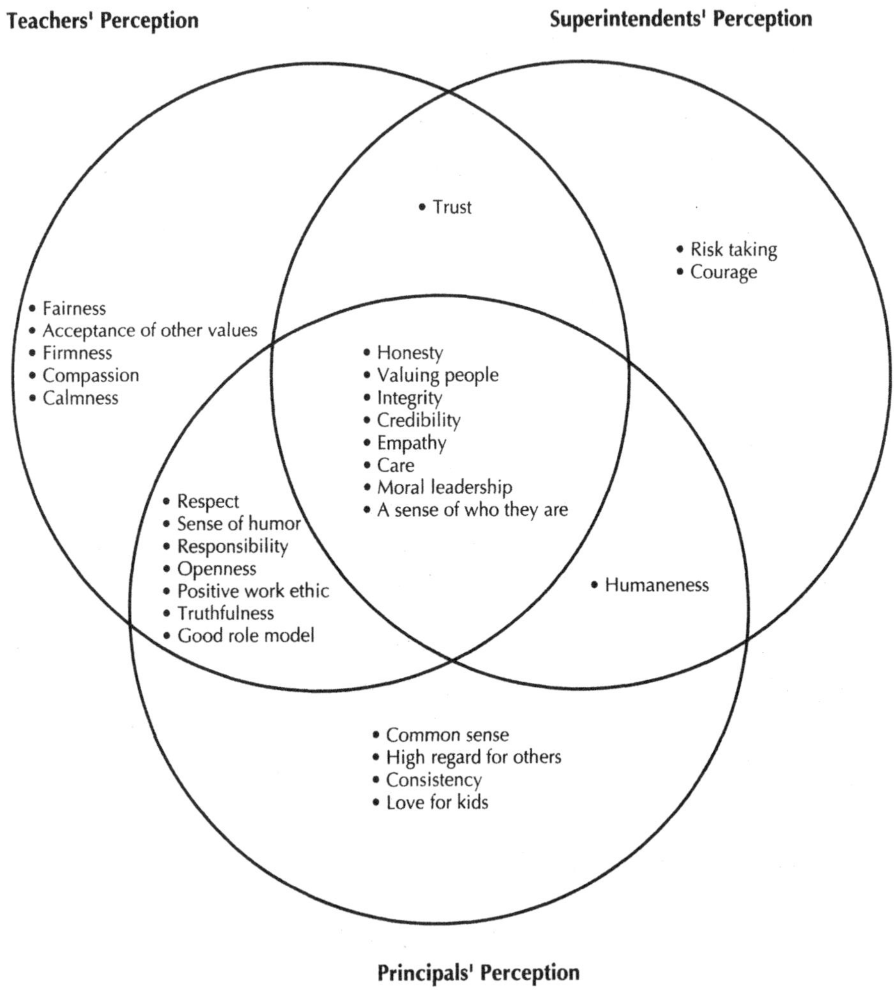

FIGURE 9.3. Values for Educational Leaders as Mentioned by the Three Groups.

The results in Table 9.1 supported those in Figure 9.3. The most important values that were agreed upon by teachers, principals, and superintendents were honesty and integrity. In addition to honesty and integrity, teachers also held that the most important values for a good educational leader include fairness, care, trust, morality, being a good person, and credibility; Principals mentioned care, common sense, empathy, and respect; and superintendents also discussed valuing people. The analysis of teachers', principals', and superintendents' similarity and difference in the most important values suggested that their views were similar and not as associated with their positions in the school system as in the cases of the skill and knowledge domains.

Discussion

The data indicated both similarities and differences among the teachers', principals', and superintendents' groups. The results show more differences in skill and knowledge domains than in value domain. Since education is fundamentally a moral enterprise (Goodlad, Soder, & Sirotnik, 1990; Hodgkinson, 1991; Shen, 1993), superintendents, principals, and teachers have a similar value system. However, the three groups differ, to a great extent, in skill and knowledge domains; and the difference appears to be due to their leadership positions in the school system.

Superintendents have to work with the community and different kinds of interest groups, and struggle in the power structure. On one hand they view leadership as a process of negotiation, bargaining, and exchange (Bush, 1995) because they have to keep the school system running; on the other hand, they view leadership through identifying the values of governing their actions (Craig & Norris, 1991) and developing moral visions to guide the practice (Carlson, 1996). Overall, the results suggest that superintendents tend to view leadership from the political and moral perspectives.

Principals have to work with the superintendent as well as teachers and students. Therefore, on one hand, they view leadership through monitoring and maintaining values and carrying out practical tasks in a school system (Bush, 1995); on the other hand, principals feel that a leader's personality—traits, attitudes, and behaviors—plays an important role in leadership (Shen, 1997). Overall, the data seem to indicate that principals view leadership from the managerial, personality, and moral perspectives.

Teachers work with students all the time. The most important thing for teachers is to be an effective instructional leader. They perceive leadership at the personal level instead of the organizational level; that is, they tend to see leadership as a function of the leader's personality—clever, firm, knowledgable, dependable, organized, adaptable to situations, fluent in speaking and writing, and alert to social environment (Hersey, Blanchard, & Johnson, 1996). By knowing the leader's personality, people can predict what the leader will do in a given situation (Boles & Davenport, 1975). They also view leadership from the moral perspective. Overall, the data seem to suggest that teachers view a good educational leadership from the personality and moral perspectives. It is also interesting to note that teachers basically use "they" rather than "we" when discussing the skill, knowledge, and value of a good educational leader. It appears that the concept of "teacher as leader" has not materialized in the practice.

Therefore, the moral perspective is common for all, but the three groups also differ on other aspects, with teachers emphasizing the personality perspective, principals stressing the managerial and personality perspectives, and superintendents accentuating the political perspective. These findings have theoretical and practical implications. Theoretically, the findings can explain why there are some tensions between teachers, principals, and superintendents when leadership is concerned. In other words, some of the issues in school leadership arise from that fact they have different conceptions of good educational leadership. It appears that conceptions of leadership change when teachers are promoted to principalship and principals to superintendents, instructional matters are de-emphasized and managerial and political affairs are emphasized as a person is promoted to a higher position in the school system.

Practically, the findings pose a challenge to the education of school leaders. Ultimately school leadership is to facilitate teaching and learning in the classroom. But principals and superintendents tend to de-emphasize instructional leadership. With the promotion within the school system, school leaders shift their attention to non-instructional matters. Ideally, principals' conception of leadership should be more inclusive than that of teachers—preserving the focus on teaching and learning, but going beyond teachers' conceptions to include those associated with leading the whole school. In the same token, superintendents' perception of leadership should move beyond that of principals to include those aspects related to leading the whole school district. Therefore, we are facing the following challenge: when educating school leaders, how to make them aware of new aspects of leadership necessary for leading the school system without losing focus on instructional matters.

This is a qualitative study with small samples. However, the study illustrates "an image of the possible" (Grossman, 1990), i.e., the possible difference in perception of leadership between teachers, principals, and superintendents. As was discussed in the foregoing, the empirical findings on the similarity and difference in teachers', principals' and superintendents' conception of leadership have implications for explaining leadership phenomenon and educating future school leaders.

References

American Association of School Administrators. (1993). *Professional standards for the superintendency*. Arlington, VA: Author.

Bass, B. M. (1990). *Bass & Stogdill's handbook of leadership: Theory, research, and managerial applications*. New York: Free Press.

Boles, H., & Davenport, J. (1975). *Introduction to educational leadership*. New York: Harper & Row Publishers.

Bolman, L. C., & Deal, T. E. (1991). *Reframing organizations*. San Francisco, CA: Jossey-Bass.

Bush, T. (1995). *Theories of educational management*. London: Paul Chapman Publishing.

Carlson, R. V. (1996). *Reframing and reform: Perspectives on organization, leadership, and school change*. White Plains, NY: Longman.

Cheng, Y. C. (1996). Relations between teachers' professionalism and job attitudes, educational outcomes, and organizational factors. *Journal of Educational Research, 89* (3), 163–171.

Cheng, Y. C., & Shum, L. C. (1997). Perceptions of women principals' leadership and teachers' work attitudes. *Journal of Educational Administration, 35* (2), 165–184.

Cohen, J. (1960). A coefficient of agreement for nominal scales. *Educational and Psychological Measurement, 20*(1), 37–46.

Council of Chief State School Officers (1996). *Interstate School Leaders Licensure Consortium: Standards for school leaders*. Washington, DC: Author.

Craig, R. P., & Norris, C. J. (1991). Values perception and future educational leaders. *Journal of School Leadership, 1*(3), 222–234.

Daresh, J. C. (1994). Restructuring educational leadership preparation: Identify needed conditions. *Journal of School Leadership, 4*(1), 28–38.

Goodlad, J. I., Soder, R., & Sirotnik, K. A. (Eds.). (1990). *The moral dimensions of teaching*. San Francisco, CA: Jossey-Bass.

Grossman, P. L. (1990). *The making of a teacher: Teacher knowledge and teacher education*. New York: Teachers College Press.

Hersey, P., Blanchard, K. H., & Johnson, D. E. (1996). *Management of organizational behavior: utilizing human resources*. Upper Saddle River, NJ: Prentice Hall.

Hodgkinson, C. (1991). *Educational leadership: The moral art*. Albany: State University of New York Press.

Kerry, T., & Murdoch, A. (1993). Education managers as leaders: Some thoughts on the context of the changing nature of schools. *School organization, 13*(3), 221–230.

Malen, B. (1994). Enacting site-based management: A political utilities analysis. *Educational Evaluation and Policy Analysis, 16*(3), 249–267.

Michigan Department of Education. (1997). Michigan education directory. Lansing, Michigan: Author.

Morgan, D. L. (1988). *Focus groups as qualitative research*. Newbury, CA: Sage.

Sergiovanni, T. J., & Starratt, R. J. (1993). *Supervision: A redefinition*. New York: McGraw-Hill.

Shen, J. (1993). "Teaching as a moral enterprise" revisited. *Review of Education, 15* (3–4), 333–339.

Stakenas, R. G. (1994). Program reform in administrator preparation: The process of change. *NASSP Bulletin, 78*(559), 28–32.

Stewart, D. W., & Shamdasani, P. N. (1990). *Focus groups: Theory and practice*. Newbury Park, CA: Sage.

Thomson, S. D. (1992). National standards for school administrators. *International Journal of Educational Reform, 1*(1), 54–58.

Weiss, C. H., & Cambone, J. (1994). Principals, shared decision making, and school reform. *Educational Evaluation and Policy Analysis, 16*(3), 287–301.

Wohlstetter, P., Smyer, R., & Mohrman, S. A. (1994). New boundaries for school-based management: The high involvement model. *Educational Evaluation and Policy Analysis, 16*(3), 268–286.

·10·

Jianping Shen, Van E. Cooley,

Connie D. Ruhl-Smith, and Nanette M. Keiser

QUALITY AND IMPACT OF EDUCATIONAL LEADERSHIP PROGRAMS: A NATIONAL STUDY

The school reform movement has impacted the way universities prepare prospective administrators. There has been a growing trend to base educational leadership programs on a "practice-based, practice-driven" curriculum rather than social science theory (National Association of Elementary School Principals, 1990; National Commission for the Principalship, 1990). Descriptions of these new types of programs have been referenced in the literature (Carter, 1994; Chapman, 1990; Coleman, 1991; Cordeiro & Sloan, 1996; Daresh & Playko, 1993; Geltner, 1993; Holdaway & Riordan, 1996; Jacobson, 1996; Katz, 1991; Kim, 1996; Peel & Wallace, 1996; Place & Reitzug, 1992; Pohland, 1986; Reed & Hannaford, 1991; Smith, 1990; Twale & Short, 1989). These experiential programs included components such as mentoring, field participation, paid internships, and practice-oriented curricula. However, current research has failed to answer the questions of whether these "new" programs are meeting the needs of participants and having the intended effect on administrators now entering the workplace (Jacobs, 1991).

Literature Review

Delivery of educational leadership programs by colleges and universities and the impact of traditional curricula on prospective administrators continues to be debated and scrutinized. The literature review was organized around three major areas which included program relevance or practicality, student satisfaction with their program, and the perceived quality of mentoring experiences. Previous research focused on the impact of educational leadership programs on administrative practices. Earlier inquirers typically surveyed participants' perceptions of the impact of educational leadership program experiences on actual administrator practices. Sample sizes of these studies were limited, ranging from 10 to 120 participants. With one exception, the programs studied involved universities in the United States.

Previous studies examined participants' satisfaction in regard to their experiences with specific courses and/or the program (Cordeiro & Sloan, 1996; Jacobson & Woodworth, 1990; Kim, 1996; Reed & Hannaford, 1991; Montgomerie, Peters, & Ward, 1991; Smith, 1990). Participants reported satisfaction levels ranging from dissatisfaction for rural administrators (Jacobson & Woodworth, 1990) to positive satisfaction with the courses and/or their programs (Cordeiro & Sloan, 1996; Kim, 1996; Montgomerie, Peters & Ward, 1991; Reed & Hannaford, 1991; Smith, 1990). Smith (1990) found that graduates of a nontraditional (practice-based) program expressed a higher level of satisfaction with their programs than did those who had graduated from traditional (theory-based) programs. Cordeiro and Sloan (1996) indicated practicing administrators recounted internships and practica as the most significant portion of their educational training; both mentors (practicing administrators) and interns (prospective administrators) indicated they learned and benefited from the internship experience. Wylie and Clark (1994) stated that master's level students rated internships as the most beneficial and least academically demanding of all activities. This reflection raised issues regarding the organization, quality, and supervision of internships. Cordeiro and Sloan (1996) identified mentor selection, organization of opportunities, theory-practice links, and definitive stages of internship development as considerations for program developers. Peel and Wallace (1996) stated internships were significant experiences in the careers of practicing administrators, noting that administrators who participated in internships credited these early field experiences to their administrative success.

Several related studies examined the quality of administrative internship programs (Heller, Conway, & Jacobson, 1988; Jacobson & Woodworth, 1990; LaCost & Pounder, 1987; Peel & Wallace, 1996). Participants in Heller, Conway, and Jacobson's (1988) study reported their programs were impractical.

Mixed ratings were also attributed to such program components as on-the-job training through internships, assessment centers, workshops, and staff development programs. However, the participants in Peel and Wallace's (1996) study considered their program to be of excellent quality. In the 1988 *Executive Educator* study involving 1,123 practicing school administrators, 44.6% of rural administrators, 47% of suburban, and 48.3% of urban administrators believed graduate preparation programs failed to provide adequate preparation for administrative positions. Coincidentally, 55.5% of the administrators viewed on-the-job training as the most significant part in training for their current positions (Jacobson & Woodworth, 1990). Field experiences utilizing adult learning theory resulted in collaboration, reflection, and a link to challenges faced by practicing administrators. LaCost and Pounder (1987) revealed the experiential programs helped to fuse the discrepancy between theory and practice.

Closely associated with quality is the relevance of educational leadership program components to administrators' positional requirements. Jacobson and Woodworth (1990) identified problems in administrator preparation, with rural, urban, and suburban administrators all expressing concerns about the relevance of university curriculum. Several researchers have examined the effect of academic programs on the student performance in administrative positions (Chapman, 1990; Jacobs, 1991). A majority of administrators reported the major areas of their educational leadership programs as relevant to their current position (Chapman, 1990). Administrators recognized the most adequate program components as (a) meeting the legal responsibilities of the school, (b) using findings of research and exemplary practice in decision making, and (c) articulating the role and purpose of education in contemporary society. Jacobs (1991) identified gender as a factor that affected administrators' perceptions of components most relevant to on-the-job success. With the exception of theoretical foundations of practice, female administrators reported the program was generally inadequate in assisting them with on-the-job success. However, male administrators responded that the program adequately supported on-the-job experiences.

Previous studies focused on the components and needs of educational leadership programs (Montgomerie, Peters, & Ward, 1991; Peel & Wallace, 1996). Participants identified program components and activities that simulated actual administrative tasks such as role playing and internships (Peel & Wallace, 1996). Participants have also suggested how educational leadership needs could be better served (Montgomerie, Peters, & Ward, 1991). These included (a) offering more practical courses such as conflict management and public relations, (b) providing courses in the local area, and (c) using distance education.

The purpose of this chapter was to contribute to this line of research. As Murphy (1992) stated, sound conclusions about an educational leadership program can only be made when its strengths and weaknesses were closely examined. This investigation included a larger sample than previous studies, examined program strengths and weaknesses as perceived by participants, and explored student perceptions of educational goals and schooling functions prior to and following their exposure to educational leadership courses. The new data, in conjunction with existing knowledge in the literature, provide additional information regarding the quality and impact of educational leadership programs on prospective school administrators.

Research Purposes and Questions

The purpose of the study was first to inquire into how students enrolled in educational leadership programs perceived the quality of their programs. A second purpose was to investigate the impact of leadership programs on students' perception of educational goals and schooling functions. The study focused on the following two sets of research questions: (a) How do students in educational leadership programs perceive the importance of the curriculum for their future success as administrators? How would educational leadership students change the emphasis of curriculum if they were to redesign the it? To what extent are students satisfied with the program? (b) After enrollment in the programs, have students changed their views of educational goals and the schooling function? Since entering the program, has the student's enthusiasm for the program and a future administrative position changed? If so, how has it changed? The study provides an empirical basis to discuss the nature and impact of the leadership program on prospective school leaders.

Methods

Sample

Data for the current study were collected during the Study of Education of Educators (SEE), a large, multi-method inquiry into the education of teachers and administrators conducted by John I. Goodlad and his colleagues in the Center for Educational Renewal, University of Washington. Researchers selected a representative sample of 29 colleges and universities based on factors including institutional type (according to The Carnegie Foundation for the Advancement of Teaching, 1987), geographic location (according to Bureau of the Census), religious or nonreligious affiliation, and the public or private sector. SEE surveyed education faculty members and students in teacher education or educational leadership programs, among other data sources. Data for this study were limited to students in educational leadership programs.

The questionnaire was distributed to 994 students enrolled in educational leadership programs in selected colleges and universities throughout the United States. Surveys were completed and returned by 457 participants or 46% of the respondents. According to Babbie's (1989) rule of thumb regarding the return rate, the data were adequate for analysis. Since the current study inquired into the impact of leadership programs, it appeared to be meaningful to select the informants who were at least halfway through their program. As a result of this selection, there were 417 informants in the sample. Among the 417 informants, 42 were "about halfway through the program," 63 "about three quarters of the way through the program," and 312 "at or near completion of the program." Among those in the final sample, 82% of the informants were pursuing certification for principalship.

A demographic breakdown of the sample by gender, race, age, and degree attainment revealed a diverse sample, consisting of 37.2% male and 62.8% female, 74.8% white and 25.2% minority. Age distribution of the informants was as follows: 24 or younger, 0.7%; 25–29, 4.6%; 30–34, 16.4%; 35–39, 31.6%; 40–49, 41.4%; and 50 or older, 5.3%. As to the highest academic degrees earned, 25.9% held bachelor's degrees, 67.6% possessed master's degrees, and 6.5% had doctorates including Ph.D., Ed.D., M.D., and J.D. (Doctor of Jurisprudence—doctorate for lawyers).

Instrument

The questionnaire was designed to collect data related to biographic and career information, informants' perceptions of schooling and education, and their views of the educational leadership programs. This study utilized data related to their perception of quality and impact of the program. Since this study used many items and different measurement scales, it seemed more efficient to describe the items in detail when reporting the findings in the results section.

Data Analysis

Descriptive statistics such as mean and percentage were widely used in this study. When the informants' perceptions before and after entering the program were compared, *t*-tests for repeated measures were used if the focus was on means, and Spearman's rank order correlation was employed if the attention was on the rank order. Data analyses were performed by using SPSS.

What We Found

Perceptions of the Leadership Program

Perception of the coursework. The informants were asked to rate "How much of a contribution do you expect these courses will make to your future success as an administrator?" by using a 7-point Likert scale ranging from "1 = no contribution at all" to "7 = a very great contribution." The means were displayed in the column labeled "mean" in Table 10.1. Supervision/evaluation, leadership/decision making, school law, human relationships, with means greater than 6.0, were considered the most important. The second tier of courses with means between 5.54 and 5.97 included curriculum and instruction, school management, personnel management, internship, school finance, and organizational theory and change. The least important courses, with means less than 4.74, included special areas (including guidance, special education, gifted/talented, ESL, multi-ethnic, etc.), educational psychology, integrative seminars (including review, synthesis, theory into practice, etc.), and foundations (including history, philosophy, and sociology of education; current educational issues; multicultural/multiethnic studies; etc.). It appeared the informants valued skill- and practice-oriented courses more than theory-oriented offerings.

TABLE 10.1. The Importance of the Courses for Future Success and the Intention to Emphasize or De-emphasize the Courses

		Emphasis			
Course	Mean*	More**	Same	Less	Eliminating
Supervision/evaluation	6.24	46.3	51.7	1.8	0.3
Leadership/decision making	6.24	46.0	51.9	1.6	0.5
School law	6.04	27.0	70.7	2.1	0.3
Human relations	6.03	41.7	54.4	2.3	1.6
Curriculum and instruction	5.97	39.2	57.0	3.4	0.5
School management	5.95	42.1	55.5	1.8	0.5
Personnel management	5.87	42.2	54.0	3.2	0.5
Internship	5.79	31.5	61.0	5.1	2.4
School finance	5.72	25.6	67.9	5.7	0.8
Organizational theory and change	5.54	22.6	66.5	8.8	2.1
Special areas	4.74	21.6	68.7	6.9	2.8
Educational psychology	4.69	21.3	60.4	11.7	6.6
Integrative seminars	4.61	26.1	63.1	6.0	4.8
Foundations	4.16	11.7	63.7	16.3	8.3

* Mean of the contribution of these courses to their future success on the 7-point scale with increasing importance.

** Percentage of respondents who indicated that more emphasis should be placed on the course.

The informants were also asked whether they would give these courses more, same, less emphasis, or eliminate them all together if they were to redesign a new program. The percentages of the responses were presented in Table 10.1. The general pattern in the data was that when they perceived courses important for their future success, they hoped that more emphasis would be placed on them, and vice versa. Therefore, more than 40% of the informants indicated that supervision/evaluation, leadership/decision making, human relations, school management, and personnel management should have more emphasis. However, more than 10% of the informants suggested that educational psychology, organizational theory and change, and integrative seminars should be given less emphasis or eliminated all together. As many as 24.6% of the informants recommend foundation courses be given less emphasis or eliminated all together.

Evaluation of the program. When the informants were asked "Overall, how would you rate the teaching by your professors in the Administrator Education Program as compared with that of professors you have had in other departments?", 50.9% chose "better than in other departments," 44.7% "about the same as in other departments," and 4.4% "worse than in other departments." As to the question "Overall, how do you think the Administrator Education Program compared with other departments on campus in terms of *status* and *prestige*?", 28.6% indicated "higher than other departments," 52.8% "about the same as other departments," and 18.6% "lower than other departments." When the informants were asked to give an overall rating of the program, the distribution of their answers were as follows: A, 45.2%; B, 43.7%; C, 9.6%; D, 1.5%; and Fail, 0%. The data seemed to suggest the informants were satisfied with their programs.

Impact of the Program

Changes in perceptions of educational goals. Table 10.2 displayed the data comparing how informants perceived educational goals at the time when the questionnaire was administered and before they entered the program. The informants were asked to rate their perceptions of the importance of each educational goal on a 7-point Likert scale, ranging from "1 not at all important" to "7 extremely important." Several patterns emerged from the data in Table 10.2. First, for each of the educational goals there was an increase in the mean from before entering the program to after entering the program; the increase for each educational goal was statistically significant at .001 level. Statistics of Cohen's *d*, a measure of effect size, ranged from .20 to .36. According to Cohen's (1988) criteria that .2, .5, and .8 represent small, medium, and large effects, respectively, the impact of educational leadership programs was within the small to medium range. The data seemed to indicate that after entering the program, the informants perceived each educational goal as more important and, therefore, participants had a more comprehensive view of educational goals. Second, areas with the largest increases were critical and independent thinking (0.45), citizenship and civic responsibilities (0.43), enculturation (0.41), and interpersonal understandings (0.40). In contrast, the areas with the least increases included basic skills education (0.20), moral and ethical character (0.24), and intellectual development in disciplines (0.25). It appeared that the leadership program had more impact on the informants' perceptions of social goals than on academic goals. Third, if ranks were assigned to each goal according to the size of the mean, there was a statistically significant positive correlation between perceptions before and after entering the program ($r_s = .90$, $p < .001$). This suggested that although the means for each goal increased after entering the program, the relative importance of each goal remained unchanged in informants' perceptions.

Changes in perceptions of the functions of schooling. There have been different schools of thought on the functions of schooling (Goodlad, 1994; Su, 1992). Goodlad and his colleagues summarized the relevant literature and formulated four schools of thought, ranging from the conservative to the liberal. The informants were requested to rate their agreement or disagreement with the four schools of thought, which were defined as follows:

A. Schools should produce educated young people who are ready to take their place in society to help maintain *order* and *stability* in the social, political, and economic fabric of society.

TABLE 10.2. Perceptions of the Importance of Educational Goals Before and After Entering the Leadership Program

Educational Goal	Mean Before	Mean After	Mean Difference	*t*	*P*	Cohen's *d*
Interpersonal understandings/human relations	6.56	6.16	0.40	7.09	<.001	.35
Critical and independent thinking	6.43	5.98	0.45	7.27	<.001	.36
Self-realization	6.31	5.95	0.35	5.94	<.001	.30
Moral and ethical character	6.29	6.05	0.24	4.66	<.001	.23
Basic skills education	6.18	5.98	0.20	4.17	<.001	.20
Emotional and physical well-being	6.05	5.66	0.39	5.93	<.001	.30
Enculturation	5.71	5.30	0.41	6.30	<.001	.31
Career, vocational and life preparation	5.68	5.37	0.31	4.81	<.001	.23
Citizenship and civic responsibility	5.60	5.17	0.43	6.30	<.001	.31
Intellectual development in the disciplines	5.57	5.32	0.25	5.22	<.001	.26
Creativity and aesthetic expression	5.43	5.10	0.32	5.56	<.001	.28

B. Schools should concentrate on children and youth as *individuals*, helping them develop their *interests* and *abilities* to their full potential.
C. Schools should educate young people to be aware of human conditions, social purposes, and societal concerns, and to think creatively and constructively and be willing and able to participate in *improving society* for the better.
D. Schools should educate young people to challenge unjust societal conditions and practices and join with others in reconstructing and *transforming* the existing social order into a more *just* and *equitable* society.

The Likert-type scale ranged from "1 strongly disagree" to "7 strongly agree." Informants' perceptions before and after entering the program were displayed in Table 10.3. The following patterns emerged. First, there were increases in means for each school of thought from the perception before entering the program to after enrollment in the program. However, the increase was statistically significant only for "to improve society for the better" ($t = 5.15$, $p < .001$, Cohen's $d = .25$). The data seemed to indicate that the program made an impact in making informants realize that "to improve society for the better" is an appropriate function of schooling. Second, the rank order of the means provided additional information for the impact of the program. From perceptions before to after entering the program, "to improve society for the better" moved from second place to first. As a matter of fact, the Spearman's rank order correlation indicated that the rank order of the perceptions before entering the program was statistically different from the rank order of the current perceptions ($r_s = .80$, $p = .20$). It appeared that the program broadened the informants' perspective by encouraging them pay more attention to the function "to improve the society for the better," on one hand, and still cherish the function of schooling "to develop individual interests and abilities," on the other.

The informants were also asked to indicate which school of thought was most representative of their perceptions. The data displayed in Table 10.4 suggested that from perceptions before entering the program to the current ones, there was an increase in percentages of informants who perceived "to improve society for the better" most representative of their thoughts while

TABLE 10.3. Perceptions of the Importance of Schooling Functions Before and After Entering the Leadership Program

Schooling Function	Mean Before	Mean After	Mean Difference	*t*	*P*	Cohen's *d*
To maintain social order and stability	5.18	5.14	0.04	0.86	.39	.04
To develop individual interests and abilities	6.15	6.11	0.04	0.96	.34	.05
To improve society for the better	6.16	5.95	0.21	5.15	<.001	.25
To transform the society	4.88	4.77	0.11	2.18	.30	.11

TABLE 10.4. Percentage of Respondents Indicating the Schooling Function as the Most Representative of Their Views Before and After Entering the Program

Schooling Function	Before	After
To maintain social order and stability	15.9	20.4
To develop individual interests and abilities	42.8	42.5
To improve society for the better	37.4	31.2
To transform the society	4.0	5.9

the percentages for "to develop individual interests and abilities" remained basically the same. The data seemed to support the findings in the previous paragraph.

Changes in perceptions regarding the leadership program and the profession. Informants were questioned "how likely do you think it would be that a person who knows the field of education could be a reasonably good administrator *without* going through this Administrator Education Program?", and the informants indicated their response by using a 7-point Likert scale ranging from "1 extremely unlikely" to "7 extremely likely". The means for before and after entering the program were 3.86 and 3.32, respectively, $t\ (403) = 5.46, p < .001$, Cohen's $d = .27$. Therefore, after entering the program the informants felt that it was less likely to be a reasonably good administrator without going through the program, but the change was relatively small as suggested by Cohen's *d*. However, the mean of the current perception was 3.32 on the 7-point scale, an indication that there was still a strong feeling that it was possible to be a reasonably good administrator without participating in the program. Finally, when the informants responded to the question whether their enthusiasm for becoming administrators changed as they progressed through the leadership program, 7.2% reported that their enthusiasm declined, 35.8% remained about the same, and 57.0% increased.

Discussion

The findings of the study revealed a sophisticated portrait of the informants' perceptions of the nature and impact of the leadership program. The informants identified a number of positive aspects of educational leadership programs. First, the informants appeared to be satisfied with the program, instructors, and courses. Of the informants, 81% responded that the educational leadership program was better than or the same as other departments on campus in terms of status and prestige; 95% indicated that professors of the educational leadership program were better than or about the same as those in other departments; 89% rated the educational leadership program "A" or "B"; and 93% felt that their enthusiasm for becoming administrators increased or remained about the same as they progressed through the program.

The second positive aspect of the educational program as revealed in the survey was that after enrollment in the leadership program, the informants developed a more comprehensive understanding of educational goals and increased their appreciation for schooling to improve society for the better. The importance of each educational goal escalated with the completion of educational leadership courses. Thus, the informants' understanding of educational goals increased as they were finishing educational leadership programs. A similar pattern was observed when examining the perceptions of schooling functions. The educational leadership program appeared to make two impacts on informants as related to the perception of educational goals and the functions of schooling: (a) The educational leadership curriculum increased the informants' consciousness of educational goals and schooling functions and, therefore, made a subliminal or indirect effect on the value and mindset of prospective administrators; (b) the leadership program motivated informants to move beyond the notion that schooling should develop individuals—an ideal usually associated with their teaching experience in the classroom—and begin to pay more attention to the social function of educational institutions in improving society.

Nonetheless, the data also pointed out informants' dissatisfaction with some aspects of the leadership program. Respondents valued skill- and practice-oriented courses more than theory-oriented offerings, and felt that the leadership program should be changed to accommodate their preference. There was also a strong sentiment that it is possible for someone who knows education to be a reasonably good administrator without going through a leadership program.

Some very important issues and challenges underlie the informants' aforementioned dissatisfaction with some aspects of the leadership program. The first challenge is the need to address what successful educational leadership entails. Until now we—the profession which educates school leaders—have not satisfactorily addressed the question of what contributes to successful educational leadership. Therefore, it is difficult for us to design and defend an educational leadership program. We have much to learn from other professions. For example, in the medical profession, there is a core of knowledge and skill on which the medical education is based. In the area of business leadership, Kouzes and Posner (1995) attempted to arrive at a set of qualities which are indispensable for successful business leadership. Even in the area of teaching—a profession close to ours—there have been attempts to conceptualize the knowledge base of teaching (e.g., Grossman, 1990; Shulman, 1987) or to investigate the nature of the profession (Pratte & Rury, 1991). If we want to develop a defensible program in educational leadership, we must address the question of what successful educational leadership entails.

The second challenge we face is the desire and practice of moving toward a field-based, internship-centered program in educational leadership, which the informants of the study prefer. There are merits in these field-based programs as they provide necessary experiences. However, to move the whole program into the field, as was advocated by some in teacher education, might be moving too far to the other extreme.

There are several reasons for arguing against moving toward a totally field-based program of educational leadership. First, historically speaking, when Flexner (1910) reformed the medical education in the beginning of this century, he recommended that those proprietary medical schools be discontinued and the medical schools be housed on university campuses. It was the intellectual and knowledge base that required the medical school to be a part of the university. The same argument could be made for the educational leadership program. As the data of the study revealed, theoretical studies helped the informants develop a more comprehensive and balanced perspective on educational goals and schooling functions. Secondly, the field tends to be conservative and self-perpetuating. It can be persuasively argued that practicing administrators have failed to meet the challenges faced by students and the communities they serve. The general view of politicians and reformers portraying schools as ineffective institutions suggests a need to reform educational leadership. Therefore, prospective school leaders should be exposed to exemplary rather than complacent practices. Finally, as to the component of the field experience, there is still an issue of how to organize the experience. As some researchers argued, field experience per se could be miseducative (Feiman-Nemser & Buchmann, 1987).

The final challenge for us, as revealed in the data, is to integrate theory and practice. A high percentage of the informants felt that they could be good school leaders without going through the educational leadership program. University personnel might characterize this "learning by doing" as an anti-intellectual bias perpetuated by practitioners who criticize the incorporation of theory and validated practice into the administrative milieu. As a matter of fact, university faculty's observations and comments of dated administrative practices occasionally fuels the tension between the school and university personnel. This tension, if accompanied by constructive dialogue, provides the framework for amalgamation of theory into practice which potentially results in substantive school change.

Merging theory with practice offers a viable solution that promises to provide students with a meaningful program which offers an external laboratory experience closely associated with theory. An argument for crafting educational leadership field experiences supported by the school and university personnel provides a workable solution to the problems in educational leadership. University faculty must begin to bridge the gap between the university and field by increasing their understanding of challenges faced by practitioners. This might mean university personnel working with school on a more regular basis, creating exchange programs, and taking other measures to increase collaboration between the university and the field. Results of the study suggest an efficacy on the part of students on the importance and influence of educational leadership courses in developing a knowledge base and philosophy of educational leadership. It is the interaction between the theory and practice—the kind of dynamics discussed by Dewey (1904)—that offers the best hope of improving educational leadership.

The study reported in this chapter is not without limitation. The primary limitation is that the inquiry was confined to the informants' perceptions of educational goals, schooling functions, and their enthusiasm for becoming administrators. Future studies should investigate other measures of program quality and impact. Second, the study used a cross-sectional approach to studying the impact of the leadership program. It would be interesting to take a longitudinal approach—i.e., to measure their perception actually before and after entering the program—to validate the findings of the study. Finally, the existing data set does not allow the authors to distinguish those studying for different types of certification. Otherwise, we would be able to detect the possible variations among subsamples—such as principals, superintendents, and school business officials—in their perceptions of the nature and impact of the program. This is an interesting area worth further research.

An extensive literature review while conducting the study indicated that currently the quality and impact of the educational leadership program is mainly an issue in North America. However, educational leadership programs are being developed and instituted in other parts of the world. For example, the government in the UK is initiating the qualification requirement for headmasters—a program called National Preliminary Qualification for Headship. With the development and institution of educational leadership programs, the quality and impact of the programs will become an increasingly important topic for research and debate.

References

Babbie, E. (1989). *The practice of social research*. Belmont, CA: Wadsworth.

Carter, D. S. (1994). A curriculum model for administrator preparation and continuing professional development. *Journal of Educational Administration, 32*(2), 21–24.

Chapman, P. (1990). *Survey of school administrator preparation programs.* (ERIC Document Reproduction Service No. ED 340 091)

Cohen, J. (1988). *Statistical power analysis for the behavioral sciences* (2nd ed.). Hillsdale, New Jersey: Lawrence Erlbaum Associates.

Coleman, D. (1991, May). *Innovation in administrator preparation.* Paper presented at the Superintendents' Conference on School Services Research and Applied Technology. (ERIC Document Reproduction Service No. ED 335 735)

Cordeiro, P. A., & Sloan, E. S. (1996). Administrative interns as legitimate participants in the community of practice. *Journal of School Leadership, 6*(1), 4–29.

Daresh, J. C., & Playko, M. A. (1993, February). Benefits of a mentoring program for aspiring administrators. Paper presented at the annual meeting of the American Association of School Administrators, Orlando, FL. (ERIC Document Reproduction Service No. ED 354 603)

Dewey, J. (1904). The relationship of theory to practice in education. In C. C. McMurry (Ed.), Third yearbook of the National Society for the Scientific Study of Education. Chicago: University of Chicago Press.

Feiman-Nemser, S., & Buchmann, M. (1987). When is student teaching teacher education? *Teaching and Teacher Education, 3*(4), 255–273.

Flexner, A. (1910). *Medical education in the United States and Canada.* New York: Carnegie Foundation for the Advancement of Teaching.

Geltner, B. B. (1993, October). *Integrating formative portfolio assessment, reflective practice, and cognitive coaching into preservice preparation.* Paper presented at the annual convention of the University Council for Educational Administration, Houston, TX. (ERIC Document Reproduction Service No. ED 365 702)

Goodlad, J. I. (1994). *What schools are for* (2nd ed). Bloomington, IN: Phi Delta Kappa Educational Foundation.

Grossman, P. L. (1990). *The making of a teacher: Teacher knowledge and teacher education.* New York: Teachers College Press.

Heller, R. W., Conway, J. A., & Jacobson, S. L. (1988). Here's your blunt critique of administrator preparation. *Executive Educator, 10*(9), 18–21.

Holdaway, E. A., & Riordan, G. P. (1996). A field experience model in a doctoral administrator preparation program. *Journal of CAPEA, 8,* 67–78.

Jacobs, H. L. (1991). Gender differences in the program effects of administrative preparation. *Planning and Changing,* 22(1), 46–64.

Jacobson, S. L. (1996). School leadership in an age of reform: New directions in principal preparation. *International Journal of Educational Reform, 5*(3), 271–277.

Jacobson, S. L., & Woodworth, B. E. (1990). Preparing rural administrators: What do they need? What do they want? *Research in Rural Education, 6*(3), 33–42.

Katz, M. (1991). Putting the holistic educational leadership puzzle together. *Planning and Changing,* 22(1), 13–22.

Kim, L. (1996). CLSA's effort to walk the talk for beginning administrators. *Journal of CAPEA, 8,* 21–28.

Kouzes, J. J., & Posner, B. Z. (1995). *The leadership challenge.* San Francisco: Jossey-Bass.

LaCost, B., & Pounder, D. (1987, October). *The internship: An alternative model.* Paper presented at the University Council for Educational Administration meeting, Charlottesville, VA.

Montgomerie, C., Peters, F., & Ward, K. (1991). *Educational leadership in Alberta: A Study conducted on behalf of the consortium.* (ERIC Document Reproduction Service No. ED 332 317)

Murphy, J. (1992). *The landscapes of leadership preparation: Reframing the education of school administrators.* Newbury Park, CA: Corwin Press.

National Association of Elementary School Principals. (1990). *Principals for 21st century schools.* Alexandria, VA: Author.

National Commission for the Principalship. (1990). *Principals for our changing schools.* Fairfax, VA: Author.

Peel, H. A., & Wallace, C. (1996). *Improving leadership preparation programs through a school, university, and professional organization partnership.* Paper presented at the annual meeting of the National Council of Professors of Educational Administration, Corpus Christi, TX. (ERIC Document Reproduction Service No. ED 402 671)

Place, A. W., & Reitzug, U. C. (1992). Educational administration research, practice, and preparation: Lessons from woodworking and American Indian philosophy. *Journal of School Leadership,* 2(4), 396–409.

Pohland, P. A. (1986, April). *Administrator preparation models and the impact of practice context.* Paper presented at the annual meeting of the American Educational Research Association, San Francisco, CA. (ERIC Document Reproduction Service No. ED 271 256)

Pratte, R., & Rury, J. L. (1991). Teachers, professionalism, and craft. *Teachers College Record, 93*(1), 59–72.

Reed, D. B., & Hannaford, M. E. (1991, October). *Practitioners as case researchers and writers.* Paper presented at the annual meeting of the University Council of Educational Administration, Baltimore, MD. (ERIC Document Reproduction Service No. ED 344 307)

Shulman, L. S. (1987). Knowledge and teaching. Foundations of the new reform. *Harvard Educational Review,* 57(1), 1–22.

Smith, J. M. (1990, August). *Experiential learning in a nontraditional setting: Are the needs of preservice principals truly being fulfilled.* Paper presented at the annual meeting of the National Council of Professors of Educational Administration, Los Angeles, CA. (ERIC Document Reproduction Service No. ED 328 964)

Su, J. Z. X. (1992). What schools are for: An analysis of findings from a US national study. *International Review of Education, 38,* 133–153.

Twale, D. J., & Short , P. M. (1989). Shaping school leaders for the future: Innovation in preparation. *Planning and Changing,* 20(3), 149–157.

Wylie, V. L., & Clark, E. H. (1994). Personal observations of using peer coaching to improve the administrative internship. *Journal of School Leadership,* 5, 543–556.

·11·

Van E. Cooley and Jianping Shen

WHO WILL LEAD? THE TOP 10 FACTORS THAT INFLUENCE TEACHERS MOVING INTO ADMINISTRATION

Who will lead the schools during the 21st century? Approximately 60 percent of the principals currently holding administrative posts reach retirement age by 2006 (Parkay & Currie, 1992). The problem is exacerbated by the declining number of teachers seeking administrator certification and the fact that many who are studying for the degree do not plan to seek an administrative position after completing degree requirements (Jordon, 1994).

Researchers have concluded that the diminished pool of candidates is related to positional demands, the extended school work day, inadequate compensation, ongoing conflict, and criticism from parents, teachers, board members, and business and industrial leaders (Abrell, 1984; Craven, 1989; McCormick, 1987; Pawlas, 1989). Teacher reluctance to enter administration coupled with the number of administrator retirements present a significant challenge to boards, superintendents, and communities.

Finding a Solution

To help find a solution to this problem, a study was conducted of 189 master's students enrolled in a midwestern university's educational leadership program. Students completed a survey identifying factors that influenced their decision to apply for an administrative position. Area superintendents encouraged the investigation. Several superintendents suggested they had not filled administrative positions because they could not find a suitable candidate.

Although there are always candidates for vacant administrative positions, finding candidates who can address today's complex issues and demands is extremely difficult for many school officials. The top 10 factors that influence teachers applying for administrative position suggest a complex list of "wants and needs" for this new generation of school leaders. The factors listed in Table 11.1 have implications for retaining and recruiting school leaders.

Factor #10: Nature of the Work

Nearly 62 percent of the educational leadership students listed the nature of the work as a consideration in applying for an administrative position. Administrative job responsibilities for most entry-level positions include discipline, attendance, teacher evaluation, supervision of co-curricular activities, and a myriad of other assignments. Student discipline, drug and alcohol abuse, teacher-administrator conflict, and increased public skepticism continue to complicate the administrator's role, responsibilities, and the nature of administrative work. The demands of a modern society have complicated and intensified the administrator's work responsibilities.

Factor #9: Poor Working Conditions

Working conditions relate to a number of interconnected issues, including the wealth of the district, size of the district, administrator-student ratios,

TABLE 11.1. Top 10 Factors Teachers Consider in Applying for Administrative Positions

Rank	Item	Percentage*
10.	Nature of the work—e.g., relationship with parents and students	61.5
9.	Poor working conditions (paperwork, long hours, little time and freedom, etc.)	62.3
8.	Emotional aspects (stress, boredom, frustration, burnout, lack of fulfillment, etc.)	65.7
7.	Location of district	68.0
6.	Reputation of the superintendent	70.3
5.	Impact of administrative position on home life	72.0
4.	Quality of life in the community (housing, cultural activities, recreation, etc.)	72.1
3.	Community support	75.8
2.	Salary commensurate with responsibilities	76.0
1.	Relationship among the board, administration, and teachers	84.4

* Percentage of respondents who rated the item "important."

composition of students, and board and community expectations. More than 62 percent of the teachers identified "poor working conditions" as a factor they would consider in applying for an administrative position.

Respondents also perceived administrators as having little freedom and discretion in completing administrative responsibilities. These conditions included excessive paperwork, long hours, and little discretionary time and freedom. The administrative work week in many instances exceeds 65 hours, with administrators often working three or four nights per week. After shadowing an administrator, one teacher noted that the dynamics and demands of the school environment forced the principal to complete paperwork and reports after regular school hours. The demands of administration often discourage teachers from seeking an administrative position.

Factor #8: Emotional Aspects of Administration

Emotional aspects related to administration include stress, burnout, and frustration. More than 65 percent of the respondents suggested that the emotional aspects of administrative were a major consideration in applying for an administrative position. Teachers often question if the extra compensation and prestige is worth being second-guessed and criticized by both internal and external stakeholders. Teachers recognize stress as a critical part of administration.

Factor #7: Location of the District

Sixty-eight percent of the respondents identified district location as a factor in applying for an administrative position. Teachers preferred to work in rural and suburban districts. Respondents also considered the proximity of the district to a metropolitan area when applying for an administrative position. Although district location is important, prospective administrators are willing to consider a variety of educational settings. Surprisingly, only 20 percent of the teachers indicated they would seek a position in the district in which they currently taught.

Factor #6: Reputation of the Superintendent

More than 70 percent of the respondents indicated that the reputation of the superintendent was a key factor in applying for an administrative position. Educational leadership students suggested that the superintendent's leadership style, accessibility, and his or her rapport with faculty and staff influenced a teacher's decision to enter administration in a particular district. The diminished pool of qualified administrative candidates illustrates the importance of the superintendent's reputation and leadership style. This is especially true in districts that experience significant geographic and financial disadvantages, as compared to their more affluent and progressive counterparts.

Factor #5: Impact of administrative position on a person's home life

The long work day, politics, a lack of job security, and ongoing conflict all have an impact on an administrator's home life. Seventy-two percent of the teachers stated they will consider the impact of administration on their home life when applying for an administrative position. It seems clear that the position and its perceived impact on the family constitutes a significant barrier to teachers entering administration.

Factor #4: Quality of Community Life

Teachers expressed concern for quality housing, cultural activities, and recreation in communities where they might seek an administrative position. There are communities in which teachers do not want to live and work. More than 72 percent of the teachers identified quality of life issues in the community as a consideration in applying for an administrative position. This certainly places a burden on boards, administrators, and communities as school district officials attempt to recruit the best and most capable educational leaders. Regrettably, school officials and community leaders have little discretion in terms of quality of life in the community.

Factor #3: Community Support

Teachers applying for administrative positions are acutely aware of the importance of community support. Seventy-five percent of the respondents identified community support as a factor in applying for an administrative position. Issues such as school funding, violence, student drug and alcohol use, community politics, and parental involvement in schools affect teachers' decision whether or not to apply for an administrative position. Community support has a critical impact on the administrator's capability to lead, develop programs, and meet the needs of faculty, staff, students, and the communities they serve. Community support also influences the administrator's perception of job security within the school-community.

Factor #2: Salary Commensurate with Responsibility

Seventy-six percent of the teachers indicated that the administrator's salary must be commensurate with responsibilities. While an administrator's contract may approach 240 days with the salary superior to that of teachers, the reality is that the daily rate may be equal to or less than that of teachers who are at the top of the salary scale. The teacher's official workday is defined by the master contract, while the administrator must participate in a number of evening activities. The daily and after-school responsibilities of administrators demand that boards re-examine salary and benefits provided to administrators.

Factor #1: Relationship Among the Board, Administration, and Teachers

The number 1 factor that teachers consider in applying for an administrative position is the relationship among the board, administration, and teachers. More than 84 percent of the respondents stated that the relationship among board members, administrators, and teachers represented the most important consideration in applying for an administrative position.

Teachers witness discord between the board, superintendent, principals, and teachers. Teachers might be reluctant to seek a position in a district that has a history of teacher-administrator strife and board tendencies to micromanage. No one wants to uproot their family and move to a district with ongoing conflict between board members, teachers, and administrators. The reality is that in school districts where boards, teachers, and administrators work together, boards and superintendents are more likely to attract and retain quality administrators.

Concluding Comments

The top 10 factors illustrate the issues teachers consider when applying for an administrative position. Admittedly, a number of the factors at first glance seem outside the control of the board and superintendent. For example, some school district locations are obviously more desirable that others. Housing and community cultural activities may be lacking in some rural areas. Funding for teacher and administrator salaries may be limited by the tax base. Urban areas may be plagued by student violence, drug and alcohol abuse, and a general apathy toward education.

Results of the study strongly suggest that aside from salary, organizational relationships, more than other factors, affect a teacher's willingness to seek an administrative position in a particular district. Boards must be willing to compensate fairly administrators who seek employment in their district. Furthermore, dispersing power and responsibilities, and the development of harmonious relationships between community stakeholders represent issues that take time and patience. Leaders must demonstrate a willingness to re-engineer ineffective management and leadership practices.

Prospective administrators identified board, teacher, and administrator relationships; community support; quality of life in the community; and the reputation of the superintendent as critical issues in applying for administrative positions. Many boards, administrators, and teachers seem to have subconsciously created a climate and work environment that is perceived by administrator candidates as undesirable. Attention must also be given to the nature of administrative work. Do we ask administrators to do too much? Administrative workload and work conditions must be closely examined and, if unreasonable, the administrator's role must be modified.

There are always individuals who will seek administrative positions. Unfortunately, many of them do not possess the skills to provide the necessary leadership for the 21st century. Some districts, however, will continue to recruit and retain "blue chip" educational administrators. These districts will continue to enjoy a competitive advantage over their less progressive counterparts. The result is that students, teachers, and school communities will prosper from hiring and retaining exceptional leaders. The 10 factors present a complex profile of issues that contribute to the administrative shortage. Until these issues are addressed, the impending crisis is likely to continue.

References

Abrell, R. (1984). Leading by stepping down (problem of burnout in school administrators). *The Clearing House* 57, 351–52.

Craven, L. *The supply and demand trends of public secondary school administrators in South Carolina from 1978 through 2002*. Paper presented at the Annual Meeting of the Southern Regional Council on Educational Administration, Columbia, S.C., 1989. (ERIC Document Reproduction Service No. ED 313 799)

Jordan, D. W. (1994). *The supply and demand trends of public school principals and administrators in southwestern Louisiana: 1993–1997*. ERIC Document No. ED 375 525, 1994.

McCormick, K. C. (1987). The vaunted school executive shortage: How serious is it?" *The Effective Executive*, *9*, 18–21.

Parkay, F. W., & Currie, G. (1992). Sources of support for beginning principals. In G. W. Parkay and G. E. Hall (Eds.), *Becoming a principal: The challenges of beginning leadership*. Boston: Allyn and Bacon.

Pawlas, G. (1989). Supply and demand trends for elementary school administrators in South Carolina from 1977 through 2002. Paper presented at the Annual Meeting of the Southern Regional Council on Educational Administration, Columbia, S.C. (ERIC Document No. ED 320 194)

·12·

Jianping Shen, Van E. Cooley, and Gary L. Wegenke

FACTORS INFLUENCING APPLICATION FOR THE PRINCIPALSHIP: A COMPARATIVE STUDY OF TEACHERS, PRINCIPALS, AND SUPERINTENDENTS

Introduction

The inability to attract quality candidates for an increasingly large number of educational administrative positions represents a serious crisis facing school board members, superintendents, and community leaders (McCormick, 1987). One study indicates that a declining number of teachers were seeking administrator certification and that less than half of those who obtained administrative certification planned to enter administration within the foreseeable future (Jordan, 1994). Another factor contributing to the administrator shortage is the under-representation of women and minorities (Wendel, 1994; Yewchuk, 1992). Coleman (1996) characterized women administrators as disproportionate to the number of female educators. In a 1998 study, 35% of the superintendents reported a need to increase the number of minority administrators (Educational Research Service, 1998). The administrator shortage is accentuated by a large number of administrator retirements. Approximately 60% of all administrators reached retirement age prior to the year 2000. Over half of current principals were over 50 years of age. The average age of principals in 1993–94 was 47.7 (Educational Research Service, 1998). The Bureau of Labor Statistics (1996–1997) projected a 10–25% increase in the number of administrative positions by 2005.

Administrator retirement, coupled with steady growth of student population, the reluctance of many teachers with administrative certification to enter administration, and the under-representation of minorities and females, has resulted in a possible leadership vacuum. The shortage of qualified educational leaders will continue to impact on educational quality and threaten many of the educational gains attained during the past decade. The educational community must continue to identify factors and solutions to address the growing problem of attracting new members into educational leadership.

The study investigated (a) the factors influencing those applying for principalship and (b) the possible differences among teachers, principals, and superintendents in their perceptions. Through the study we intended not only to identify the importance of the factors that influence the application of principalship, but also to establish a foundation for developing balanced policies so that the focus of the policies will not be misplaced.

Literature Review

A review of the literature provides an overview of the reasons for the diminished pool of qualified administrative applicants. The nature of the work, the elongated administrator work-day, the relatively comparable compensation of teachers to administrators, continuous conflict, and criticisms from both internal and external stakeholders represented significant obstacles to teachers applying for leadership positions (Abrell, 1984, Craven, 1989; McCormick, 1987; Pawlas, 1989; Portin & Shen, 1998; Portin, Shen, & Williams, 1998; Shen, Rodriguez-Campo, & Rincones-Gomez, 2000). In a Wisconsin study, Price (1994) found the impact of an administrative position on an individual's home life, stress, politics, the nature of administrative work, and board directives contributed to a teacher's reluctance to enter administration. A study conducted by the Educational Research Service (1998) revealed that reasons for teachers not seeking administrative positions included inadequate compensation, stress, excessive time commitment, disgruntled parents and community members, and a number of societal problems that compromised the educational process.

A variety of motivating and restraining factors also influenced teachers as they give thought to pursuing an administrative position. Motivating factors included the excitement of the position, the opportunity to work with teachers, the desire to make a difference by affecting the lives of teachers and students, and a change from classroom routine (Shen, Cooley, & Ruhl-Smith, 1999). Restraining factors involved night responsibilities for supervising sports events and other activities, excessive hours, politics, and answering to a number of publics (Albright, 1997). Other conditions contributing to the scarcity of administrators included limited mobility, inequitable salaries, escalating responsibilities, and little or no job security (Bowles, 1990).

Pressures from politicians and business and industrial leaders to deliver quality education have raised administrators' frustration and discontent (Ginty, 1995). The demands of the principalship with its associated frustrations force many teachers to pause and contemplate the benefits of principalship. Chubb and Moe (1990) and Portin (2000) summarized the changing role of the principal as a powerless position mired in a bureaucracy and characterized by bickering, infighting, and nonexistent teamwork between teachers and administrators.

Differences in job satisfaction among teachers and administrators may influence career paths of teachers and administrators. Herzberg's (1968) seminal work on motivation identified two factors—motivators and hygiene or maintenance factors—as influencing workers' productivity. According to Herzberg's theory, once a certain level is obtained, hygiene or maintenance factors do not motivate workers to higher performance. Hygiene or maintenance factors include, for example, salary and work conditions. However, motivators, which include achievement, challenging work, increased responsibility, and recognition, can lead to higher performance. Derlin and Schneider (1994), relying on research of Hertzberg (1968) and Maslow (1954), studied job satisfaction and reported differences between urban and suburban administrators and between teachers and administrators. Urban principals expressed concern with compensation and extrinsic factors; suburban principals were more likely to value a positive work environment. Teacher job satisfaction differed from their administrators and increased with involvement in decision-making, recognition, and support. Several studies pertaining to what workers want from their jobs have been replicated over several decades (Hersey & Blanchard, 1996). Workers sought appreciation for completed tasks, input into decision-making, opportunities for promotion and growth, job security, and good wages.

The literature suggests that a number of diverse factors affect a candidate's decision to apply for an administrative position in education. These internal and external factors often create an unappealing work environment for many of today's candidates for school administrative positions. Although we are able to find in the literature some factors that influence teachers when applying for administrative positions in education, there is no evidence of systematic inquiry into the topic. Furthermore, the existing literature focuses more on teachers' perspectives rather than on those of the principals and superintendents. It is certainly important to investigate teachers' perspectives because they are the potential candidates for principalship. However, it is also important to inquire into the perspectives of principals and superintendents. Principals are currently experiencing the principalship positions, it is important to compare teachers' and principals' perspective because teachers' ideas about what principalship entails might not be entirely accurate. Further, principals and particularly superintendents will be heavily involved in developing policies for recruiting and retaining principals. It is important to know the perspectives from all three groups so that the emphasis of the policies will not be misplaced. This study inquired into (a) the factors influencing those applying for principalship and (b) the possible differences among teachers, principals, and superintendents in their perceptions as to these factors.

Research Purpose and Questions

The study investigated the reasons why teachers are reluctant to seek principalship positions. The following three questions guided the study.

1. What are the major factors influencing teachers to apply for principalship positions?
2. Are there distinguishable differences between teachers, principals, and superintendents in rating the importance of these factors?
3. In terms of the perspectives or factors influencing the application for principalship positions, are there any dimensions along which teachers, principals, and superintendents can be reliably distinguished?

Methodology

Sample

The sample of the study consisted of 198 teachers, 306 principals, and 370 superintendents in the state of Michigan, with a total of 874 respondents. All the respondents worked in public schools. As to the sub-sample of superintendents, a random sample of 551 superintendents was selected from *The Directory of Michigan Educational Administration Association*. Questionnaires were then mailed; 370 returned usable data, resulting in a return rate of 67.2%. As to the principals, 493 questionnaires were sent to a random sample of principals. The names were also selected from *The Directory of Michigan Educational Administration Association;* 370 returned usable data, with a return rate of 75.1%. The sub-sample of teachers was constructed from the surveys of current students and graduates from the Department of Educational Leadership, Western Michigan University. The return rates for the current student survey and the graduate survey were 100% and 49%, respectively, with a weighted return rate of 64.5%. Among the current students and graduates surveyed, only those who were public school teachers at the time of the survey were extracted to form the sub-sample of teachers. All the surveys were conducted in late 1998. There were two postcard follow-ups for the graduates and principals, and one postcard follow-up for superintendents. The survey of current students was conducted during regular class sessions, and 100% return rate was achieved without any follow-up procedure. According to Babbie's (1989) rule, the return rates for all three sub-samples are good. Because private schools and public schools are functioning in two different contexts in terms of student population, school organization, and requirements for principalship, this study focused on the public school arena. All teachers, principals, and superintendents in the sample of the study worked in public schools.

Instrument

Teachers, principals, and superintendents were asked to rate, on a 6-point scale, the importance of 30 items influencing application for principalship position, with "1" meaning "not important at all" to "6" "extremely important". As illustrated in the literature review section, we developed the 30 survey items from a comprehensive review of the relevant literature. The survey items include, among others, the nature of the job (such as "stress of the position," "poor working condition"), the nature of the school district and community (such as "reputation of the school district" and "quality of life in the community"), compensation (such as "salary must be commensurate with responsibilities"), and reasons for applying for the principalship (such as "opportunities for professional advancement" and "autonomy in a leadership position"). For a list of all 30 items, please refer to "Table 12.1. Results of Factor Analysis." Teachers, principals, and superintendents responded to the same set of items.

Data Analysis

Corresponding to the three research questions, there were three major steps in the data analysis process. First, a factor analysis was conducted to collapse the 30 items into factors influencing the application for a principal position.

Second, based on the results of factor analysis composite scores for each of the factors were constructed by averaging across the items in each factor. One-way ANOVA was then conducted to investigate whether there were differences among teachers, principals, and superintendents on each of the factors; and if so, Scheffe's post-hoc multiple comparison was conducted to investigate which group(s) differed from which one(s). Based on the mean of each factor, Spearman's rank-order correlation was also conducted to inquire into whether the three groups differed from each other from the perspective of the rank order of those factors. Finally, in order to have a concise picture of the possible differences among the three groups, discriminant function analysis was conducted to investigate along which dimensions(s), if any, the three groups could be reliably distinguished.

Results

Results of the Factor Analysis

The results of the factor analysis are displayed in Table 12.1. Principal components extraction, eigenvalue greater than 1.0, and varimax rotation were employed to collapse the 30 items. The factor analysis identified eight factors related to the application of principal positions. The eight factors include (a) workload and compensation, (b) macro-constraints of the position, (c) the impact of the position on the individual and family, (d) intrinsic rewards which include the individual's status within the community, opportunity for advancement, and the degree of position autonomy, (e) work environment, (f) school district characteristics which include the location, size, and reputation of the district, (g) community characteristics, and (h) safety and support. These eight factors, identified through the factor analysis, present a comprehensive profile of the factors influencing the application for principalship positions.

Results of ANOVA, Multiple Comparison, and Rank Order Correlation

The mean and rank for each factor, ANOVA results, and multiple comparisons are presented in Table 12.2. The ANOVA on each factor was statistically significant at the .05 level, except for "intrinsic rewards." For the factors where statistical significance was found among the three groups, the effect sizes, as measured by eta squared, tended to be small and in the following descending order: "safety and support," "work load and compensation," "macro constraints for the job," "work environment," "impact of the job," "characteristics of the school district," and "characteristics of the community."

TABLE 12.1. Results of Factor Analysis

Factor and Item	Loading
Work load and compensation	
length of contract days	.71
time required for supervising extra-curricular activities	.67
administrator's daily rate significantly exceeds teacher's daily rate	.58
length of work days	.54
diversity of the job responsibility	.52
salary must be commensurate with responsibilities	.50
length of the administrative contract	.48
Macro constraints of the job	
lack of respect for educators	.67
school board micro-management in the school district	.65
labor related issues	.64
Impact of the job	
stress of the position	.72
emotional aspects	.64
impact of administrative position on family life	.63
political nature of administration	.54
poor working condition	.51
Intrinsic reward	
administrator's status in the educational community	.74
opportunities for professional advancement	.71
autonomy in a leadership position	.59
Work environment	
relationship between the board, administration, and teachers	.68
reputation of the superintendent	.54
nature of the work	.54
community support	.53
Characteristics of the school district	
location of the district	.81
size of the school district	.79
reputation of the school district	.48
Characteristics of the community	
finding a suitable position for spouse	.79
wealth and prosperity of the district	.56
quality of life in the community	.42
Safety and support	
personal safety	.74
lack of support for administrators	.45

TABLE 12.2. Results of *F*-test and Scheffe's Post-hoc Multiple Comparisons

Factor	Teacher		Principal		Superintendent					
	Mean	Rank	Mean	Rank	Mean	Rank	*F*	*P*	Eta squared	Scheffe's*
Work environment	5.01	1	4.99	1	4.80	1	20.2	.00	.04	T>S, P>S
Impact of the job	4.73	2	4.98	2	4.70	2	13.9	.00	.03	P>S, P>T
Safety and support	4.62	3	4.37	5	3.69	8	50.0	.00	.10	T>S, P>S
Characteristics of the school district	4.36	4	4.21	7	4.17	5	3.2	.04	.01	T>S
Work load and compensation	4.24	5	4.54	4	4.18	4	21.3	.00	.05	P>S, P>T
Intrinsic reward	4.11	6	4.23	6	4.14	6	0.7	.48	.00	
Macro constraints for the job	4.02	7	4.55	3	4.41	3	21.6	.00	.05	P>T, S>T
Characteristics of the community	3.86	8	3.97	8	3.99	7	5.9	.00	.01	P>T, S>T

* Scheffe's post-hoc multiple comparisons statistically significant at .05 level; T=teacher, P=principal, and S=superintendent.

Based on the results of Scheffe's post hoc multiple comparison, it is clear that teachers and principals rated "work environment," "impact of the job," "safety and support," "characteristics of the school district," and "work load and compensation" higher than did superintendents. There was a statistically significantly positive correlation between how principals and superintendents rank-ordered these factors ($r_s = .83$, $p = .01$). However, no association was found between teachers and principals ($r_s = .64$, $p = .09$) and between teachers and superintendents ($r_s = .48$, $p = .23$).

Results of Discriminant Function Analysis

Table 12.3 displays the results of the discriminate functional analysis. On the basis of all eight predictors, there was reliable association between groups and predictors, χ^2 (16) = 295.6, $p < .001$. After the removal of the first function, reliable association remained, χ^2 (7) = 65.2, $p < .001$. The two discriminant functions accounted for 79.6% and 20.4%, respectively, of the between-group variability in discriminating among groups. The first function, which was basically a dimension of the work context, distinguished superintendents, on one hand, and teachers and principals, on the other. An inquiry into the group centroids indicated that teachers and principals rated the context of work more important than did superintendents. Due to the nature of their jobs and the location of their offices, superintendents rated safety and work environment less important than did teachers and principals.

TABLE 12.3. Results of Discriminant Function Analysis

	Item to Function Correlation	
Factor	Function 1	Function 2
Work load and compensation	.12	.85
Macro constraints for the job	–.25	.61
Impact of the job	.08	.62
Intrinsic reward	–.01	.25
Work environment	.35	.39
Characteristics of the school district	.14	–.08
Characteristics of the community	–.10	.10
Safety and support	.59	.32
Canonical correlation	–.49	.27
Group Centroids		
Teacher	.86	–.28
Principal	.12	.38
Superintendent	–.56	–.16

The second discriminant function, which was essentially a dimension of the nature and impact of the leadership position, distinguished principals, on one hand, and teachers and superintendents, on the other. The group centroids suggested that principals rated this dimension more important than did teachers and superintendents. It appears that due to the daily discharge of their responsibilities, principals paid more attention to the nature and impact of the leadership position than did teachers and superintendents.

Discussion

A Variety of Factors Influencing the Application for Principalship

This study identified eight major factors influencing teachers applying for principal positions. "Workload and compensation" includes hours and the number of contract days worked, time required to supervise extracurricular activities, diversity of administrative tasks, and a salary commensurate with responsibilities. "Macro constraints" relate to political and organizational factors and consist of respect, labor issues, and school board micromanagement. "The impact of the job" focuses on work conditions, the emotional aspects of the position, and the overall effect of administration on one's family life. "Intrinsic rewards" reflect the autonomy of a leadership position and the opportunities for advancement. "Work environment' involves community support, the nature of work, the reputation of the superintendent and the relationship between the board, administration, and teachers. "School district characteristics" include the location, size, and reputation of the school district whereas "community characteristics" include quality of life issues, wealth and prosperity of the district, and the ability to find employment for a spouse. "Safety and support" encompasses personal safety issues and the support given to administrators.

Two interesting patterns emerge from the list of factors influencing the application for principalship. First, the variety of factors based on the results of factor analysis—"work load and compensation," "macro constraints of the job," "impact of the job," "intrinsic reward," "work environment," "characteristics of the schol district," "characterisitcs of the community," and "safety and support"—points to the complexity of the issue of addressing principal shortage. Second, it is also interesting to note that the list of factors is dominated by those related to "extrinsic rewards" rather than "intrinsic rewards." As a matter of fact, seven out of eight factors are related to different aspects of extrinsic rewards.

Similarity and Difference among Teachers, Principals, and Superintendents

The analyses found some similarities among the three groups. As far as rank is concerned, all three groups rated "work environment" and "impact of the job" as the two most important factors influencing the application for principalship. Interestingly, all three groups rated "characteristics of the community" among the least important. As far as the mean is concerned, there is no difference among teachers, principals, and superintendents in rating "intrinsic reward" and "characteristics of community."

However, the analyses also found some differences among the three groups on the following aspects. First, "safety and support" was rated the third ($M = 4.62$) by teachers, but it was rated the fifth ($M = 4.37$) by principals and the eighth ($M = 3.69$) by the superintendents. "Macro constraints for the job" was rated the third by both principals ($M = 4.55$) and superintendents ($M = 4.41$), but the seventh by teachers ($M = 4.02$). It is clear that these differences are due to the nature of their current position. Teachers, who are in constant contact with students, are more aware of the safety issues, while principals and superintendents are more concerned about the leadership environment. Second, both the multiple comparison and the discriminant function analyses indicated that principals are more concerned about the nature and impact of the administrative positions. As was found in a survey in the state of Washington, principals reported that there had been an increasing demand for them to interact with parents, write grants, and implement new legislation and rules (Portin, Shen, & Williams, 1998). The overall pattern of the difference among the three groups is that their perspectives on factors influencing the application for principalship are closely associated with their current positions. In others words, teachers pay more attention to factors related to their immediate environment such as "safety and support" and "work environment;" principals rate "work load and compensation" and "impact of the job" highly; and both principals and superintendents feel that the factor "macro constraints for the job" is very important.

Policy Implications

A multi-faceted policy issue. The factor analysis of this study indicated that there are many factors influencing the application for principalship, ranging from "(a) workload and compensation" to "(h) safety and support." The range of the factors suggests that we need to develop a multi-faceted policy to address the issue of shortage of qualified applicants for the principalship. To focus on any one factor will not suffice.

A redefinition of the principalship. The list of factors influencing the application for principalship is dominated by factors related to "extrinsic rewards" such as "work environment," "the impact of the job on family life," "safety and support," "characteristics of the school district," and "workload and compensation." Although one factor is related to the "intrinsic reward," those factors related to the "extrinsic rewards" were usually rated higher than the "intrinsic reward" factors. This leads to the question as to whether or not the principalship needs to be restructured. As research indicates (e.g., Portin & Shen, 1998; Portin, Shen, & Williams, 1998; Shen, Rodriguez-Campo, & Rincones-Gomez, 2000), the principalship (a) has become more layered (i.e., more and more responsibilities placed one on top of the other), (b) has demonstrated a shift from leadership to management (due to more management tasks, many of which have legal consequences), and (c) has become more complex and ambiguous when working with the school system's decentralization agenda (e.g., site-based management issues) and simultaneously addressing the centralization agenda (e.g., state mandates, high-stakes state tests, and district-wide accountability measures). As a result, the morale of the principalship work force has been negatively impacted. Therefore, potential principal applicants are paying more attention to the factors related to "extrinsic rewards" rather than "intrinsic rewards." Among other things, we need to redefine the major responsibilities of the principalship and restructure it to make the job more attractive to potential candidates.

Balancing perspectives when developing policies to address principal shortage. As discussed in the previous section, the study also found that some differences exist among teachers, principals, and superintendents regarding their perspectives on the factors influencing the application for principalship positions. Their perspectives are essentially determined by their thoughts and views stemming from their current positions. For example, "safety and support" was ranked the third by teachers, the fifth by principals, and the eighth by superintendents in terms of its importance in the decision to apply for principalship. On the other hand, "macro constraints for the job" was rated the third by both principals and superintendents, but the seventh by teachers. It is not surprising that teachers', principals', and superintendents' perceptions are associated with the views of the principalship from their current positions. However, the finding does point to the importance of balancing teachers', principals', and superintendents' perspectives when we develop policies designed to address the principal's role and responsibilities so that future principal shortage can be alleviated. If we do not balance the perspectives when developing the policies, the emphasis on the policies will be misplaced given the differences among the three groups. In other words, policies based on principals' and superintendents' perspectives will not effectively address teachers' concerns.

Strengthening the leadership preparation for those teachers who aspire to be principals. The differences among teachers, principals, and superintendents also point to the need to improve the leadership preparation experiences for those teachers aspiring to be principals. It is important to take into account classroom teachers' perspectives based on their experiences. It is also imperative to educate aspiring teachers in terms of what makes an effective school leader so that they, in turn, are forward looking as to what the principalship entails. The rank order correlation analysis, the post-hoc multiple comparisons, and the discriminant function analysis indicated that principals' and superintendents' perceptions are very closely aligned. However, teachers' perceptions are not similar to those of principals and superintendents. Generally speaking, teachers rated job-related factors such as "work load and compensation" and "macro constraints for the job" much lower than did principals. This points to the need to educate those teachers who aspire to be principals to have knowledge and understanding of the factors that confront principals in their work environment. The lack of a realistic perception of a principal's job will not only prohibit some teacher applicants from applying for the position, but may also increase the attrition rate after a teacher applicant accepts the principalship position. In both cases, the issue of the principal shortage will be accelerated. One solution is to strengthen the internship component of educational leadership programs (Mullen & Cairns, 2001). This will allow potential applicants to see and experience first hand the job complexities found in the principalship.

Conclusion

The principal shortage continues to be a serious issue facing the educational community in the US. The data collected from 198 teachers, 306 principals, and 370 superintendents indicate (a) that a variety of factors influence candidates applying for the principalship, (b) that there are differences among teachers, principals, and superintendents in their perceptions of the importance of the factors influencing the application for principalship, (c) that the factors are more related to "extrinsic rewards" than "intrinsic rewards," and (d) that teachers need to know "first hand" more about what the principalship entails. The findings point to (a) the need to address the principalship shortage as a multi-faceted policy issue, (b) the urgency to redefine the principalship to make it more understandable and less complex, (c) the need to balance teachers', principals', and superintendents' perspectives when developing policies to address the principalship shortage so that the emphasis will not be misplaced, and (d) the importance of strengthening the educational leadership preparation programs for teachers who aspire to become principals. As professional educators concerned about the future, we are challenged to improve the principalship—both to educate our principalship candidates well and to recruit and retain the best candidates. Our communities are depending on us. We have a challenge ahead of us.

References

Abrell, R. (1984). Leading by stepping down (problem of burnout in school administrators). *The Clearing House, 57*, 351–352.

Albright, L. (1997). Is it time to move into administration? *School and Community, 83* (3), 8–12.

Babbie, E. (1989). *The Practice of social research*. Belmont, CA: Wadsworth.

Bowles, B. D. (1990). The silent crisis in educational leadership. *The Educational Digest, 55*, 12–14.

Chubb, J. E., & Moe, T. M. (1990). *Politics, markets, and America's schools*. Washington DC: The Brookings Institute.

Coleman, M. (1996).Barriers to career progress for women in education: The perceptions of female headmasters. *Educational Research, 38*, 317–332.

Craven, L. (1989). *The supply and demand trends of public secondary school administrators in South Carolina from 1978 through 2002*. Paper presented at the annual meeting of the Southern Regional Council on Educational Administration, Columbia, South Carolina. (ERIC Document Reproduction Service No. ED 313 799).

Derlin, R., & Schneider, G. T. (1994). Understanding job satisfaction, principals and teachers, urban and suburban. *Urban Education, 29*, 63–68.

Educational Research Service. (1998). *Is there a shortage of qualified candidates for openings in the principalship? An exploratory study*. Arlington, Virginia: Author.

Ginty, E. F. (1995). Supporting the success of the aspiring and beginning school leader. *NASSP Bulletin, 79*, 34–41.

Hersey, P., & Blanchard, K. H. (1987). *Management of organizational behavior: Utilizing human resources* (5th ed.). Englewood Cliffs, NJ: Prentice Hall.

Herzberg, F. (1968). One more time: How do you motivate employees? *Harvard Business Review, 46*, 53–62.

Jordan, D. W. (1994). *The supply and demand trends of public school principals and administrators in southwestern Louisiana: 1993–1997*. (ERIC Document Reproduction Service No. ED 375 525).

Maslow, A. (1954). *Motivation and personality*. New York: Harper & Row.

McCormick, K. C. (1987). The vaunted school executive shortage: How serious is it? *The Effective Executive, 9*, 18–21.

Mullen, C., & Cairns, S. S. (2001). The Principal's apprentice: Mentoring aspiring school administrators through relevant preparation. *Mentoring & Tutoring 9* (2), 125–152.

Parkay, F. W., & Currie, G. (1992). Sources of support for beginning principals. In G. W. Parkay & G. E. Hall (Eds.), *Becoming a principal: The challenges of beginning leadership* (pp. 70–84). Boston: Allyn and Bacon.

Pawlas, G. (1989). *Supply and demand trends for elementary school administrators in South Carolina from 1977 through 2002.* Paper presented at the annual meeting of the Southern Regional Council on Educational Administration, Columbia, South Carolina. (ERIC Document Reproduction Service No ED 320 194)

Portin, B. S. (2000). The changing urban principalship. *Education and Urban Society, 32* (4), 492–505.

Portin, B. S., & Shen, J. (1998). The changing principalship: Its current status, variability, and impact. *The Journal of Leadership Studies, 5* (3), 93–113.

Portin, B., Shen, J., & Williams, R. (1998). The changing principalship and its impact: Voices from principals. *NASSP Bulletin, 82* (602), 1–8.

Price, J. (1994). *The school administrator supply and demand report.* Wisconsin State Department of Instruction, Bureau for Teacher Education, Licensing, and Placement, Madison. (ERIC Document Reproduction Service No. ED 369 164).

Shen, J., Cooley, V. E., Ruhl-Smith, C. (1999). Entering and leaving school administrative positions. *International Journal of Leadership in Education,* 2 (4), 353–367.

Shen, J., Rodriguez-Campo, L., & Rincones-Gomez, R. (2000). Characteristics of urban school principals: A national trend study. *Education and Urban Society, 32* (4), 481–491.

Wendel, F. C. (1994). *Supply and demand of school administrators in Nebraska.* Lincoln, NE: National Council of School Administrators. (ERIC Document reproduction Service No. ED 367 064)

Whitaker, K. S. (1996). Exploring causes of principal burnout. *Journal of Educational Administration, 34* (1), 87–94.

Wooster, M. W. (199 1). First principals: The leadership vacuum in American schools. *Policy Review,* 57, 55–61.

Yewchuk, C. (1992). *Gender issues in education.* (Eric Document Reproduction Service No. ED 371553)

·13·

Connie D. Ruhl-Smith, Jianping Shen, and Van E. Cooley

GENDER DIFFERENCE IN REASONS FOR ENTERING AND LEAVING EDUCATIONAL ADMINISTRATION

As Burns (1978) pointed out two decades ago, leadership is a ubiquitous but little understood phenomenon. Leadership and gender is even a more complicated topic (Banks, 1995; Bass, 1990; Shakeshaft, 1989). This study contributes to the discussion on leadership and gender by inquiring into whether males and females decide to enter and possibly leave educational leadership positions for different reasons.

With the belief that effective leadership has swung from "military-style authoritarian management in favor of an approach that supports and empowers people thereby increasing both productivity and profits" (Aburdene & Naisbitt, 1992, p. 63), many believe that women are advantaged by this change. Such authors argue that women generally approach leadership in a much more developmental, supportive, and collaborative nature than men (Hall, 1993; Ozga, 1993; Rosener, 1990; Shakeshaft, 1989). To offer this argument is to support the notion that gender-related differences do, in fact, exist.

In interviews conducted by Rosener (1990), it was found that women leaders frequently mentioned their desire to involve others and to share both power and information. She also discussed that these same women encouraged open communication in the workplace. Pearson (1981) discovered a difference in speech patterns and styles of communication with women using a less autocratic, less coercive style of speech than men. Other researchers have also reported differences in leadership style between men and women. Gross and Trask (1976) indicated that female administrators were much more concerned about teachers' professional activities than male administrators. Charters and Jovick (1981) found female administrators to be more trusting and considerate than their male counterparts. In fact, Helgesen (1990) went so far as to state that an organization led by women is more inclusive, a place where "the value for connectedness is nurtured" (p. 224).

A difference in career paths in administration between men and women has also been documented (Al-Khalifa, 1992; Gray, 1989; Hall, 1993; Ozga, 1993; Shakeshaft, 1989). As pointed out by Ortiz (1982), women move into administration at a much later point in their career than men. Meskin (1978) reported women to be approximately ten years older than men when they assume their first administrative positions. It was also discovered that most women move into administrative positions at the elementary level and express a reluctance to advance any further (Gross & Trask, 1976). In addition, Gross and Trask discovered gender-related differences in reasons for moving into administration. Men usually move into the administrative position for the purpose of occupational and social mobility and to increase their income; women, on the other hand, move into an administrative position only after the support and encouragement of a mentor or as a result of a "fortuitous accident" (Ortiz, 1982).

The body of research that has been cited throughout this section is not without its critics. Bass (1981), after an investigation of research conducted on the leadership styles of females and males, believed that there is no clear pattern of difference between the two. Nieva and Gutek (1981) arrived at a similar conclusion. In an effort to further the examination of gender differences related to administration, this study inquired into whether males and females decide to enter and leave educational administration for different reasons.

Methods

Sample

Data for the current study were extracted from the Study of Education of Educators (SEE), a large, multi-method study of the education of teachers and administrators conducted by John Goodlad and his colleagues in 1989. SEE surveyed education faculty members, students in teacher education and school administration programs, among other data sources. Researchers first selected a representative sample of 29 colleges and universities based on factors which included institutional type (according to The Carnegie Foundation for the Advancement of Teaching, 1987), geographic location (according to Bureau of the Census), religious or nonreligious affiliation, and the public or private sector, and then sampled all those in school administration programs in the 29 institutions. For more detailed methodological information regarding SEE, please refer to Goodlad (1990) and Sirotnik (1989).

The questionnaire was distributed to 994 students enrolled in school administration programs in the 29 selected colleges and universities throughout the United States. Surveys were completed and returned by 457 participants, or 46% of the sample. Among the respondents, 79% of them were seeking the principal certificate and 47% were after certificates for superintendency and other central office positions. As we can infer from the aforementioned two percentages, some respondents were studying simultaneously for multiple certificates. However, most of them were studying for principalship. More than 90% of the respondents were teaching before entering the school administration program; among them 30% taught more than 15 years, 26% 10–15 years, 22% 5–10 years, and 13% 0–5 years.

A demographic breakdown of the sample by gender, race, age, and degree attainment revealed a diverse sample consisting of 37.6% male and 62.4% female, 75.3% white and 24.7% minority. Age distribution of the respondents was as follows: 24 or younger, 0.7%; 25–29, 4.9%; 30–34, 16.9%; 35–39, 31.2%; 40–49, 40.9%; and 50 or older, 5.4%. As to the highest academic degrees earned, 26.5% held bachelor's degrees, 67.3% possessed master's degrees, and 6.3% had doctorates including Ph.D., Ed.D., J.D., and M.D.

Instrument

The questionnaire was designed to collect data related to biographic and career information, participants' perceptions of schooling and education, and their views of the educational administration program. This study used data from two sets of items focusing on reasons why they chose to enter and possibly leave administration (See Table 13.1 for specific items). As to the reasons for entering administration, respondents were asked to indicate the importance of each factor in their seeking an administrative position using a 7-point Likert scale ranging from "1" (not at all important) to "7" (extremely important). Participants also responded to reasons that would motivate them to leave administration by using a 7-point Likert scale ranged from "1" (extremely unlikely) to "7" (extremely likely).

Data Analysis

Two discriminant function analyses were conducted to inquire into whether there are differences between males and females in their reasons for entering and leaving administration. If they differed, the question became along which

TABLE 13.1. Results of Discriminant Function Analysis

Item	Men		Women		Univariate	Item to function
	M	SD	M	SD	F	correlation
Reasons for entering administration						
I didn't know what else to do with my college education	1.54	1.09	1.52	1.20	0.03	−.02
I didn't know there was another career open to me	1.59	1.22	1.61	1.32	0.02	.02
To have a backup job while pursuing another career	1.60	1.20	1.60	1.30	0.06	.03
I was influenced by others (family, friend, etc.)	1.86	1.88	2.75	1.96	0.32	−.07
To have job security and a steady income	4.18	1.89	4.26	2.06	0.13	.04
To work in a noble, moral, and ethical profession	4.44	1.68	4.55	1.90	0.40	.07
To have a high paying job	4.70	1.70	4.90	1.60	0.97	.12
To pursue an interesting career with interesting colleagues	4.67	1.67	5.15	1.68	6.94**	.31
I like to work with adults	4.81	1.57	5.24	1.67	6.76**	.31
To manage the affairs of a school	5.20	1.40	5.20	1.50	0.01	.01
To make a contribution to society	5.20	1.40	5.70	1.30	12.46***	.42
To work with teachers in school improvement efforts	5.40	1.35	6.04	1.08	27.14***	.62
To help children and/or young adults	5.70	1.30	5.90	1.30	1.70	.15
To have a personally satisfying job	5.60	1.40	6.20	1.20	22.08***	.56
I like children and/or youth	5.95	1.20	6.00	1.27	0.16	.05
To have an impact on program quality	6.08	1.07	6.28	1.01	3.38	.22
To provide effective leadership	6.20	0.94	6.30	0.93	0.35	.07
Group centroids						
Men −.53						
Women .34						

TABLE 13.1. *(continued)*

Item	*Men* M	*Men* SD	*Women* M	*Women* SD	Univariate F	Item to function correlation
Potential reasons for leaving administration						
Inadequate, low salary	3.77	2.04	3.54	2.08	1.17	.22
Student-related problems	3.96	1.70	3.60	1.79	4.20*	.41
Parent/community-related problems	4.19	1.53	3.89	1.71	3.11	.35
Lack of respect	4.20	1.67	4.10	1.86	0.29	.11
No chance for advancement	4.07	1.93	4.27	1.96	1.00	−.20
Faculty-related problems	4.29	1.60	4.17	1.70	0.59	.15
Poor working conditions	4.77	1.77	4.78	1.90	0.01	−.01
Administration-related problems	5.04	1.61	4.69	1.73	4.09*	.40
Emotional aspects (boredom, stress, frustration, etc.)	4.88	1.75	4.77	1.91	0.35	.12
Opportunity to do something else more rewarding	5.23	1.70	5.72	1.66	8.10**	−.57
Group centroids						
Men .32						
Women −.19						

*$p < .05$. **$p < .01$. ***$p < .001$.

dimension they differ. Discriminant function analysis is a multivariate technique that identifies the combination or combinations of variables (i.e., functions) that best separate (i.e., discriminate between or among) groups. In this study, discriminant function analyses were conducted on items rather than on composite factors resulting from factor analysis because the correlation coefficients between items were generally small, and analysis on items rather than composite factors had a potential to have a more revealing discriminant function. Data analyses were performed using SPSS 6.1. Results of the discriminant function analyses were presented in Table 13.1, in which the following statistics were displayed: mean, standard deviation and univariate F test for each item, item to function correlation coefficient, and group centroid.

What We Found

Reasons for Entering Administration

There was one statistically significant discriminant function to distinguish males and females on reasons for entering administration [$\chi^2(17) = 64.36, p < .001, R_c = .39$], and 70% of the respondents were correctly classified by the discriminant function. An examination of group centroids and item-to-function correlation coefficients indicated that this discriminant function separated males from females on the following variables: "to work with teachers in school improvement efforts," "to have a personally satisfying job," "to make a contribution to society," "to pursue an interesting career with interesting colleagues," and "I like to work with adults." Females gave higher ratings to all these five variables than males did. Since these five variables focused on collegiality and intrinsic reward of the job, the discriminant function analysis indicated that females decided to enter administration more because of collegiality and the intrinsic reward of the job than their counterparts. Previous research indicates that females tend to teach a longer period of time than males before seeking administrative positions, an important factor which makes females emphasize more collegiality and the intrinsic reward of the job than males.

Potential Reasons for Leaving Administration

There was also one statistically significant discriminant function to distinguish males and females on reasons for leaving administration [$\chi^2(10) = 24.28, p < .001, R_c = .24$], and 67% of the respondents were correctly classified by the discriminant function. The discriminant function separated males from females on the following variables: "opportunity to do something else more rewarding," "administration-related problem," and "student-related problem." An examination of group centroids and item to function correlation coefficients indicated that in comparison to males, females were less likely to leave administration because of administration-related problems and student-related problems, but they were more likely to leave because of the opportunity to do something else more rewarding. The results seem to indicate that females are more resistant to student and administration-related difficulties because they contemplate entering administration for a long period of time and they enjoy the intrinsic rewards of the profession. However, females are more likely to leave because of the opportunity to do something more rewarding. It appears nowadays those females who decide to be administrators have a stronger desire to advance.

Discussion

The results of the study indicate that males and females can be statistically distinguished by their reasons for deciding to enter and possibly leave educational administration. Collegiality and the intrinsic reward of the job of building-level administration are rated much more highly by females than males as reasons for entering administration. As is stated in the literature, "Women enter teaching with clear educational goals, supported by a value system that stresses service, caring, and relationships" (Shakeshaft, 1989, p. 200). This often carries into the leadership roles of women. It is believed that females focus on using power to empower others and to motivate them to create change through collaborative efforts (Bennis, 1990). This interest in collegiality and teamwork leads female administrators to join professional organizations in larger numbers than males (Pharis & Zachariya, 1979). Men, on the other hand, begin their careers in education with less commitment to teaching (Shakeshaft, 1989), move into administrative positions sooner than women (Paddock, 1980), and move up the administrative hierarchy more quickly. Males, in fact, view advancement into an administrative role as a status symbol (Reynolds & Elliot, 1980) and tend to be more dedicated to the formal hierarchy and personal power needed to advance further up the career ladder.

When examining reasons for leaving administration, it is found that women are less likely to leave due to administration- or student-related problems. In reviewing female work behavior in schools, Shakeshaft (1989) noted that relationships with others, student performance and learning, and involvement with faculty, staff, and students are some of the most important factors surrounding the lives of female administrators. Meskin (1974) found that women usually advance into administrative roles after gaining a strong background in teaching and learning and becoming familiar with the "ins and outs" of the profession. Hughes and Robertson (1980), however, reported that females are more likely to have conflict with central office administration than males. The speculation on the part of these researchers was that women are more interested in their roles as instructional leaders at the building level and, in turn, are less concerned about the politics of central office. As was mentioned earlier in this paper, women are perceived to be more participatory than men, a factor that may well lead to less conflict with faculty, staff, and others at the campus site.

On the other hand, results indicating that women are more likely to leave administration to do something more rewarding appear to be inconsistent with the existing literature. According to the profile, most females move into administrative positions only after much encouragement. Women are more likely to remain in that position for an extended period of time, if not for the rest of their professional career (Gross & Trask, 1976; Meskin, 1974). Two possible arguments could be offered to rationalize these findings. One explanation might be that women moving into leadership roles today may be approaching the role differently from females of the past (Rosener, 1990). This may result in females not only moving into administrative positions earlier than previously but also in their choosing to lead differently from what was traditionally expected. Another explanation centers on the age of the respondents. As was discussed by Barnett and Baruch (1979), women typically begin to gain a feeling of self-worth at mid-life. The majority of respondents in this study ranged in age from 35 to 49. This demographic characteristic might account for the difference between the findings of the study and the existing literature.

Studies often lead to additional research questions for further investigation. Inquiry into males' and females' reasons for entering and leaving administration can be developed along varying dimensions. First, participants of the study were those in educational administration programs. Consequently, it would be beneficial to investigate how preservice administrators differ from practicing administrators. Second, data of this study were cross-sectional. In order to gain a more thorough picture of the dynamics related to school administrators' entering and leaving the profession, longitudinal data should be collected to determine if different entry and exit patterns exist based on such factors as age and career stage. There is still much need for additional investigation in this area.

References

Al-Khalifa, E. (1992). Management by halves: Women teachers and school management. In N. Bennett, M. Crawford, & C. Riches (Eds.), *Managing change in education: Individual and organizational perspectives*. London: Paul Chapman.

Aburdene, P., & Naisbitt, J. (1992). *Megatrends for women.* New York: Villard Books.

Banks, C. A. M. (1995). Gender and race as factors in educational leadership and administration. In J. Banks & C. A. M. Banks (Eds.), *Handbook of research on multicultural education* (pp. 65–80). New York: Macmillan.

Barnett, R. C., & Baruch, G. K. (1979). *Multiple roles and well being: A study of mothers of preschool age children* (Working Paper No. 3). Wellesley MA: Wellesley College Center for Research on Women.

Bass, B. M. (1981). *Stogdill's handbook of leadership: A survey of theory and research* (rev. ed.). New York: Free Press.

Bass, B. M. (1990). *Bass & Stogdill's handbook of leadership: Theory, research, and managerial applications* (3rd. ed.). New York: Free Press.

Bennis, W. G. (1990). *Why leaders can't lead: The unconscious conspiracy continues.* San Francisco: Jossey-Bass.

Burns, J. M. (1978). *Leadership.* New York: Harper & Row.

Carnegie Foundation for the Advancement of Teaching. (1987). *A classification of institutions of higher education.* Princeton, NJ: Author.

Charters, W. W. Jr., & Jovick, T. D. (1981). The gender of principals and principal/teacher relations in elementary schools. In P. A. Schmuck, W. W. Charters, Jr., & R. O. Carlson (Eds.), *Educational policy and management: Sex differentials* (pp. 307–331). New York: Academic Press.

Goodlad, J. I. (1990). Studying the education of educators: From conception to findings. *Phi Delta Kappan, 71*, 698–701.

Gray, H. (1989). Gender considerations in school management: Masculine and feminine leadership styles. In C. Riches & C. Morgan (Eds.), *Human resources management in education.* Milton Keynes: Open University Press.

Gross, N., & Trask, A. E. (1976). *The sex factor and the management of schools.* New York: John Wiley.

Hall, V. (1993). Women in educational management: A review of research in Britain. In J. Ouston (Ed.), *Women in educational management.* Harlow: Longman.

Helgesen, S. (1990). *The female advantage: Women's ways of leadership.* New York: Doubleday.

Hughes, L. W., & Robertson, T. A. (1980). Principals and the management of conflict. *Planning and Changing, 11*(1), 3–16.

Meskin, J. (1974). The performance of women school administrators: A review of the literature. *Administrator's Notebook, 23* (1), 1–4.

Meskin, J. (1978). Women as principals: Their performance as educational administrators. In D. A. Erickson & T. L. Reller (Eds.), *The principal in metropolitan schools* (pp. 323–347). Berkeley, CA: McCutchan.

Nieva, V. F., & Gutek, B. A. (1981). *Women and work: A psychological perspective.* New York: Praeger.

Ortiz, F. I. (1982). *Career patterns in education: Men, women, and minorities in public school administration.* New York: Praeger.

Ozga, J. (1993). *Women in educational management.* Milton Keynes: Open University Press.

Paddock, S. C. (1980). Women principals: The rule or the exception? *NASSP Bulletin, 64* (4), 1–4.
Pearson, S. S. (1981). Rhetoric and organizational change: New applications of feminine style. In B. L. Forisha & B. H. Goldman (Eds.), *Outsiders on the inside* (pp. 54–74). Englewood Cliffs, NJ: Prentice Hall.
Pharis, W. L., & Zachariya, S. B. (1979). *The elementary principal in 1978: A research study.* Washington, DC: National Association of Elementary School Principals.
Reynolds, B., & Elliot, B. (1980). *Differences between men and women in their aspirations for careers in educational administration.* Unpublished manuscript.
Rosener, J. B. (1990). Ways women lead. *Harvard Business Review, 68* (6), 119–125.
Shakeshaft, C. (1989). *Women in educational administration.* Newbury Park, CA: Sage.
Sirotnik, K. A. (1989). *Studying the education of educators, technical report No. 2.* Seattle: Center for Educational Renewal, College of Education, University of Washington.

·14·

Bradley S. Portin and Jianping Shen

THE CHANGING PRINCIPALSHIP

Introduction

In 1993 Hopkins and Ainscow wrote, "We now live in a change rich environment, where multiple policy initiatives and innovation overload are the norm" (p. 303). Even to the casual observer, the demands for educational reform and school improvement are apparent and loud. For those within schools, the clamor of this "change-rich environment" is having an effect. In the first case, principals in schools report that their role is changing (DuFour & Berkey, 1995; Ford & Bennett, 1994; Williams & Portin, 1996). Simultaneously, observing the policy domain reveals a progression of legislation, regulation, and general political attention to educational improvement (Spring, 1998). Finally, the social context of schools, particularly urban schools, often reveals an environment that is increasingly complex, diverse and needy.

In recent years, a number of changes have been initiated in Washington State public schools. These changes have included increased centralization of curriculum direction, funding realignment, and new forms of school management which include a greater degree of staff and community participation. The common paradox of centralizing academic standards and testing while devolving responsibility in the name of "empowerment" (Anderson & Dixon, 1993) characterizes some of the legislated actions in Washington state.

At the same time that legislated changes have occurred, sociological changes have continued to press upon many schools. These sociological changes are characterized by practitioners as an increased range of student needs within a diverse student population. A greater number of students seem to be needing special educational assistance, behavioral intervention, and social and family support. Murphy (1992) notes, "Immense new social and economic challenges have been added to the leadership agenda. The fabric of American society is being rewoven in some places and unraveling in others, resulting in changes that promise to have a significant impact on schooling" (p. 122).

This chapter examines the changing role of the school principal in this dynamic context. In the sections that follow, research aimed at assessing the perceptions of those who are school principals is explained and survey data are analyzed in order to illuminate the features of role change and whether the effects are being uniformly felt throughout the principal ranks. While referring to the role of the principal, we recognize that school leadership, especially in secondary schools, includes the leadership and responsibility extended to assistant principals as well.

The article concludes with a discussion of the policy implications arising from these changes. As the impacts are not the same, differential policy intervention may be needed in order to best enable school principals to meet the needs in their school communities.

Washington State Education Reform

Education reform in Washington State includes many pieces of legislation over a period of years. Beginning in the late 1980s, the state government began to address perceived weaknesses in the state's education system, particularly in preparing students for the work force.

The process of education reform has been described as follows:

> Washington has embarked on a process of improving its schools which began with the Schools for the 21st Century (1988), found voice in the Governor's Council on Education Reform and Funding (1991), and culminated in a series of education reform legislation (1992–1996). Why was it necessary to change our schools? Washington's leaders responded to concerns from parents, business, and community leaders. The world was changing, and they were concerned that our children were not being prepared for those changes. They wanted schools that would help all students meet high international standards. They also wanted reduced regulation, more local control, increased accountability, and closer connections between schools and their communities. This led to many initiatives. (Office of the Superintendent of Public Instruction, 1997a)

The centerpiece of educational change in Washington state was the passage of ESHB 1209 (Engrossed Substitute House Bill 1209, 53rd Legislature, 1993), the state education reform legislation. The changes initiated by ESHB

1209 are not unlike those that have occurred in a number of states and could be viewed as representative of the types of reforms that are being implemented elsewhere around the country and in other nations (Swanson, 1989; Tyack, 1990). The central instructional components of this legislation, and subsequent legislation included: the establishment of a statewide "performance-based" education system with student learning goals and corresponding specific "essential learning requirements"; performance standards and a student assessment system; and a required "certificate of mastery" of the essential learning requirements in order to earn a high school diploma (Office of the Superintendent of Public Instruction, 1997b).

A number of new commissions and departments of the Office of the Superintendent of Public Instruction have been established for the purpose of overseeing efforts to improve education in Washington State. These state offices, in cooperation with the state organizations for teachers, administrators, school boards, and parents have worked collaboratively in order to support the early stages of the statewide plan for improving student learning. Implementation plans for education reform are reported to be on a positive path (Plecki et al., 1997) although the education policy environment remains volatile and subject to the continuous debate between the political parties.

In addition to educational reform legislation, largely aimed at teaching and learning, one other legislative enactment has significantly impacted the principals and assistant principals in Washington State. Commonly called the "Becca Bill" (Engrossed Second Substitute Senate Bill 5439), truancy legislation was passed by the 1995 legislature. The provisions of the bill were designed to tighten attendance and truancy recording and reporting in the wake of a highly publicized case of a runaway who was murdered while truant. The provisions of the new law establish a complex system of attendance reporting by the school to parents and truancy intervention by the courts. The legislation has had a significant impact particularly on urban secondary administrators (Williams & Portin, 1997), although effects are experienced across all schools. This specific legislation was included in the study because of information provided in focus groups at the planning and pilot stage of the study. Few legislative acts have had more significant impact on school administrator time.

The Important Role of Principal Leadership

The school effectiveness research of the last twenty years repeatedly affirms the role of principal leadership in school success (Austin & Reynolds, 1990; ERIC, 1981; Leithwood & Montgomery, 1986; Lipham, 1981; Sergiovanni, 1991; Taylor & Valentine, 1985). Principals remain key individuals as instructional leaders, initiators of change (Fullan, 1991), school managers, personnel administrators, problem solvers, and boundary spanners for the school (Goldring, 1990; Vandenberghe, 1995).

The principal is in the center of multiple demands to reform schools and to meet the challenges of future leadership. As Leithwood, Begley, and Cousins (1994) state,

> If education, in general, and schools, in particular, are seen as tools for social change, educational leaders are assumed to be among the most critical artisans. This assumption is widely held by the public-at-large, as well as by education professionals (e.g., Schlechty, 1990). It is also an assumption warranted by relevant evidence (e.g., Immegart, 1988). Indeed, the "leadership effect" becomes increasingly prominent the more one focuses attention on schools as opposed to other types of organizations. (pp. 5–6)

New models of shared leadership and teacher empowerment have cast leadership responsibilities more widely, but the principal remains the singular individual at the nexus of leadership in the school. It is the very fact of increasing complexity of schools and school administration that reaffirms the essential role of the school principal—a mandatory responsibility for tomorrow's leaders (Murphy, 1992). The unique role of the principal includes both instructional, organizational, and statutory leadership.

As an instructional leader, the principal is expected to retain knowledge of effective instructional practice, both curricular and pedagogical. The role of the principal as evaluator of instruction underlines the organizational leadership expected. In addition, the traditional labor/management dichotomy of unionism also keeps leadership largely vested on the side of the principal, particularly in the area of teacher evaluation for instructional improvement (Schlecty, 1990, p. 10).

Finally, the importance of the principal's role is vested in statute, code, and policy. As a result, principals are given responsibility for most school operations. For new models of leadership to occur, significant statutory and policy change would have to occur. Until that time, at least by law, principal leadership occupies the role of the "middle manager" in a large school district organizational structure.

Traditionally, public schools in America are slow to change. As a "system" (Cohen, 1995) it is almost impervious to change. The growing literature on teacher empowerment (Hart & Reyes, 1990; Lieberman, 1992; Wasley, Hampel, & Clark, 1997) and shared decision making (Leithwood, Begley, & Cousins, 1994; Sackney & Dibski, 1994) indicate the way ahead. The slow-to-change nature of public schooling means that old roles are slow to shift.

However, as with other social institutions, the schools continue to reflect national norms and desires. As the participatory process of governance infuses other public entities, it is likely that decision making in schools will change as well.

The Current State of Understanding Principal Role Change

Much attention has been given to the impact of school policy and societal changes on teachers, parents, and students. It is assumed by policy makers, parents, teachers, and the public-at-large that principals have the capacity to lead and supervise the implementation of new programs and regulations while continuing to provide previously assigned responsibilities (e.g., provide instructional leadership, manage resources, assure a safe school environment, and respond to parent and community requests).

A number of studies on the role of the principal, and the barriers to principals serving as instructional leaders, suggest the public's expectations might not be realized (e.g., Kowalski, 1979; Morris, Crowson, Porter-Gehrie, & Hurwitz, 1984; Peterson, 1984; Evans, 1994). As noted in the literature, numerous factors have been identified that contribute to the ways in which principals spend their time. Analyses of the principals' role reveal constant interruptions, lack of planning time, fragmentation of activities, compliance with numerous rules and regulations. Clearly, the role of the principal is changing as more is expected of them (Richardson, Short, Prickett, & Flanigan, 1991).

The data for this study were gathered with the participation and support of the Association of Washington School Principals (AWSP). This professional association, in response to their members' increasing concerns over mounting pressure and increased responsibilities on principals, formed an advisory committee. The committee was interested to know the scope and reasons for escalating principal discontent. University researchers agreed to work with the committee to design a study to gather these data and provide a report on the changing role of the principal. This chapter further explores the data from this original study. This chapter utilizes this data from principals and assistant principals in Washington state in order to provide a deeper understanding of the impact of changing roles on the principals who work in public schools.

Research Questions

This study has three related research questions. First, to what extent do principals perceive that the principalship has changed in the last five years? Second, does the changing principalship vary by school level and the geographic location of the school? Third, what is the impact of the changing principalship on principals' working hours, level of frustration, and enthusiasm toward their job? An inquiry into these questions has implications for understanding the current principalship for the purposes of preparing, recruiting, and retaining principals.

Methods

Sample

A total of 2,431 questionnaires were mailed to the AWSP members and 840 useful questionnaires were returned resulting in a 34.6% response rate. Among those who returned the questionnaire, 687 had been principals or assistant principals for at least five years and they became the subjects of the study. An analysis of those who returned questionnaires indicated that the suburban respondents were slightly over-represented, and the rural respondents were slightly under-represented. There was not a significant difference between expected and observed frequencies of respondents by level. Generally, the respondents represented the AWSP membership in terms of school level and geographic location of the school.

Instrument

During the preparatory stage of the study, a series of focus-group discussions were conducted with school principals from around the state attending the principals' association summer conference. The focus-group discussions identified several issues and topics, which provided a list of topics to be covered in the questionnaire of the current study. An initial questionnaire was then developed, field tested, reviewed by the AWSP sponsoring committee and subsequently revised—a process which resulted in a 55-item questionnaire. The questionnaire asked for the respondents' perceptions about ways the principalship had changed in the last five years. Accordingly, only data from those with at least five-year experience in principalship were included in the study.

The 55 items on the questionnaire were grouped by general topics identified in focus-group discussions. The main question areas were:

- Has your school district delegated to your school more decision making responsibility than was the case five years ago?
- Does compliance with the "Becca Bill" truancy legislation require a moderate to significant amount of attention in your school? (The Becca Bill aims to reduce truancy. It requires schools to determine each day which student absences are excused, to take prescribed steps to report students who are

unexcused, and if student attendance does not improve, to accompany students to a judicial hearing.)
- Would you say that the breadth of student diversity in your school (e.g., ethnic, economic, social, language groups) has changed in the last five years in a way that has had an important impact on your school?
- Some districts are utilizing school site councils as part of an overall decentralization plan. Has your district directed or encouraged the establishment of site-based councils?
- Have interactions with parents regarding individual pupils or general school concerns increased in a manner you would consider moderate or significant in the last five years?
- Do you find that administrative requirements for special education have required a disproportionate amount of administrative time and attention?
- Do you find that you spend more time and energy considering and planning for issues of public relations and school presentation to an external community?

All above items were answered as "yes" (coded as "1") or "no" (coded as "0") except for the penultimate item—the one on special education—which was answered on a 5-point scale, ranging from "strongly disagree" (coded as "1") to "strongly agree" (coded as "5"). The current study also utilized four items related to the impact of above changes on the principalship:

- Changes in the principal/assistant principal role have meant that I am working more hours than I was five years ago.
- The changes in the principal/assistant principal role in the last five years have increased my level of frustration.
- The changing principalship has provided me with more opportunities for leadership.
- I feel more enthusiastic about my job than I did five years ago.

All these four items were answered by using a 5-point scale, ranging from "strongly disagree" (coded as "1") to "strongly agree" (coded as "5").

Data Analysis

Consistent with the three research questions, the current study took the following three major steps for data analysis. First, in order to reveal to what extent the principalship changed in the last five years, percentages of those who felt or did not feel the aforementioned changes were examined. Second, chi-square tests were conducted to inquire into whether there is any association between school level and geographic location and the changing principalship. Finally, multiple regression analyses were conducted to investigate the impact of the changing principalship on principals' work and their feelings about their job.

What We Found

The Changing Principalship

As illustrated in Table 14.1, the survey data supported the pattern of the changing principalship identified in the focus-group discussions before the state-wide survey. Of the subjects, more than three quarters reported that in the last five years they have had more responsibility for site-based decisions, monitoring truancy, dealing with the impact of student diversity, interacting with parents, improving school-community relationships, and administering special education programs.

It is interesting to note that several seemingly incompatible trends are embedded in the changing principalship. First, principals are encouraged to make site-based decisions and the mechanisms for site-based decision making—such as the school site council—have been established in many cases. All these seem to raise the professional status of principals as decision makers rather than mere decision implementers. Second, principals are also asked to make more efforts to monitor truancy and administer special education programs, both of which are mandated by legislation. Third, in addition to more site-based decision making and more legislation, the immediate work environment for principals has also changed. They are now faced with the challenges

TABLE 14.1. Percentage of Principals Who Agreed or Disagreed with the Statement

	Response	
Item	Yes	No
More decentralization	90.9	9.1
More efforts on monitoring truancy	79.0	21.0
Impact of increasing student diversity	76.3	23.7
Establishing site-based council	77.6	22.4
More interaction with parents	82.5	17.5
More efforts on school-community relation	83.5	16.5
More efforts on special education program	77.3	12.5

Note: "More efforts on special education program" is rated on a five-point scale; 77.3% of the subjects strongly agreed or agreed with the statement, 12.5% strongly disagreed or disagreed with the statement, and 10.2% were undecided.

associated with the further diversity of the student population; they have to interact more with parents; and they also have to make more efforts to present and market their schools to the community at-large.

All these seem to suggest that principals are expected to provide more leadership, on one hand, and to take on more managerial responsibilities, on the other. There appears to be a growing tension between the leadership and managerial imperatives of the job. The combination of more decentralization and more interaction with the school's immediate environment also points to the increasing ambiguity and complexity of the principalship. The principalship has simply become more challenging.

Variability in the Changing Principalship

The data presented in the foregoing support the observation that the principalship has changed to a great extent in the last five years. The next logical step in data analysis was to inquire into whether the changing principalship occurs invariably between elementary and secondary principals, and among urban, suburban, and rural principals. Findings on the variability of the changing principalship have implications for the preparation, recruitment, and retention of principals.

Table 14.2 presents statistics on whether there are any differences in the changing principalship between elementary and secondary schools. The statistics include actual frequency, expected frequency denoted by parenthesis, and chi-square statistics.

The statistics in Table 14.2 suggest that there is no difference between elementary and secondary schools in decentralization ($\chi^2 = 0.94, p > .05$), the impact of increasing student diversity ($\chi^2 = 1.7, p > .05$), interaction with parents ($\chi^2 = 0.24, p > .05$), efforts on school-community relationships ($\chi^2 = 1.37, p > .05$), and efforts on special education programs ($\chi^2 = 3.7, p > .05$). However,

TABLE 14.2. Percentage of Principals Who Gave Affirmative Answers: A Comparison Between Elementary and Secondary Principals via Chi-square Tests

Item	Elementary	Secondary	χ^2	p
More Decentralization	91.9%	89.8%	0.94	> .05
More Efforts on Monitoring Truancy	65.4%	92.4%	73.8	< .001
Impact of Increasing Student Diversity	78.1%	74.7%	1.7	> .05
Establishing Site-based Council	81.3%	87.1%	4.9	< .05
More Interaction with Parents	81.8%	83.2%	0.24	> .05
More Efforts on School-Community Relation	81.7%	85.1%	1.37	> .05
More Efforts on Special Education Program	74.8%	79.8%	3.7	> .05

they do differ on efforts to monitor truancy and site-based decision making. A higher percentage of secondary principals reported that they made more efforts on monitoring truancy than did their elementary counterparts ($\chi^2 = 73.8$, $p < .001$). Since truancy is anecdotally reported as a greater problem in secondary schools than in elementary schools, this finding is not unexpected. A higher percentage of elementary principals reported that they established site-based councils than did secondary principals ($\chi^2 = 4.9$, $p < .05$). This might be due to the complexity of secondary school operation or to the greater parental involvement in elementary programs than is the case in secondary schools.

Table 14.3 displays the statistics on the relationship between the changing principalship and school's geographic location. There are no differences among urban, suburban, and rural schools in the impact of increasing student diversity ($\chi^2 = 1.7$, $p > .05$), interaction with parents ($\chi^2 = 1.3$, $p > .05$), and efforts expended on special education program ($\chi^2 = 6.1$, $p > .05$). However, a higher percentage of urban and particularly suburban principals, reported more decentralization ($\chi^2 = 8.2$, $p < .05$), establishing site-based councils ($\chi^2 = 75.8$, $p < .001$), and more effort on school-community relations ($\chi^2 = 13.0$, $p < .005$) than was reported by rural principals. This suggests that urban principals, and particularly suburban principals, are affected more by the changing principalship than are their rural counterparts. Given the demographic complexity in urban areas and the demands from middle-class-dominated suburbs, the findings are congruent with our everyday observations. As to monitoring truancy, a higher percentage of urban and rural principals reported more efforts than did suburban principals ($\chi^2 = 11.7$, $p < .005$).

The Impact of the Changing Principalship

The final step of data analysis for the current study inquired into the impact of the changing principalship by conducting multiple regression analyses, i.e., by

TABLE 14.3. Percentage of Principals Who Gave Affirmative Answers: A Comparison Among Urban, Suburban, and Rural Principals via Chi-square Tests

Item	Urban	Suburban	Rural	χ^2	p
More Decentralization	95.4%	92.8%	87.1%	8.2	< .05
More Efforts on Monitoring Truancy	89.5%	74.0%	81.7%	11.7	< .005
Impact of Increasing Student Diversity	77.7%	78.3%	74.2%	1.7	> .05
Establishing Site-based Council	93.0%	87.8%	60.5%	75.8	< .001
More Interaction with Parents	86.2%	82.8%	81.0%	1.3	> .05
More Efforts on School-Community Relation	84.1%	88.4%	77.3%	13.0	< .005
More Efforts on Special Education Program	76.14%	79.26%	75.09%	6.1	> .05

regressing criterion measures—working more hours, becoming more frustrated, becoming more enthusiastic about the job, and providing opportunities for more leadership, respectively—on variables representing different aspects of the changing principalship. On the base of face validity, attempts were made to collapse working more hours and becoming more frustrated into one factor, and becoming more enthusiastic about the job and providing opportunities for more leadership into the other. However, Cronbach's alphas were .47 for the former and .36 for the latter. Therefore, no composite scores were formed, and four standard multiple regressions were conducted. The results are displayed in Table 14.4.

Working more hours. The variables related to the changing principalship account for 13% of the variance in the variable of working more hours. The size and direction of the regression coefficients indicate (a) that the following variables in the changing principalship—more efforts on special education program, more efforts on school-community relations, more interaction with parents, and more decentralization—are statistically significant predictors of principals' working more hours; and (b) that the more subjects perceived the

TABLE 14.4. Results of Multiple Regression Analyses: Standardized Regression Coefficients (Beta) and Multiple R

	Criterion Measure			
Aspects of the Changing Principalship	Working more hours	More frustration	More leadership	More enthusiastic
More Decentralization	.01*	.01	−.02	.01
More Efforts on Monitoring Truancy	.05	.01	−.06	.06
Impact of Increasing Student Diversity	.03	.02	.02	−.03
Establishing Site-based Council	.06	−.02	−.02	−.05
More Interaction with Parents	.11**	.15**	−.01	−.03
More Efforts on Special Education Program	.22**	.24**	−.21**	−.17**
More Efforts on School-Community Relation	.13**	.07*	−.05	−.02
F	13.40	11.30	5.55	3.81
P	<.001	<.001	<.001	<.001
Multiple R	.35	.33	.24	.20
R Square	.13	.11	.06	.04

Note: ** $P < .01$; * $P < .05$.

changing principalship in the aforementioned aspects, the more time they felt they spent on the principalship than five years prior. It appears that more efforts on special education programs, more efforts on school-community relations, more interaction with parents, and more decentralization lead to principals working more hours.

More frustration. The second multiple regression analysis inquires into whether the changing principalship is associated with the frustration that principals experience. The analysis indicates that variables in the changing principalship explain 11% of the variance in more frustration in the last five years, and that more efforts on special education programs, more interaction with parents, and more efforts on school-community relationships are significantly and positively associated with principals' reports of increasing frustration.

More leadership. The third multiple regression analysis examines whether the changing principalship provides opportunities for more leadership. The analysis suggests that the changing characteristics of the principalship accounts for 6% of the variance in the variable of providing more leadership. A further examination of the size and direction of regression coefficients reveals that more efforts on special education programs appear to lead to the exercise of less leadership. All these suggest that the changing principalship in the last five years is marginally related to the opportunity to provide more leadership, and the marginal relationship seems to indicate that the changing principalship increases managerial activity rather than leadership.

More enthusiastic about the job. The final multiple regression investigates whether the changing principalship is related to principals being more enthusiastic about their job. The results indicate that the changing principalship explains 4% of the variance in being more enthusiastic about the principalship, and the only significant predictor—more efforts on special education programs—is negatively correlated with more expressed enthusiasm toward the job. Therefore, the changing principal is marginally related to being more enthusiastic about the job, and the direction of regression coefficients indicates that the changing principalship leads to being less enthusiastic about the job.

The multiple regression analyses suggest that the changing principalship contributes, to a certain extent, to working more hours and becoming more frustrated in the last five years. Among the various aspects of the changing principalship, more efforts on special education programs, more efforts on interaction with parents, and more efforts on school-community relations are predictors of working more hours and becoming more frustrated. Besides, more decentralization is also positively associated with working more hours. Among the variables positively correlated with working more hours and becoming more frustrated, more efforts on special education programs is the most important one. Therefore, it appears that more support should be given to principals for implementing special education programs, and principals should also receive support in interaction with parents and strengthening school-community relationships.

The associations between the changing principalship and providing more leadership or becoming more enthusiastic about the job are weaker than those between the changing principalship and working more hours or being more frustrated. The multiple regression analyses seem to indicate that the changing principalship does not make them more enthusiastic about their jobs and does not provide more opportunity for leadership. On the contrary, many aspects of the changing principalship—particularly more efforts on special education—lead to less enthusiasm and less leadership. In sum, the changing principalship seems to contribute to principals working more, becoming more frustrated, eliciting less enthusiastic about their job, and providing less opportunity for crucial leadership in the school. Therefore, this study suggests the changing principalship has a negative impact on principals' work and their feelings about their job.

Discussion

The data of the study indicate that the principalship has changed in the last five years, and some aspects of the changing principalship vary for elementary and secondary schools, and for urban, suburban, and rural schools. Ninety-one percent of the principals indicated they are in districts that are decentralizing decision making to the local school site, 76 percent were in districts that were initiating or encouraging the use of site councils, 79 percent indicated the need to establish school/business partnerships. A higher percentage of secondary principals reported more efforts on monitoring truancy and a higher percentage of elementary principals indicated more efforts on establishing site-based council. A higher percentage of urban and particularly suburban principals indicated more decentralization, establishing site-based councils, and more efforts on school-community relations than did rural principals. These additional responsibilities are being assumed in a shifting context. Seventy-six percent reported working in sites with increased student diversity that has had an important impact on the school, 83 percent increased interactions with parents that have had a significant impact on their work, 91 percent reported it was important to consider "client satisfaction" when making decisions.

As to the impact of the changing principalship, the study found that the changing principalship, particularly more efforts on special education programs in the last five years, appears to have had negative impacts on principals' work and their feeling about the job. Some issues arise from the aforementioned findings.

Each principal has her or his own specific view of the impact of the changes. Still, it is generally clear that the role of the principal in Washington State has changed in important ways.

There are a number of ways to draw conclusions from the findings of this study, and a number of audiences who should be interested in these findings. The conclusions which we draw are largely aimed at those whose actions impact the continuing effectiveness of school principals, namely policy makers at a district and state level, and those engaged in principal preparation and inservice for practitioners.

As we interpret the data, several themes or trends emerge. These themes have also been discussed in Williams and Portin (1996, 1997).

Layering

Each of the changes noted in this article require the principal to take on additional responsibilities; these responsibilities can be perceived as being "layered" one on top of the other. This layering is often reported by principals as taking a "disproportionate amount of time and attention." One interpretation of the disproportionality is that as new responsibilities are added, time must be taken from another previously allocated responsibility in order to meet the changing demands. At the same time, principals have not been relieved of other duties and responsibilities that have traditionally been a part of their job, e.g., building maintenance and repair, instructional leadership, maintaining a safe and secure environment, responding to teacher and staff requests, conducting legally required teacher evaluations, managing the budget, and maintaining discipline.

The layering of responsibility does not always come with corresponding authority. Whereas a school may have the added responsibility of a site council for local decisions, that decision making is often constrained by state legislation, district policy, and negotiated agreements with bargaining units. The responses suggest that this is one of the pressures which principals and assistant principals feel with layered responsibility.

Shift from Leadership to Management

It is useful to think of the principal's role as being a balance between leadership and management. Leadership covers the important role of supervising the curriculum, improving the instructional program, working with the staff and parents to identify a vision and direction for the school, and building a close and congruent working relationship between the school and its community. Management, which is also important, includes managing the budget, maintaining the building, completing and submitting required reports, complying with legislative mandates and state and district regulations. Because the management tasks are often more explicit, and because not complying with them becomes very visible to district administrators and can have legal consequences, it is understandable that principals give high priority to attending to managerial responsibilities, often at the expense of leadership responsibilities. There simply is not enough time to do both.

Ambiguity and Complexity

These changes and additional responsibilities often are accompanied by considerable ambiguity. Many principals view districts as decentralizing decision making to the local school without clear guidelines about which responsibilities rest with the principal and which remain with the district. This same lack of clarity exists with regard to district instructions to utilize site councils. Some principals report they lack the necessary skills required for success in some aspects of the changing role, e.g., marketing the school and dealing with an increasingly diverse school population. The complexity comes from trying to balance these diverse new responsibilities in a context of increasingly critical constituencies.

In addition, there appears to be a growing paradox that contributes to the ambiguity and complexity of principal roles. Grace (1995) describes a similar phenomenon of decentralization of responsibility, coexisting with centralization of authority for the key purposes of schooling. Grace describes this paradox in England as experienced by headteachers as, "a much more complex and contradictory matrix of changes which had involved the simultaneous impact of increased central control and bureaucracy, on the one hand, with moves towards a deregulated education market on the other" (p. 207).

This links with the previously noted themes of layering and the shift from leadership activities to the managerial responsibilities which often associate with devolved responsibility.

Declining Morale and Enthusiasm

Many of the principals reported feeling greater frustration, less secure, and less enthusiastic about their work. It is important to note that these attitudes do not reflect an attitude that these changes are unnecessary, or that they wish to return to some "golden age." For the most part they welcome these changes, as evidenced by their optimism toward the Washington State school reform effort, their general support of greater parent involvement in the schools, and their recognition of the benefits of decentralized decision making. A noted exception to their support of these changes is their skepticism about the eventual effectiveness of the truancy legislation.

Their decline in morale and enthusiasm stems, instead, from their inability to carry out both their management and leadership functions effectively and efficiently, and their preference to provide leadership. One response to the additional "layering" of duties has been for them to work longer hours. Many principals report work weeks of 50 to 70 hours. This, of course, takes its toll on both their professional and personal lives. Many are reaching the limit of the number of hours they can, or are willing to devote to the job and they are being forced to make choices about where they will spend their time and attention.

Another source of frustration is the shift to managerial rather than leadership responsibilities. While they recognize that managing the building is a necessary function for principals, they receive great satisfaction out of their role as instructional leaders, spending time with teachers, students, and parents improving the school's program for student learning. Yet many find it increasingly difficult to fulfill that role because of the more immediate managerial responsibilities that press down on them.

Still another source of frustration, which surfaced in discussions with principals when planning this study, is the seeming lack of appreciation principals feel for the contributions they are making in the schools. They sense a popular attitude that administrators are a major impediment to school improvement and that school reform would flourish if we just got rid of principals. What principals find missing in the public debate about school improvements is appreciation that the many changes that are taking place in our schools carry with them mandated administrative responsibilities and duties. Principals report working longer hours and dealing with considerable frustration and complexity. They would like to be thought of as important partners with teachers, central administrators, and policy makers in efforts to improve the schools in Washington State.

Implications

We set out in this article to answer three important questions for the principalship: First, to which extent do principals perceive that the principalship has changed in the last five years? Second, does the changing principalship vary by school level and the geographic location of the school? Third, what is the impact of the changing principalship on principals' working hours, frustration level, and enthusiasm about their job?

The findings suggest that the principals in Washington State do perceive a significant change in their role, that changes vary along certain criteria for principals at different levels and in different demographic areas, and, finally, that the impact of a number of these changes is serving as a detriment to their sense of efficacy in educational leadership. From the findings, we suggest three implications for practitioners, policy makers, and principal preparation and support.

Targeted Assistance

The impact of policy decisions, either at a state or school district level, lack uniformity in a number of cases. For instance, the implementation of truancy reduction legislation has had remarkably different effects whether a school is elementary or secondary, or found in an urban or suburban area. The implications for principal and assistant principal time are enormous. However, the legislation fails to account for the full differential outcome in the school setting. This is one example where state level policy makers could provide further targeted assistance, in this case in the form of administrative support for the increased time of complying with the legislation.

At a school district level, the responsibilities and extra time commitment of establishing a system of site-based decision making, often through a site council process, is reported as being more complex and time consuming for elementary, urban, and suburban schools. The data do not provide specific insight into why this is so, but the implication for school district directors is that the rush toward site-based decision making, in many cases, in not equally affecting schools and is presenting more challenges to layered responsibility for some principals than others.

Special Educational Needs

No other factor was reported as having more consistent effect on principals' time, enthusiasm, their ability to lead their schools, and their frustration level than was special education. There are several parts to this factor that were reported in the data. Seventy percent of the respondents believe that special education programs are more difficult to implement than most programs; 77% believe the administrative requirements for special education have required a disproportionate amount of time and attention. One contributor to this level of frustration has been decreased funding levels for special education. In fact, 77% reported that changes in special education funding levels have required the reallocation of regular education funds.

What seems to be contributing to the weight of responsibility is a reported perception (90%) that more students are requiring special services than was the case five years prior. In addition, programs such as inclusions models received mixed reviews from the respondents.

Principals expressed a desire to lead to best meet the needs of students. However, their responses indicated a growing sense of being "overwhelmed" by the need, the managerial responsibility of reporting, compliance, and program management, decreased resources, and the rising tide of students being presented for special education services.

Bridging the Constituencies

Principals are in a unique role to act as a bridge between the school and external constituencies, or as Goldring (1990) identifies them, as "boundary spanners." Principals serve as the individuals who market the school, who interpret the school's program to the parents and community. Increasingly, principals are being called upon to form partnerships with the business community, and to enter the discussion and debate regarding future policy directions for the state's schools.

The principals who serve, and will serve in future schools, will need to be prepared for this important role. The time of schools operating in professional isolation and autonomy is fading, if not extinguished. Schools exist in a social milieu and the leaders who serve will need particular skills in forming new alliances and working with multiple constituencies to meet needs in complex society. The challenge is not easy, and the environment of critique of public education means that principals who serve need not only support and understanding, but those preparing for leadership need particular training in the skills necessary to, as Murphy (1992) writes, "learn to lead not from the apex of the organizational pyramid but from the nexus of a web of interpersonal relationships" (p. 124).

Who Will Provide Leadership to Our Schools?

Clearly the principals are saying that they are approaching the limits of the amount of time they can dedicate to the job. Those who are proposing additional changes that will impact the school and the principal's role should realize that for many principals their capacity to take on additional duties is severely limited. In addition to the time restraints, the principals, because of external priorities, are increasingly becoming managers rather than instructional leaders. If this trend continues, we all will have to address the question, who will provide leadership to our schools?

For everyone, policy makers, district administrators, parents, school staffs, and the public, the principals are seeking some appreciation for the very difficult and demanding leadership responsibilities they are carrying. They work very long hours, often experiencing considerable conflict from various groups that insist that their demands be met. They find the specific responsibilities of their job are becoming increasingly ambiguous as they assume tasks never before required of them. Nonetheless, a large percentage, at least at this time, seem quite prepared to continue providing leadership for our schools. In fact, 72% reported that given the choice they would choose the principalship again.

Role change for principals in Washington State, and elsewhere, is occurring. Importantly, as the data from this study show, the changes are not occurring in a uniform manner and the implications for principal effectiveness is that their leadership is being compromised. If school-based reform is to continue as an overall strategy of educational improvement, addressing these reforms, continuing to aim research at the changing role, and developing programs and policy to support leadership in schools will remain a vital concern.

References

Anderson, G., & Dixon, A. (1993). Paradigm shifts and site-based management in the United States: Toward a paradigm of social empowerment. In J. Smyth (Ed.), *A socially critical view of the self-managing school* (pp. 49–61). London: Falmer.

Austin, G., & Reynolds, D. (1990). Managing for improved school effectiveness: An internations survey. *School Organisation, 10* (2), 167–178.

Cohen, D. K. (1995). What is the system in systemic reform? *Educational Researcher, 24* (9), 11–17,31.

DuFour, R., & Berkey, T. (1995). The principal as staff developer. *Journal of Staff Development, 16* (4), 2–6.

ERIC. (1981). *Schools—and their principals—do make a difference* (Research Action Brief No. 20). Eugene, OR: ERIC Clearinghouse on Educational Research. (ERIC Document Reproduction Service No. ED 213 068).

Evans, R. (1996). *The human side of school change.* San Francisco: Jossey-Bass.

Ford, D., & Bennett, A. L. (1994). The changing principalship in Chicago. *Education and Urban Society, 26* (3), 238–247.

Fullan, M. (1991). *The new meaning of educational change* (2nd ed). New York: Teachers College Press.

Goldring, E. B. (1990). Elementary school principals as boundary spanners: Their engagement with parents. *Journal of Educational Administration, 28* (1), 53–62.

Grace, G. (1995). *School leadership: Beyond educational management.* London: Falmer.

Hart, A. W., & Reyes, P. (Eds.). (1990). *Teachers and their workplace: Commitment, performance and productivity.* Newbury Park, CA: Sage.

Hopkins, D., & Ainscow, M. (1993). Making sense of school improvement: An interim account of the "improving the quality of education for all" project. *Cambridge Journal of Education, 23*(3), 287–304.

Kowalski, T. J. (1979). The principal's role in curriculum development: What are the barriers? *Contemporary Education, 50* (1), 150–161.

Leithwood, K. A., & Montgomery, D. J. (1986). *Improving principal effectiveness: The principal profile.* Toronto: Ontario Institute for Studies in Education.

Leithwood, K., Begley, P. T., & Cousins, J. B. (1994). *Developing expert leadership for future schools.* London: Falmer.

Lieberman, A. (Ed.). (1992). *The changing contexts of teaching.* Chicago: National Society for the Study of Education.

Lipham, J. M. (1981). *Effective principal, effective school.* Reston, VA: National Association of Secondary School Principals. (ERIC Document Reproduction Service No. ED 207 131).

Morris, V.V., Crowson, R. L., Porter-Gehrie, C., & Hurwitz, E., Jr. (1984). *Principals in action: The reality of managing schools.* Columbus, OH: Charles E. Merrill.

Murphy, J. (1992). *The landscapes of leadership preparation: Reframing the education of school administrators.* Newbury Park, CA: Corwin.

Office of the Superintendent of Public Instruction. (1997a, August 13). *A framework for excellence: Improving education in Washington state* [On-line]. Available Internet: http://www.wa.gov/ospi/contents.htm.

Office of the Superintendent of Public Instruction. (1997b, August 13). *Engrossed substitute House bill 1209* [On-line]. Available Internet: http://cisl.ospi.wednet.edu/cisl/legislative/ALL1209OLD.html#PART_II.

Peterson, K. D. (1984). Mechanisms of administrative control over managers in educational organizations. *Administrative Science Quarterly, 29*, 573–597.

Plecki, M. L., Koppich, J. E., Kirst, M. W., Guthrie, J. W., Hayward, G. C., & Florio, D. H. (1997). *Conditions of education in Washington state 1997.* Seattle: University of Washington, Institute for the Study of Education Policy.

Richardson, M. D., Short, P. M., Prickett, R. L., Flanigan, J. L. (1991, November). *The changing roles of the school principal: A research synthesis.* Paper presented at the Annual Meeting of the Mid-South Educational Research Association, Lexington, KY.

Sackney, L. E., & Dibski, D. J. (1994). School-based management: A critical perspective. *Educational Management and Administration, 22* (4), 104–111.

Schlechty, P. (1990). *Schools for the twenty-first century.* San Francisco: Jossey-Bass.

Sergiovanni, T. J. (1991). *The principalship: A reflective practice perspective* (2nd ed.). Boston: Allyn & Bacon.

Spring, J. (1998). *Conflict of interests: The politics of American education* (3rd ed.). Boston: McGraw-Hill.

Swanson, A. D. (1989). Restructuring educational governance: A challenge of the 1990s. *Educational Administration Quarterly, 25* (3), 268–293.

Taylor, A., & Valentine, B. (1985). *Effective schools: What research says about series* (Data-Search Report No. 1). West Haven, CT: National Education Association. (ERIC Document Reproduction Service No. ED 274 073).

Tyack, D. (1990). "Restructuring" in historical perspective: Tinkering toward utopia. *Teachers College Record*, *92*(2), 170–191.

Vandenberghe, R. (1995). Creative management of a school: A matter of vision and daily interventions. *Journal of Educational Administration*, *33*(2), 31–51.

Wasley, P., Hampel, R., & Clark, R. (1997). The puzzle of whole-school change. *Phi Delta Kappan*, *78*(9): 690–697.

Williams, R. C., & Portin, B. (1996). *The changing role of the principal in Washington state*. (Available from the Association of Washington School Principals, 1021 8th Ave. S.E., Olympia, WA 98501-1500).

Williams, R. C., Portin, B. (1997, April). *The changing role of the principal in Washington state*. Paper presented at the annual meeting of the American Educational Research Association, Chicago, IL).

INDEX

FSC
www.fsc.org
MIX
Papier | Fördert gute Waldnutzung
FSC® C083411

Kolibri 360 GmbH
Ferdinand-Jühlke-Straße 7
99095 Erfurt, Deutschland
produktsicherheit@kolibri360.de

Druck:
CPI Druckdienstleistungen GmbH
im Auftrag der
Kolibri 360 GmbH
Ferdinand-Jühlke-Str. 7
99095 Erfurt